SUPERCHIC

James Brady

SUPERCHIC

Little, Brown and Company
Boston—Toronto

FIRST EDITION

T 11/74

LIBRARY OF CONGRESS CATALOGING IN PUBLICATION DATA

Brady, James, 1928–
  Superchic.

  Autobiographical.
  1. Brady, James, 1928–   I. Title.
TT505.B7A34   746.9'2'0924 [B]   74-13303
ISBN 0-316-10593-7

Designed by Barbara Bell Pitnof

*Published simultaneously in Canada by Little, Brown & Company
(Canada) Limited*

PRINTED IN THE UNITED STATES OF AMERICA

For Florence, Fiona, and Susan

Contents

SUPERCHIC

1

Arrogant Opinions

American women invest a great deal of passion and some twenty-five billion dollars a year in their clothes. To guide their choices they rely on the so-called women's pages of their daily newspapers and on a half-dozen slick magazines. Of all the fashion publications in this country, the three most powerful, though not the largest in circulation, are *Vogue, Harper's Bazaar,* and *Women's Wear Daily.* From 1964 through 1972 I was the publisher of two of them, first *WWD* and later *Bazaar,* and I competed vigorously throughout those eight years with the third, *Vogue.*

Coco Chanel used to tell me that fashion worked when it caused you to notice the woman, that it failed when you noticed what she was wearing. Looking at clothes bores the hell out of me. And so does ponderous talk about "significant" fashion. Fashion is a serious business but I find myself impatient with people who take it too seriously. Clothes that make you look good and feel better are fine things to have but I could never be pious about it. Yet although I am indifferent to clothes, I am drawn to the women who wear them, the men and women who sell them, and especially to the designers who create them. People *are* more interesting than things, and the most stimulating people in fashion are the designers. I have known fashion designers touched with genius, others who were petty and stupid, several who were crooks, drunks, and liars, men of monumental conceit, of saintly humility, at least one flagellant, numerous other perverts, and a few who were clearly quite mad. None of them was ever dull. Fashion journalism, whether in newspapers or trade papers or in the slick magazines, achieves distinction when it focuses on such creative people and uses their designs to illuminate the craft.

John Fairchild once traveled to Moscow in the late fifties when the Maison Dior was invited to show its wares in Russia. I was in Washington then and knew nothing of fashion, but I remember reading Fairchild's cables. Instead of describing the fashion show, the clothes that these Russian women were seeing for the first time in their lives, he described the women's faces, how their eyes followed the line and color and spirit of the French couture clothes they would never wear but very clearly had dreamed about. He wrote about the women who watched and by writing with care and sensitivity about people, Fairchild succeeded very nicely indeed in describing the clothes without even mentioning them.

It is nonsense to elevate clothes to the level of art objects. Clothes are body coverings. It was Yves Saint Laurent, perhaps the greatest contemporary designer, who told me fashion was not an art, that "art" was too grand a word, but a craft like any other, *un métier*. Its distinction came from its being a poetic métier, superior to plumbing or carpentry only in the amount of poetry a gifted designer might contribute. Like a beautiful house or a classic automobile, well-designed, competently manufactured clothes provide additional dimensions:

comfort, sensual pleasure, security, variety, refreshment, and, for the insecure, status. During the years I reported on fashion and wrote about it, I always preferred talking fashion with an intelligent man like Saint Laurent, a dedicated craftsman like Emanuel Ungaro, or the quotable, wicked, and unique Chanel, to sitting on a straight-backed little gilt chair watching their clothes paraded before me. I enjoyed the creators more than their creations.

All journalism is flawed. It is in the nature of writing to deadline that it be imperfect. But in most branches of journalism there is a striving for excellence. Much of the fashion journalism committed in this country is swill. Of course, I make exceptions. There are diligent professionals writing about fashion as honestly and sometimes as gracefully as Red Smith writes about sports or Tony Lewis the law. And there are editors who insist on good writing and accurate reporting. But there are hundreds of women, and a few men, who make their living writing about clothes on the fashion pages of American newspapers who rarely compose an accurate sentence. What they write is not really journalism at all but advertising puffs in the guise of critical reports. They do this on behalf of the local retail stores that stock, and anxiously hope to sell, the clothes being puffed. Since local department and specialty stores are the major advertisers in local newspapers you stand a gaudy chance of ever reading that a dress being promoted by one of those stores is badly cut or poorly made or in execrable taste. Even if your average provincial fashion editor were qualified to make such outrageously critical judgments.

You might reasonably expect the quality of fashion magazine reportage to be somewhat higher. After all, magazine editors presumably know something about clothes. A few of them actually go to see, with their own eyes, the clothes on which they report. But such rash initiatives, bordering on hysteria, are frowned upon by more responsible, senior editors.

For in the arch and breathless style of writing favored by our great fashion periodicals, factual information has never been considered much of an asset. As with the newspapers, there is always the pressure of advertisers. In the magazines it is national advertising pressure, sometimes overt, more frequently assumed by the top editors who parcel out the fashion pages among their major advertisers month after month lest an advertiser discover he is being shortchanged and go away sobbing. At the first editorial meeting I ever had at *Harper's Bazaar* in 1971 I was informed that of a total of sixty pages of fashion pictures in an upcoming issue, "forty-five are for the advertisers." The ad department of this great and respected national magazine had allotted more than two-thirds of the fashion pages to advertisers, or potential advertisers, without even consulting with the fashion editors ostensibly being paid to make such judgments.

This would be laughable stuff if the fashion pages of American dailies and the slick fashion magazines existed solely for titillation, for the amusement of idle women with nothing to do between sessions of filing their nails. But the women's pages and the fashion books parade themselves as accurate and honest guides to what women should wear this year, this season, this very night, to be more attractive, more desirable, more fashionable. The blatant sellout was most dramatically exemplified a couple of years ago when perhaps 90 percent of the women's pages in the country attacked and ridiculed that season's new fashion, the longer skirt lengths variously lumped together under the name "midi." It doesn't matter whether the longer lengths had any innate value. They *were* fashion news. And fashion news was supposed to be what the fashion pages were delivering. But not, I hasten to assure you, while the local stores and the big manufacturers still had in their inventories millions of mini skirts they had to get rid of before the buying public was to be permitted to develop enthusiasm for skirts below the knee.

Such insights did not come to me miraculously, like the Lady's voice at Lourdes. I learned them painstakingly at *Women's Wear Daily*, that breezy and irreverent tabloid read every business day by retail executives, fashion designers, and other professionals in the fashion *apparat*. Despite its belligerent willingness to call a fashion spade a spade, even at the risk of losing the occasional ad, *WWD* makes a substantial profit. *Bazaar* and *Vogue*, slick monthly magazines with a combined readership of about five million affluent women, do not. When I moved from *WWD* to *Bazaar* I attempted to introduce the same caliber of aggressively honest fashion reporting to its slicker pages. Given the journalistic training I had had, there was no other choice. Before becoming *WWD*'s publisher late in 1964, I had been first a Washington correspondent, then a foreign correspondent for two years in London, then for four years in Paris a reporter who specialized in covering and writing about the business and the aesthetics of fashion and about the people who made it work.

This, then, is an account of those years. Since I fell into fashion journalism *par hasard* instead of, as might have happened, being hired by the *Wall Street Journal* to cover finance, or the *Sporting News* to compile batting averages, this is a story about fashion and about fashionable people. It is as true and accurate an account as I can make it of how it was to be a young American newspaperman, often naïve and uninformed, in an alien and sophisticated setting. It is the story of a heterosexual in a frequently homosexual milieu, of a critic who, unlike other critics, had to go back again next day to interview creators whose latest work he had just pilloried, and of a journalist who was at first a tentative, and later an arrogantly self-confident, arbiter of taste, of style, of elegance. It is the firsthand account of a mere man whose healthy young conceit permitted him to make responses to that most frequently asked, and difficult to answer, question of millions of American women: "What shall I wear?"

I've not set out to do an exposé of fashion, the seamy side of the business, the Seventh Avenue manufacturers providing buyers with theater tickets and free meals and girls. That is dull and vulgar stuff long since packaged in any number of trashy novels, and no more unique to the fashion business than to the frozen food industry or the machine tool trade. Instead, this is the story of fashion and fashion journalism, written from the inside, a story that ranges from Marion Davies's perfumed, monogrammed toilet paper to Jacqueline Kennedy Onassis's passion for clothes, a story of models and artists, of a genius named Chanel who would have been memorable had she never designed a dress, of White House feuds and tantrums by Princess Margaret, of master Balenciaga surrounded by his little monks in their little smocks, of a poor Italian boy called Valentino who now eats off gold plate in his villa on Capri, of journalists on the take and others so palpably honest you know they will die poor, of cosmetic monarchs like Charles Revson and Estée Lauder, and of a rugby player named Courrèges who became violent if you suggested that anyone but he had convinced women they could wear pants. It is the story of designers like Luis Estevez whose companies are always going bust and yet who continue to live in great houses and drive Rolls-Royces. It is an account of a brilliant innovative journalist called John Fairchild, of the doddering nepotism of the Hearst Corporation, of writers who ought to be certified mad lest they run amok and damage the furniture, of politicians and storekeepers, of photographers and beautiful women, of the great chemical empires such as Du Pont and Celanese and Monsanto, of lovely clothes and abominable taste, of jealousy and generosity, of my own triumphs and follies.

Episodic and gamy, frustrating and rewarding, this is how

it was in that splendid, irritating, chaotic, absurd and some-times wonderful world of fashion and the fashionable. Or to lapse without delay into the hyperbole that is fashion's language, the regions of the Superchic.

2

Korea, Washington, London

In the summer of 1952 I came home to New York from Korea, a twenty-three-year-old Marine lieutenant who had survived for nearly a year the best efforts of the Chinese army. In justice, the Chinese had also survived mine. An advertising copywriting job awaited me at Macy's, and, equipped with a new Chevrolet convertible and a Brooks Brothers suit, I made the transition to civilian life without realizing it was supposed to be difficult. It never occurred to me that the war had been anything more than an interlude, generally pleasant, certainly maturing, occasionally terrifying, and within a month I was writing captions for that year's Christmas catalogue. There was a woman copy chief with whom I did not get on, but instead of sending me packing she rather sensibly had me transferred to a job helping to edit the Macy house organ, a biweekly called the *Macy Star*. I had worked on newspapers while in college and the assignment was child's play. For most of the next year I interviewed assistant buyers, covered Communion breakfasts and men's smokers, and passed one memorable afternoon taking down *mots* as they fell from the lovely lips of Miss Ava Gardner, who for some obscure reason was making a personal appearance at the store. I was impressed not only by Miss Gardner's beauty but by her ability to consume great drafts of chilled vodka without becoming smashed.

During that year there was a strike by Macy's house union, a normally compliant organization called Local 1-S. In the weeks leading up to the strike, store executives were notified that they would be expected to man stockrooms, wrap packages, and sell toasters if the union pulled out its people. Although I was making perhaps eighty dollars a week I was considered an executive, but after a somewhat tortured examination of conscience, I decided the proposed strike was a valid bargaining tactic and I would refuse to become a strikebreaker. I would report to work but only to do my own job. When I informed my superiors of this admittedly complicated decision, they muttered darkly and warned me I was endangering a brilliant future at the store. The strike was called, I went to work, was jostled and hissed as I passed through the picket line with what I hoped was poise, and for an hour or two fiddled with papers on my desk and read the newspaper. I was summoned by one of the senior executives, told that in a strike you were either with management or against it, and sent home. The strike was over by noon and I returned to work the next day. Nothing more was said and it was months later that I learned the strike had actually been settled in the pre-dawn hours but that the union had asked the store's permission to pull the workers anyway for a brief demonstration. Macy's management, being fond of this particular union and not wishing to encourage a more aggressive one, was delighted to agree. It was a valuable early lesson in skepticism for a young man about to enter journalism full time.

Working in a retail store, I was aware of the existence of *Women's Wear Daily*. I did not read it, of course, but I knew it was out there, a sort of *Variety* of the soft goods business. John Fairchild, grandson of one of its founders and son of its then president, was a blond young man recently out of Princeton who had been assigned to cover retail news in the city. In the course of writing a feature article on Macy's he had interviewed me about the store's newspaper, and since we hit it off and I seemed knowledgeable about the retail business, he suggested I go to work for his family's paper. After an interview with the personnel people, and an impressive lunch with John and his father at the University Club, I went off to Mexico on vacation. When I got back I was informed that I had been hired, at a hundred dollars a week, to succeed John as retail news reporter in the New York metropolitan area.

I am fond of describing myself (friends think I overdo it) as an "editorial animal." Except for Macy's, and my two years as a Marine (another matter on which I am known to bore people), I had always been a newspaperman. I had done the usual things on school and college publications, had been a copyboy on the *Daily News* while in college, and put in a few months as a reporter on the now-defunct *Bronx Times*, a neighborhood throwaway of little distinction. The man who ran the *Bronx Times* sat at a large wooden desk eating peanut butter from a jar and had, according to office legend, once distributed Christmas bonuses of fifty cents a man, pleading that the paper could spare no more in those difficult times. Although the *Bronx Times* had but five employees, three of us part-time, it boasted a sophisticated battery of telephones and a switchboard operator named Richie. Richie busied himself with telephonic associates who were never seen nor fully identified. They all seemed to possess only first names and to live in Miami, Las Vegas, or Reno. In my innocence I wondered why Richie refused to place or take calls for the reporters and why a neighborhood weekly had such a staggering volume of long distance phone traffic. The riddle was solved one afternoon when Richie stepped briskly through the office window and down the fire escape just a minute or two before the New York City Police Department visited the city room.

At *Women's Wear Daily*, journalists ran things. In the city room there was a sign that reminded the staff: "Our Salvation Depends Upon Our Printing the News." Young Fairchild and his father, Louis, gave me a brief course in their brand of journalism and turned me loose on an unknowing industry. I was sent up to ask the president of one of the big stores about rumors that it was about to close down an unprofitable branch in Connecticut. The executive cheerfully acknowledged this was so but declared he didn't want the story to be published. "The employees will get upset and start looking for jobs. And I want to get the Christmas selling season in before we announce." I said I was sorry but the story had to run. "You run that story," the store president warned, "and I'll keep open until Easter to make you look like a horse's ass." We published it, of course, and the man was as good as his word, keeping the branch open until the following spring. I consoled myself with pious thoughts of the workers whose jobs I'd saved, at least temporarily.

After two years or so, John was shipped off to Paris and a year later I was dispatched to the company's Washington bureau. The notion was that we were promising young men who should be sent out from headquarters, from the protective womb of the New York office, to make our mistakes and polish our skills with less supervision than we would have in New York. Eisenhower dawdled in the White House, padding out with golf the intervals between his several, near-fatal illnesses, and, as the joke ran, was urged by Nixon, "Race you up the stairs." There was a vacuum in the White House so I was assigned to where the news was, to Capitol Hill. Those were heady days. Sam Rayburn still ruled the House. Lyndon Johnson was running the Senate and some said the country as well. Joe McCarthy had been censured and was drinking heavily but was still there, buttonholing reporters in the elevators or the cloak room with his own eccentric version of the day's truth. A spare and elegant young Jack Kennedy was making a name and being spoken of as a vice-presidential possibility. His kid brother, slim, tanned, with a curiously piping voice, was counsel for an investigating subcommittee of the Senate, and had already begun the digging that would lead to the destruction first of Dave Beck, then of Jimmy Hoffa, and of an entire pride of greater and lesser rascals. I worked under the guidance of a splendid journalist, Robert Barr, a spindly and bespectacled reporter with a file cabinet for a mind. Barr taught me my trade if anyone did.

I worked in Washington those three years as a legman. I covered committee hearings and Senate floor debates and asked questions and took notes. Years later, as a publisher, I would be dealing with power. But in Washington, as a correspondent whose beat was the Senate, I simply chronicled it, reported on those who did wield it. From January 1956 through 1958 I was a kid reporter, wide-eyed in the presence of great men, trying to get down quotes without ever having learned shorthand. Bobby Barr spared neither me nor himself as the two of us covered as many as twenty hearings a day, kept track of the floor debate in both Houses, filed for three morning papers, a p.m. paper, and a couple of weeklies. Barr was the most patient of men but there were times when he blew up, chewed me out, times when I had strayed from pure reportage to try to learn something about how Washington really worked. I was taking a postgraduate course in civics, a seminar in American power, but it was Bob Barr's understanding that we were there to get congressional coverage into the Fairchild papers, not to educate ourselves. Under Barr's direction I did the job, but whenever I could I slipped away from the Southern mill lobby's plea for import relief, or the flammable fabrics labeling legislation, to sit in on one of Lyndon Johnson's fabulous bull sessions.

"Y'see," Johnson would say to the three or four reporters he could scrape together in some marbled corner of the Capitol, "some people think I should get Alaska and Hawaii statehood the same year. But I don't think that. 'Cause there are a lot of colored people in Hawaii, and they're gonna vote one way. And there are a lot of white folks in Alaska, voting the other way. Now I like to take a drink. But if I put a bottle on my head and drink it all down, next day I'm gonna be sick as hell. Same with statehood. We'll get them both in, I promise you. But we'll get one in this year and one in the next. And no one's gonna feel like hell next morning."

It wasn't always so folksy. One day about twenty of us were crowded into his office listening to Lyndon hold forth on a knotty bit of legislation. Toward the back of the room his paunchy but brilliant press secretary, George Reedy, was whispering an explanation to a reporter who had missed something Johnson had said. "Goddam it, Reedy," Lyndon shouted. "You don't talk when I'm talking." Reedy said he was answering a reporter's question. "You work for me, not for him," Lyndon snarled. "If I drop my coat on the ground, you pick it up, Reedy." The abashed Reedy said yes, sir, and the briefing went on.

Three years after I left Washington, Lyndon Johnson came to Paris, no longer the powerful, assured leader of the Senate, but a Vice-president. He had been to Berlin, handing out ball-point pens to puzzled Germans, and now he was making the ritual call in Paris. De Gaulle virtually ignored him, having read American political science and understanding that Vice-presidents have no power. I went over to the Hotel Georges V to see Lyndon after he had done the usual tour. He came into the lobby with a couple of bodyguards (the French called them "gorillas") and Liz Carpenter, a plump

Texas newspaperwoman and old friend who acted as his press agent. I introduced myself, reminding him I had covered the Senate for three years. I'm sure he didn't remember me but we spoke for several minutes and then he asked if I ever got back to Washington.

"Well, from time to time," I said.

Lyndon grabbed my shoulder and shook me firmly but gently.

"You come up and see me, hear. You come up to my office and you just make it headquarters, hear. I don't want to hear you been in Washington and didn't come to see me, hear?"

Less than two years later Jack Kennedy was dead and Lyndon was President and I was still in Paris. Put it down to my native skepticism that I made no plans to situate myself in the White House next time I found myself in Washington.

I learned about politics by watching the politicians. And the political writers who watched the politicians. There were great men in the Senate press gallery then: Joe Alsop in carpet slippers; Rollie Evans with his Ivy League trousers flapping above his ankles; Bill White losing endlessly and substantially at gin to the gallery attendants; Al Drury writing *Advise and Consent* on the gallery's yellow copy paper during quorum calls; Peck Trussell, old and deaf, a Pulitzer winner hustling down marble halls after quotes from men not fit to sharpen his pencils; Harry Taylor, who would be killed in the Congo; Jack Bell of AP; Tom Wicker, who went over the Potomac's Great Falls one Sunday afternoon in a canoe and survived, though the man with him died; Tony Lewis, one Pulitzer already won, another soon to come, and Lewis just thirty.

Theodore Francis Green, the oldest man ever to inhabit the Senate, was chairman of the Foreign Relations committee, and whenever he fell asleep during the hearings, Bill Fulbright would gently nudge him to wakefulness, after a decent interval of rest the old man needed. Herman Welker of Idaho lacked Joe McCarthy's knack of handling his liquor and during evening sessions would stand there weaving at his desk, smiling amiably at his colleagues, totally unable to follow the debate. And on the last day of every session, one of the older men, I think it was Carl Hayden of Arizona, would make his single speech of the year. A procession of page boys would carry in the entire *Congressional Record* of the whole session, Hayden would point to the piled-up volumes, and lecture "the greatest deliberative body in the world" on its windiness. There were arguments in the press gallery as to whether Carl Curtis, Karl Mundt, or Roman Hruska was the dumbest man in the Senate. And it was generally conceded that the conservatives, like Barry Goldwater, were much more civil than the liberals when it came to their dealings with individual reporters.

I had studied political science in college but for three years the Senate was my postgraduate work. As for divertissement, there was no competing with it. I had a theory that they should close down the movie houses, Griffith Stadium, the museums, Uline Arena, and even the strip joints out on the Maryland line, and send everyone to the Senate each day. It was the best show in town.

I suppose my irreverence stemmed from those years. Eisenhower was known familiarly as "Bubblehead," Lyndon Johnson as "Uncle Evil," Everett Dirksen as a pious old fraud, and the drinking habits and extracurricular sexual activities of Congressmen and Senators, as well as those of Cabinet members, were conversational currency. But I also came away from Washington with a real appreciation of the system, a respect for legislators who worked, and for those with intelligence, sensitivity, and courage. I learned in those three years that the system must be a good one: it had survived so many mediocrities, produced so many decent men.

By 1959 I was married and in London. Fairchild had appointed me bureau chief, I had a staff of eight or nine people, our silver-gray poodle was in six months' quarantine, and I trekked up and down the country from Land's End to the Scottish borders. My wife found us an apartment in Mayfair, a block from Hyde Park, I learned to drive on the left, we joined the Hurlingham Club in Fulham and played tennis on grass, and the job of turning an eager young reporter into a newspaper executive was under way. The Beatles were schoolboys in Liverpool, Churchill was still alive and would dodder into the House of Commons on Budget Day, the harlots were still walking the streets of W.1., *Time* magazine hadn't yet "discovered" London, and it was a perfectly wonderful place to be.

When Fairchild sent me to Europe I was a fashion illiterate. I had never seen a fashion show and had no intention of ever seeing one. But John came over to London from Paris once I had settled in. "Come on," he said, "we're going to see some clothes." He informed me that John Cavanagh was the best of the London couture designers and that he had called Cavanagh to have him put on a show for us. I was agog that anyone could simply call a man like Cavanagh and tell him to stage a show. I had assumed that fashion designers were rather grand and distant and that you wrote them polite letters on decently watermarked bond if you wanted to meet with them. We trotted down Curzon Street to Cavanagh's. (John never simply walks; he moves at a sort of half dogtrot, half skip.) Cavanagh turned out to be a very pleasant fellow, a nice-looking, lean Irishman who'd been in British Intelligence during the war. He had scraped up a couple of model girls and while John and I sat in splendid isolation in the salon the girls came in and went out, showing us perhaps thirty or forty dresses. I didn't know whether I was seeing something good or something bad. John took down some numbers in his illegible left-hand script, I set my face at something noncommittal, between a smile and a frown, and the eager-to-please

Cavanagh hovered, in a pleasant way. When it was over John stood up and shook Cavanagh's hand.

"John, your model girls are so nice. They're so pretty. Thank you so much."

When we got out on the sidewalk I said brightly that I thought the whole thing had been terrific, that Cavanagh had great taste, that the clothes were, well, whatever good clothes were supposed to be.

"Nonsense," John said. "I used to think he had some talent but I guess I was wrong."

I asked why he'd been so effusive about the models, that I hadn't found them all that marvelous.

"Oh," said John, "you always say that when you can't say anything good about the clothes."

In the beginning I found that the clothes I liked were the classic and familiar. I was uncomfortable with the look of new designs. Such a bias in favor of the old is fatal to the critic whose job it is to discover new talents, recognize unfamiliar permutations on traditional things, and make distinctions between what has gone before and what is an original creation. I spent much of my six years in Europe learning to make such distinctions.

In early 1960 John and Jill Fairchild rented Lilli Palmer's chalet in Kitzbuhl and my wife and I flew out from London to join them for the skiing. One evening we were having cocktails with some English people and a toast was announced. Princess Margaret, the Margaret Rose we all recalled as a little girl, was to marry. Peter Townsend, the R.A.F. ace and divorced suitor, was forgotten. A photographer called Tony Armstrong Jones (the hyphen in his name came later) was the lucky man. We drank their health, wondered who this Jones chap might be, and promptly lapsed back into the usual Kitzbuhl discussion of that day's snow and whether Francel or Pepi was the better instructor. But Margaret's wedding was to give *WWD* what was, I suppose, its first great international scoop.

John was running the Paris office and, as European director, was my boss. He badgered me incessantly in London: couldn't we get some idea of what Margaret's dress would look like, couldn't we break the story, get the scoop. There were days when I wished Margaret would elope or, as princesses did in the Middle Ages when prevented from marrying their lovers, enter a convent. Norman Hartnell had been selected to design the royal wedding dress. It was a logical choice. Hartnell and Hardy Amies both had been granted the royal warrant as dressmakers to the Queen, and one of them would have to be given the job. Amies is the better designer, but Hartnell had long before mastered the sort of regal dowdiness demanded by the royal family and had the technical capability to cope with women — the Queen Mother, the Queen herself, and Margaret — who were small people with enormous bosoms. If you look closely at the British royals, and young Princess Anne can now be included in their number, you'll see they rather resemble pouter pigeons with great plump breasts that begin somewhere south of the chin and proceed downward almost to the waist. Anyway, Hartnell was enough of a technician to cope. John exhausted me with his strident queries, I drove my staff to distraction, and poor Hartnell was shadowed wherever he went. Norman is a large man, with red cheeks and an imposing bulk, and in those days his shop was in Bruton Street, W.1., administered by one Captain Mitchison, a great beefy fellow with an R.A.F. moustache and muttonchops. Captain Mitchison represented Hartnell to the world and pretty much kept me away from the great man. In short, I failed completely to get a single solid hint of what Margaret's dress would look like. Over in Paris, John was also hard at work. Most London couture fabric came from France, as did the laces and the appliqué work, many of the shoes, the veils, the bridesmaids' hats, and the like, and French artisans are incapable of keeping secrets. So it was *WWD*'s Paris fashion editor, Thelma Sweetinburgh, who listened in the right places and broke the story. John Fairchild was ecstatic. Not only did *WWD* have the story but it was his staff, not mine, that had done the deed.

The purported sketch was dispatched to me in London by courier and I was sent around to ask Mr. Hartnell to comment. Feeling somewhat like Oliver Twist asking for "more," I stood on the front steps of the Maison Hartnell and presented my case to Captain Mitchison.

"Please ask Mr. Hartnell if this is an accurate sketch of his wedding dress for Princess Margaret," I said.

Mitchison's moustache and muttonchops quivered with a proper disdain and he extended a gloved hand to take the filthy thing from me. I was not asked inside, of course, but was left on the doorstep while presumably Mr. Hartnell was shown our sketch. After a few minutes Mitchison returned, pushed the sketch into my hand, and said Mr. Hartnell would have no comment to make.

"Well, then, we're going to publish it tomorrow," I told him.

I wish I could report that Mitchison replied in words worthy of the moment — "publish and be damned," something like that — but he merely waved a gray-gloved hand in my general direction, and having thus dismissed me, disappeared again behind the polished hardwood and impressive brass of Norman Hartnell's establishment.

The sketch was wirephotoed to New York, appeared on the front page of next day's *WWD*, and by noon every British correspondent in New York had a copy of it. The following day the seven or eight London dailies played it as their major story. All of them put it on the front page (except *The Times*, which was in 1960 still running personal adverts on *its* front page). My favorite was the *Daily Mirror* which, in headline type customarily restricted to declarations of war or cricket

21

victories over Australia, shouted: YANK SPIES STEAL THE DRESS. It was *WWD*'s finest moment and I don't think Mr. Hartnell ever fully recovered.

Word leaked out of Buckingham Palace that Princess Margaret was incensed, that she wanted to have the dress changed at the last moment, that Mr. Hartnell was called on the royal carpet and rather royally abused. Tony Armstrong-Jones was said to have found the whole affair amusing, an attitude which only exacerbated Margaret's mood. Finally it was the Queen herself who was said to have convinced Margaret to be above it all, to turn a royal cheek toward the ink-stained wretches of the tuppenny press, to be as noble as we were common.

Months later, just before I was to leave London for Paris, the women's page editor of the *Daily Express*, Lord Beaverbrook's paper, invited me to an expensive lunch in one of London's better restaurants. Jill Butterfield was an attractive blonde and she saw to it that we both drank a good deal of an excellent wine. Over dessert, Jill leaned very close to me and whispered, "Tell me, just how *did* you get that sketch of Margaret's dress?"

Feeling the wine, and very much aware of Miss Butterfield's proximity, I straightened my tie and called for the check myself. It was no time to be letting down the side.

3

An American in Paris

In 1960 Paris was a magnificent but troubled city. General de Gaulle was threatening to smash the young and hopeful European Common Market over his opposition to British membership. The Algerian War droned on, a bleeding wound to a France that had lost Vietnam just six years earlier. Right-wing army officers of the O.S.S. were whispering of coups d'etat and plotting to assassinate de Gaulle. Algerians of competing persuasions were murdering one another with abandon in the industrial ghettos. And the riot police, with their traditional truncheons and weighted capes, took to carrying submachine guns on ordinary sidewalk beats in broad daylight. To John Fairchild, who had earlier lived through the 1958 coup d'etat that brought de Gaulle to power, none of this seemed to matter. He was intent on bringing the haute couture to bay and on establishing WWD's power and influence both in Paris and at home.

Knowing that John would soon return to New York and

that I would succeed him in Paris, my wife and I hired a French tutor in London and passed as many long weekends as we could afford in the Paris that would soon become our home. The first time I visited the Paris office, John introduced his secretary, a stocky and dignified woman in her late fifties. She had what seemed to be a sprained ankle and was hobbling around the office on a cane.

"This is Madame Traimond," John announced. He waved a hand airily at her injured ankle. "Her lover chased her up a ladder and she broke her leg."

Madame Traimond giggled and shook her head.

That evening we ate steak *au poivre* and *pommes frites* and drank Beaujolais with the Fairchilds at a restaurant called Chez Pauline, and John asked how the hotel was. Were the beds comfortable?

"Oh, yes, they're fine."

"I sent Madame Traimond over to bounce on the beds," John announced proudly. "You can never tell about the beds unless you bounce on them."

I put this story down to John's verbal excesses but later, when she had become my secretary, I had it from Madame Traimond that she really was sent to bounce on hotel beds whenever special guests of the Fairchilds were to descend on Paris. Fortunately, she did not always have the handicap of a sprained ankle and a cane to hinder her bouncing.

It was during that first visit to the Paris office that John showed me Madame Traimond's desk.

"Look at what she's got under here," he implored. "She's a pack rat. I don't know what to do with her. Galoshes and old shoes and these slippers and —" He picked up a stack of seedy-looking files from atop the desk. "Look at this. Can you believe it? I can't get her to throw anything away. She hoards everything."

He went to the window with a handful of files, slid it open, and tossed Madame Traimond's precious documents out into the rue Cambon where they drifted slowly earthward over the elegant eaves of the Hotel Ritz and onto the front steps of the Ministry of Justice. A bored policeman looked up to determine the source of this beneficence. John looked inordinately pleased.

"You'll see," he declared. "She'll never miss them."

Eighteen months later, when I had succeeded John and inherited Madame Traimond, I kept thinking that one desperate day some vital files would turn up missing, that the lease to the office, perhaps, or the entire staff's press credentials would be gone. But they never were, and Madame Traimond worked as effectively for me over the next few years as if her files had never been rifled.

As we were leaving Paris after that first weekend, headed back to the predictable calm of London, I asked John quietly if he expected the political thing to explode in France, if he thought de Gaulle might be assassinated or overthrown, if there would be a civil war.

He stared at me as if I were mad.

"James," he said, "you simply don't understand the French. Politics is their national game."

Within two years paid assassins were machine-gunning de Gaulle's car at a crossroads called Petit Clamart, *bombes plastiques* were going off all over Paris, the army was rising in Algeria, Arabs were slaughtered on one of those lovely, delicate bridges that span the Seine, and tanks were parked in front of the Chamber of Deputies waiting for the parachutists to arrive. Had John still been in town I'm sure he would have smiled tolerantly and put all the commotion down to the French penchant for drama or a national liver attack. "All that meat and red wine, James, to say nothing of the cheese and pastry."

As is customary in such matters, the company arranged that I be transferred from London to Paris at a time in 1960 when my wife was six months pregnant and our poodle bitch had just produced puppies. We took the boat train to Paris the first of September, and John prepared to return to New York where he would become publisher of *Women's Wear Daily*. While I was meeting my first Paris couturiers, he would be setting out to remake the family's flagship newspaper. Still grappling with French verbs, I asked John rather desperately over a farewell lunch, "Which designers are cooperative, whom can I trust, who are your best sources?"

John shrugged.

"Oh, you'll find out. I did." And he left France after five years to go home. He would run *WWD* and I would give him the sort of Paris coverage he wanted. *WWD* would never be the same.

Women's Wear Daily had been founded by the Fairchild brothers as a strike daily in 1910, giving as accurately as it could the facts about a garment industry labor dispute at a time when both management and trade union competed for the most outrageous lie. The Fairchild paper sought to provide its readers with the truth. Nothing of great import occurred to *WWD* from 1910 until 1959, when *Time* magazine saluted it as "reliable as gingham and just about as plain." Now, after ten years in the family business, John Fairchild set out to change all that, hopefully to retain the reliability but to add a panache that even he was as yet unable to define. In the months before his return to New York he had begun to spell out, in a series of memos to the then-editor of *WWD*, as we had started to call it, the kind of aggressive and exciting newspapering he intended the paper to adopt. Once John got back the unfortunate editor lasted about as long as that frock-coated gentleman Orson Welles hustled into retirement in an early reel of *Citizen Kane*. Fairchild and I were a good team. In Europe I became the cutting edge of his jugular-vein journalism.

In publishing circles it was no longer fashionable to display the sort of professional eagerness on which Fairchild insisted and which I was only too pleased to supply. In the eyes of some we were hooligans in button-down collars, type-cast for a revival of *The Front Page*. Except for our relative sobriety, we were seen as being in the grand tradition of reporters who would steal the murdered child's photograph right off the bed table of the grieving mother.

WWD had little prestige and less leverage with the haughty giants of fashion, the dozen or so major couture designers, when Fairchild became Paris bureau chief in 1955. "We were given seats on the second day in the back row along with the German buyers," he later would complain. John changed all that. He cultivated the younger designers, the anonymous assistants, discovered new talents in the ateliers, and began to write about these men and women in WWD. As they came to power, they were grateful to Fairchild for his patronage, and slipped him gossip of the rialto and advance sketches of what the new fashion direction would be.

Jules Francois Crahay, a shy Belgian with graying blond hair, was the house designer for Nina Ricci, one of the great old Paris *maisons de couture*. John admired Crahay's work, liked him as a man, and began to file long stories about this new talent on the Paris horizon. The buyers flocked and Crahay's work got instant recognition. Robert Ricci, son of the founder and a dignified executive who wore gray gloves every day of his life, demanded that Fairchild refer to Crahay, not by name, but as "the Ricci designer." John responded by banning the name Ricci from the paper and rechristening the establishment "The House of Crahay." After six months Robert Ricci capitulated, Crahay's salary was doubled or trebled, and WWD got its favored place, and exclusive sketches in advance, from the Maison Ricci.

By the time I arrived in 1960, the battle was nearly won. Over the next four years we mopped up the last few pockets

of resistance and the French couture's power over the press
was broken forever. But there was a particularly sticky hour
in the House of Dior during my first month in Paris. I had
gone to present my credentials as the new *WWD* man on the
beat to Dior director Jacques Rouet, a bulldog variety of
Frenchman who spoke English fluently but refused to do so.
He and I had our first interview through an interpreter,
Rouet's secretary. After I had completed a gracious little
speech, Rouet pounced. "Do you know," he demanded, "what
Monsieur Fairchild dared to say to me on his departure? He
said there was no use my trying to keep any secrets in the
House of Dior because he knew the way up the back stairs
and knew what was going on before I did." Rouet ranted for
the better part of an hour on the ingratitude of Americans
in general, and reporters in particular, occasionally fixing his
gaze on a formal photograph of the late Christian Dior, the
house's very special patron saint. I dropped my eyes in suit-
able reverence each time the late Dior's name was invoked.
Later I learned he had died of overeating on a voyage his
astrologer had warned him not to take.

When Yves Saint Laurent got out of the army early in
1961, I lunched with him, his partner, Pierre Bergé, and my
Paris fashion editor, Thelma Sweetinburgh. Saint Laurent
told how he was suing the Maison Dior for refusing to rehire
him. It was a rather sordid story, since for several years, when
Yves was doing successful collections, Dior had arranged to
have him deferred even though France was fighting a major
war in Algeria. Then after two collections less well received
by the buyers, poor Yves was drafted. My French was still
rather fragile, and after the heavy lunch and much wine my
attention wandered from the rapid three-way conversation
between Saint Laurent, Bergé, and Thelma. When there was
a lull I interposed a question in my carefully framed textbook
French.

"Tell me, Monsieur Saint Laurent, do you think it possible

you might one day open a couture house of your own, to compete with Maison Dior?"

Thelma looked at me blankly and in her schoolmistress tones said, "Why, Jim, that's what he's been telling us for the last half hour."

We were usually more alert, however. In Paris I came to be known as "le para," a reference to those rebellious and competent French troops who were attaching electrodes to the genitals of Algerian nationalists when they were not threatening to seize the Elysée Palace right out from under President de Gaulle. To winkle out the secrets of the Paris couture for *WWD*'s readers, our reporters were disguised as florists' assistants and smuggled into the fashion studios with bouquets of flowers for the designers, complete with florid dedications forged by me in the names of Seventh Avenue manufacturers. Two of our reporters were beauties and they were sent out to "swing the bag" on the Avenue Georges V, posing as streetwalkers while taking mental notes on what was going on behind the open windows of Balenciaga and Givenchy.

My first exposure to fashion editors en masse, sitting in the front rows of fashion shows, convinced me they had the worst legs, as a group, that I had ever seen. By and large I found the incidence of chic among fashion editors to be on a par with what you might expect at a Methodist church dinner on a hot August night in one of the lesser cities of Iowa.

The designers were another matter. Cristobal Balenciaga, considered by some to be the greatest fashion designer who ever lived, carried a clean linen handkerchief whenever he walked his dog. He would use this handkerchief to tidy up his dog's bottom after it had visited the curb. It was always difficult after learning this to be as reverential about Balenciaga as we were all supposed to be.

But at least few of them were boring. Of course, there is the story of Balenciaga and Givenchy, at a dinner party in

Paris, where the conversation was said to have gone something like this:

"Cher Cristobal, when you mount the shoulder, how does it go?"

"Cher Hubert, you must always be sure that the seam goes thus and . . ."

And so on into the night. Givenchy was once said to have taken to doing needlework during dinner parties just to fill in the gaps of conversation that might possibly pertain to matters other than fashion.

But most fashion designers, and they are the most appealing and interesting people in the whole fashion *apparat,* are people of distinctive character with traits and areas of concern all their own.

Chanel, of course, was a character who would have been a great personality had she never sewn a seam. Saint Laurent and Pierre Bergé are intelligent and sensitive men who are an integral part of the social and cultural life of Paris. The Dior designer Marc Bohan, on the other hand, is a shy and retiring chap much of whose life revolves around the education and rearing of his teenage daughter. (Bohan's wife was killed in an auto accident ten years ago.) Emanuel Ungaro, one of the brightest of the new stars, opened his house with money pledged against his girl friend's Porsche sports car and now that he's made good, spends his time cross-country skiing in Switzerland where he's built a chalet. Jacques Heim, a mediocre couturier now dead, delighted me over countless lunches with his tales of supplying Madame de Gaulle with her clothes. He was especially good at describing the old-fashioned corsets she wore, complete with strings and whalebone. Madame Grès, then and now one of the classic Paris couturiers, is a shy little woman who wears a turban every day of her life. No one I know has ever seen her without it. The assumption is that she is bald as an egg, but I cannot swear to it.

Emanuelle Khahn was a beautiful young Parisienne, a former model who had become a rather important ready-to-wear designer, and I went to her Paris walk-up apartment to do an interview. Her husband was there, a young Vietnamese who would later rechristen himself "Quasar," after the astronomic term. An empty television set, stripped of its guts, hung from the ceiling, rotating slowly on a wire. I asked about it. "It is to show our disdain for television," Quasar explained. After I looked over Emanuelle's sketches, which were very good, Quasar showed me some nude photos he had done of his wife.

Pierre Cardin is one of the most creative designers in the business, but for a time, in the early sixties, he experienced business reverses that were in no way aided by his personal financial excesses or by the fact that one of his trusted aides absconded with thousands of dollars, leaving the books in such a state of disarray that Cardin's lawyers advised against bringing an action. There was simply no way to prove there ever had been any money there in the first place. We so reported in WWD and Cardin, as might be expected, was furious. But then Cardin was generally furious at something or somebody.

A few years later Jerry Dryansky, then WWD bureau chief in Paris, had painstakingly constructed a new bridge of mutual trust and respect between Cardin and the newspaper. It had been tough, but Dryansky is resourceful and got help from Cardin's two aides, André Oliver and Nicole Alphand. Cardin permitted Jerry to preview the collection and send some sketches to New York for publication. In his cable, he used the word *dingue* (batty, wacky) to describe the mood of the clothes, a word that to Dryansky meant "colorful" and to Cardin very obviously something else. When the Cardin collection had been presented to the press, and gotten its usual applause, Dryansky was among the journalists who went backstage to congratulate Cardin. Cardin spied Dryansky, burst into tears, and, according to the newspapermen, fell weeping to the carpet. At that particularly inopportune moment, the

WWD photographer arrived at Cardin's office and innocently asked if Dryansky wanted him to take Cardin's picture now. Cardin leaped to his feet and ordered someone to call for the police to have both Dryansky and the cameraman arrested. Astonished, they backed out before the *agents de police* could arrive. I had to attend a formal dinner given for Cardin by Nicole and Hervé Alphand the next evening and, though Cardin was now under icy control, it was not the most pleasant dinner party I'd ever sat through.

Gérard Pipart, now the designer for the House of Ricci, used to be a free-lance designer for a half-dozen French ready-to-wear concerns and was always in difficulty with the French tax collectors. We lunched one day at La Truite on the Faubourg St. Honoré and I listened sympathetically to his tale of poverty and impending imprisonment, and of course picked up the check to solace poor Gérard. When we left we passed the prohibitively expensive Hermès boutique and Pipart dragged me inside. He ruffled through the silk squares, which sold for fifteen or twenty dollars apiece, selected a half-dozen and had them charged to his account. "I thought you were broke," I said. "I am, but I can't resist beautiful things. They make me forget my debts."

Pierre Balmain was put in focus for me by Coco Chanel. She said of his clothes, "Well, provincial women have to dress too." A decade ago Balmain sold out his perfume to Revlon and with the fortune it brought, purchased property on Elba where he would live out his days as a king. He became more *snob* than ever and offended anyone within reach. His salon was thronged and it was said he was on close terms with a Franciscan monk who attended in brown sackcloth and sandals. I held that the good friar was attempting to convert Balmain; others proposed more sinister motives. In any event, Balmain's fortune eventually ran out and he is today still hard at work in Paris, turning out dresses that bore the fashion press and delight his "provincial" ladies.

One of the lesser Paris couturiers, but one of the more color-ful characters, was Louis Feraud, a stocky forty-year-old with a sailor's gait and an appreciation of good-looking women. When I knew Louis, in the early sixties, he was still married to a woman who worked with him in the business. The two had been separated for some years and their total contact was during working hours. They would later divorce and Louis would marry Mia Fonssagrives, a young American boutique designer and daughter of the near-legendary model Lisa Fons-sagrives, but at the time I knew him Louis was simply a minor designer and a major playboy. His atelier and shop were on the Faubourg St. Honoré just opposite the Elysée Palace, and those were the days when both Algerian terrorists and right-wing French Army officers were interested in assassinating General de Gaulle. Since Louis's upstairs windows gave on the courtyard of the Palace, there were occasions when secur-ity police invaded his premises and sat on the windowsill until de Gaulle had come or gone and his bodyguard could relax. None of this seemed to bother Louis, a relaxed character at best. His clientele during those years consisted of the big New York store Saks Fifth Avenue, which had a contract with him, and any number of beautiful young French movie star-lets. The girls were fond of changing their clothes in front of the windows, and since they rarely wore anything but bikini pants under their dresses, the Palace guards opposite were frequently distracted from their primary role of protecting the President of the Republic. Had Feraud not been apolitical, I would have suspected him of being in league with the right-wing officers, setting up the changing rooms and the young actresses as as a blind for the anti–de Gaulle conspirators.

One night when my wife was in the United States on a visit, Louis and I went to the movies and then to the Brasserie Lipp for a late supper of *choucroute* and beer. He was just back from his first trip to California, where he had fallen in with the movie actress Kim Novak. It was not clear how Louis had met Miss Novak, but the crucial point was that he had spent some days in her beach house and was full of an understandable enthusiasm for California life-styles. Feraud rarely talked about his women, their role in his life being more implicit than expressed, and I asked him somewhat tentatively what he thought about California.

"Magnificent," Louis said, shaking his head. "Though I must admit, I saw it under rather unique circumstances."

After we left Lipp I wanted to get a cab, but it was a pleasant spring evening and Louis asked if I would walk with him to a drugstore. Inside the pharmacy he engaged in a complicated discussion of sleeping potions, was given professional advice by the pharmacist, and purchased some pills. I asked Louis what that was all about.

"Well," he said, "Kim [he pronounced it *Keem*] is flying over to visit me for a few days. She arrives day after tomorrow and I wanted to get something so I could sleep for thirty-six hours or so. I want to be rested when she comes."

Emilio Pucci lives in an old palazzo in Florence, a magnificent house that boasts, among other things, a Wedgwood dining room, walls and ceilings entirely covered in that familiar blue jasperware. When I first visited him, Pucci pointed out the room. "Josiah Wedgwood himself came over to supervise it," he told me. I allowed as how I was impressed. After dinner that evening we drove through the beautiful city and across the Arno to the Pitti Palace. We got out of the car and in the moonlight Emilio pointed out the size of the Pitti's windows. "Look at them," he told me as a lecturer would address a class. "They're so large, too large really for the façade. You see the windows are out of proportion because, when the Pitti was built, the architect was instructed to make everything larger, grander than the Palazzo Pucci. The Pitti," he sneered, "were nouveaux riches."

Valentino was still a minor figure on the Italian fashion scene when I was in Europe. Later, when I was a publisher, he had become the biggest talent in Rome and one of the half-dozen most important designers in the world. John Fairchild and I once spent a weekend in his villa on Capri for which he paid a reputed four hundred thousand dollars, putting in another quarter million's worth of decorating. We played cards around his marble swimming pool and watched the beautiful young girls and ate pizza on solid gold plate. The pizza was about what you would expect of the frozen food department of the local Safeway. But that's no matter. The plate was so splendid you were able to compliment Valentino effusively without necessarily saluting his incompetent cook.

Valentino loves parties and in Rome he entertains with brio, whatever that means. Once I spent an entire evening ogling Audrey Hepburn, who proved she could eat a dish of ice cream without ever bowing that magnificent neck. Her husband, Dr. Dotti, ignored her and talked to everyone else and when it was time to go home poor Audrey, like any ordinary housewife, stood tapping her foot in the foyer while her husband chatted, until finally she had to come back into the apartment to drag him away. It was that night, or another night (they blur one into the other) that we went to a nightclub and Valentino introduced us to the smooth young man who ran the place. When he left the table, Valentino whispered that he was the man who stole the jewels of the Vicomtesse de Ribes. Helmut Burger was with us, a marvelous-looking girl hanging onto him, and when Burger seemed to be taking more interest in me than in the girl, I dragged her off to dance.

Valentino is the only designer in Rome today who has any sort of impact on world fashion. Roberto Capucci was the Italian star a decade ago but moved his couture house to Paris, in an ill-advised attempt to reach more American buyers, and, like a delicate flower replanted in arid ground, the fragile Capucci talent withered and died. Simonetta and her husband, Fabiani, were another Italian pair who pulled up stakes and moved to Paris. Their business also fell apart, their marriage broke up, and today Simonetta attends parties and talks deeply of mysticism while Alberto Fabiani shuffles about in carpet slippers, plays bridge, and takes up young actresses. Patrick de Barentzen was a hot Italian talent for a time, played the grand seigneur with people who had earlier helped his career along, and when he went broke there were few to weep for him. Princess Irene Galitzine is a delightful and elegant woman of a certain age, but no creator, and her collections succeed or fail depending on which young designer she is able to recruit for that particular season.

Only Valentino fills the Italian fashion vacuum. Several years ago he sold his business to an American mini-conglomerate, Kenton Corporation, for a reported three million dollars in cash and a high salary and huge expense account. Although Valentino has been successful, the parent firm, Kenton, went badly into the red, sacked its founder, Robert Kenmore, and today is still in the throes of financial reorganization (and suing Valentino in the bargain). When I was running *WWD*, Valentino was most cooperative, feeding the newspaper advance sketches, calling us whenever Jackie Kennedy came picking through the racks of Valentino clothes in his suite at the Hotel St. Regis in New York. After I went to *Bazaar*, Valentino permitted a *WWD* reporter to accompany him on a trip to the West Coast. The young woman spent her time smoking pot and scribbling down bits of bitchy conversation which appeared each day in the newspaper. Valentino finally asked her to leave the tour, John Fairchild erupted, and Valentino's name was not to appear in *WWD* for six months except in a negative context ("That Rome designer who gets all his ideas from Kenzo . . ."). As always, peace was made, at least until the next time.

André Courrèges is an old rugby player from the southwest of France who to this day will be sure to attend all the big rugby matches at the Stade Colombes. When Courrèges quit the Maison Balenciaga and opened his own fashion establishment, there were Seventh Avenue manufacturers, one of them Andrew Arkin, who, having claimed to have discovered the talented Courrèges, went on to mispronounce his name as "Courageous." André took their money regardless. When last I saw him, Courrèges greeted me at the door wearing yellow vinyl knickerbockers and matching lumberjacket, with an American baseball cap perched on his head. This was what the haute couture was coming to, he seemed to be saying in that ironic way of his. Or perhaps he thought he looked dashing.

4

How Fashion Works

One of the great enduring myths about fashion is that every year, or twice a year even, a small group of wicked men gathers in a smoke-filled room to decide what that season's women's clothes are to be. The codicil to this myth is that since all fashion designers are homosexuals, and therefore hate women, they create clothes that will make women look ridiculous.

Both theories are nonsense, of course. Although it is true that many male fashion designers are homosexuals, they are also businessmen who are no more anxious to go into bankruptcy than the most *macho* heterosexual. They make clothes they think will sell, and if some of their creations are ridiculous, and sometimes they are, it is because they lack talent or timing or taste, and has nothing to do with their supposed enmity toward women.

The cabal theory, the smoke-filled-room school of fashion conspiracy, is a more complicated matter. Until I went to

Paris in 1960 and learned, really learned, how fashion came to be, I didn't myself understand how it was that in a certain season a dozen different fashion houses would drop their skirts, broaden their shoulders, and become frenetic about mohair.

"It all begins with the cloth," Coco Chanel was always telling me and anyone else who would listen. And in a very literal way, fashion does begin with fabric. In Paris there are perhaps a dozen couture houses that are truly creative. There are another couple in Rome, one or two in good years in Spain, and a number of more or less influential designers in the United States. But most new fashion ideas through the years have come from Paris, and this is how it happens that in a given season the look of clothes from competing houses are generally in the same mainstream of fashion.

There are a small handful of great fabric houses in Europe that sell to the Paris couture. These are the great silk houses of Lyon, the very special Swiss firm of L. Abraham in Zurich, several tweed suppliers from Ireland, a couple of Italian specialists, one or two British, and so on. These mills employ salesmen who sell only to the couture and who, four or five months before a new couture collection is to be shown, visit with the various couturiers and show them their new line of cloth. Although their sample bags may contain hundreds of different colors, weaves, surface textures, natural and synthetic blends, there tends to be a certain similarity of cloth in any given fabric season because the cloth-makers themselves are attuned to the same sort of cultural and subcultural influences that work on the fashion designers. The cloth-makers are aware of what sold well last year and what didn't, and they themselves watch very carefully for the prophetic fashion directions that may have been hinted at in the last collection by the most influential of the creative designers — a Balenciaga, for example, or recently, Yves Saint Laurent or Cardin.

So when the couturiers pick through the cloth samples they have already been channeled into certain preestablished directions. The good designers, Bohan of Dior, for example, will ask that certain fabrics be reserved for him, and not sold to anyone else. Or a Saint Laurent may actually design a print and ask the mill to make it up for him exclusively. But generally the designers are seeing and buying the same cloth, so from the very start there are bound to be similarities in color, texture, and even in shape, since certain weights and types of cloth dictate what you can do with them in making up a coat or a dress.

Except for a recluse like Balenciaga, couturiers live in a real world, as far removed from the ivory tower as most Parisians, and such cultural events as the current show of paintings at the Louvre or one of the big galleries, the new rage movie, or a state visit to Paris by the Shah of Iran all influence the designers. Following the student riots that shook Paris and eventually led to the fall of the de Gaulle government, several designers, especially the sensitive Saint Laurent, admitted that their next collections were powerfully influenced by the French political crisis. In the early sixties, when I was living and working in Paris, there was a film called *Les Années Folles* (The Mad Years), a series of old newsreel clips from the twenties, which every designer had to see. The next season the salons were awash with clothes inspired by the 1920's. A couple of years ago one of the several Barons de Rothschild gave a costume party inspired by Proust, and the couture prospered by making up special-order dresses for the event. The *Remembrance of Things Past* influence carried over to the following season. The return to longer skirts several years ago could very clearly be traced to the "flower children," young women wearing cheap cotton dresses to the ankle. Their dresses were badly made and in the least expensive cloth, but they were a very definite reaction against pants and the mini skirt and they influenced nearly every major couturier to drop hems in his next collection.

Another reason why clothes may look alike in any given year is that the young assistant designers tend to hang out together. Although their masters rarely socialize, being in rather bitter competition, the young assistants don't seem at all reluctant to mix. And as young men will, over wine and a meal, or in bed, they talk. Next day in the studio an assistant may let drop something he heard the night before, some new cut or color he's heard about, and without really being conscious of the fact, the designer may incorporate it in one of the models he's working on for the new collection.

And, of course, there is some outright cheating. There's been very bitter talk between the House of Dior and the House of Saint Laurent in recent years with Saint Laurent convinced that some of his ideas were being leaked to Marc Bohan at Dior. About five years ago both men came up with the safari jacket as the basis for their suit shape, and though Bohan's safari jacket looked very different, and Marc himself denied angrily that he had gotten the idea from across town, Saint Laurent could never be convinced that his Dior rival hadn't been tipped off. When we were leaving Paris to return to New York in late 1964, my wife and I gave a buffet for our special Paris friends in fashion, in the newspaper business, and in the Foreign Service. Bohan and Saint Laurent came and spent the evening in opposite corners of the room, Courrèges never left the foyer except to tiptoe in to see our sleeping daughters, and only Gérard Pipart, a delightful young man who likes everybody, circulated through the rooms to talk to everyone.

Clothes in America tend to look somewhat alike because many of the biggest manufacturers attend the Paris collections and take the ideas back to New York to be adapted or even reproduced exactly by the tens of thousands. James Galanos, the Los Angeles designer who charges up to a thousand dollars for a ready-made dress, is just about the only

American who insists he never sees a Paris couture collection. But even Galanos goes to Paris, "to sniff the air," to buy cloth and talk to the accessories houses. He sees the French designs in *Women's Wear Daily* and in the fashion magazines, and to my way of thinking, cannot fail to pick up some ideas, to be influenced subconsciously. Even Norman Norell, who died in 1972 after years of being considered the greatest of all American designers, went to Paris regularly and paid his way in to certain shows.

For although an American tourist can get in to see Cardin or Dior or Givenchy simply by having the concierge of her hotel reserve a seat, professionals must pay their way in to most Paris couture shows. The usual custom is for the couture house to charge what is called a caution. A caution may range as high as eight thousand dollars, and generally it costs twice as much for a manufacturer to get in as for a retail store buyer. The buyer or manufacturer then buys against his caution, reluctantly up to the full amount if the collection is disappointing, and eagerly over that figure if the collection is a big success. Say that Ungaro charges a two-thousand-dollar caution to a retailer such as Bonwit Teller and four thousand dollars to Originala, a manufacturer. If the Ungaro collection is just so-so, the Bonwit buyer will pick the two dresses he likes best, costing about a thousand dollars apiece, to make up his caution. But if the Ungaro collection is a triumph, Originala may come away with six or seven models, for say six to eight thousand dollars, or substantially more than the caution.

For this sort of money the American buyer actually gets a dress or a coat or a suit which is shipped by jet plane to New York several weeks after the collection is shown. If a store has made the couture purchase, the coat or dress is turned over to a manufacturer who will make it up for the store in whatever quantity the retailer thinks he can sell. The garment has all its seams opened, is taken apart, and a pattern is made in paper from which the thousands of machine-made copies are manufactured. Since cheaper cloth is used in most of the American-made copies — the buttons, linings, and trim are also cheaper — a thousand-dollar coat can be reproduced for several hundred dollars or even less. A big couture buyer such as Ohrbach's will have some of its copies made up in the original European cloth to sell for four to six hundred dollars.

During the first decade after the war, when European stores and ready-to-wear manufacturers were short of money, the couture set up a system by which they could see the collection at a much lower caution and could buy paper patterns, rather than the clothes themselves. There is still some trade in paper patterns, but the balance of buying power has shifted so dramatically that today Japan is the single biggest customer of the Paris couture and Germany probably comes next with the United States third.

Despite the high prices charged by the couture (an individual dress these days may cost closer to two thousand dollars than to one thousand dollars), it is rare for a couturier to make money on fashion. Handwork costs more, fringe benefits for French workers are roughly calculated to be just as much again as the base wage, and cloth and accessories prices have rocketed. Most great couture houses become rich through the sale of their private-label perfume. In fact, for many Paris houses the couture collection is simply an event to attract publicity, to promote the name, so that more of its own label perfume will be sold. During the past five years most of the big French couturiers have begun manufacturing their own ready-to-wear and either selling it to American stores or retailing it themselves through their own boutiques, as Saint Laurent does through his chain of Rive Gauche shops in America and in Europe. Cardin has a ready-to-wear line bearing his name which is manufactured to his specifications in the United States by the same company that produces Anne Klein.

The big American fabric mills, such as Burlington and J. P. Stevens and Lowenstein and Collins & Aikman, have never been big factors in the European couture. Their business is based on turning out tens of thousands of yards of cloth of the same design. The making of what is called short pieces, the small, exclusive trade which the couture demands, is not for them. The man-made fiber manufacturers, Du Pont, Celanese and Monsanto, on the other hand, have long worked with the couture. When Du Pont launched its new silklike Qiana a couple of years ago, it placed the fiber with all the major European fabric mills that supplied the couture, reasoning that though it was uneconomic to do so, the publicity value of having its new fiber in a Givenchy or a Dior dress more than made up for the loss.

While these are the bare bones of how the couture operates, far more interesting are the behind-the-scenes operations of the Paris fashion *apparat*. American buyers hate the caution system and many of them try to avoid paying. The strong couturiers force them to pay, the weak permit them to come in without having paid, and the houses in the middle negotiate for the best deal they can get. A Seventh Avenue manufacturer will work a deal with an American store buyer by which the store buyer pays his way in (at half what it would cost the manufacturer) and then sketches out the numbers he likes and has the models sent on to the manufacturer as soon as they get to New York. The money the manufacturer saves on the caution may be split with the store in the form of a slightly lower price for the copies he makes.

In much the same way, an American fabric mill, which is supposed to pay a caution, will get its man in as a "friend" of a Seventh Avenue manufacturer. Since the two get in for the price of one, the cloth man will trim his price for the manufacturer when they get back to New York.

These, of course, are the honest ones. There are some Americans who come to the couture whose ethical standards are not as high. There are fashion manufacturers who employ "designers" whose creative qualifications are nil but who can sit on a small gold chair for two hours, watch perhaps a hundred and sixty or a hundred and eighty numbers pass by, thirty-five or forty seconds each one, take a few notes, and go back to the Hotel Plaza Athenée or the Ritz and sketch, quite accurately, a hundred or more of the dresses in the collection. Such sketches, back in New York, will become the basis for a ready-to-wear collection that will sell, at retail, for millions of dollars. And the manufacturer for whom the retentive "designer" works will complain about the two-thousand-dollar caution he had to pay to see the couturier's collection.

Then there are the outright thieves who don't pay even the nominal caution but who get their sketches through bribery, theft, or by sending "designers" in disguised as tourists. Occasionally a marginal fashion journalist will be paid to sketch a couture collection for an unethical manufacturer, but journalists are not held in high esteem in this regard. Their memories are not up to the chore, for one thing, and as men (or women) of letters, they are inclined to elaborate, to add their own original touches. Poetry of this sort has no place among the style pirates. They want the facts, unadorned.

The couturiers don't come to this combat as innocent as the babe to the baptismal font. I remember how the buyers would rail at Pierre Cardin ten years ago. Cardin, who in those days could never say no, would smilingly sell number 227 to Macy's exclusively and then turn around and sell it to Lord & Taylor, also exclusively. And late one night, after a particularly triumphant dress rehearsal, I remember Saint Laurent's partner, Pierre Bergé, racing through the racks of dresses, revising the prices upward by several hundred dollars each so that the buyers, when they arrived next morning, would understand just how fine this collection was.

Fashion designers will argue endlessly among themselves, to the press, and indeed to anyone who will listen to such tedium, about who created what new fashion. The truth is there is very little new in fashion that has not been done before, perhaps in a different way, perhaps even for another sex (pants for women, kilts for men). Fashion is one field in which timing is perhaps more important than originality.

Antonio del Castillo, a Spanish designer in Paris who stuttered in several languages and who for a time was bankrolled by Gloria Guinness, was very fond of having me up to his flat to prove ("I have the documents!") that whatever new fashion emerged from the couture that season had been done by him five years before. He would pull out copies of sketches filed with the couture's trade association, the Chambre Syndicale de la Haute Couture, and jab a pudgy finger at the lines. "You see," he would announce triumphantly, "I did it first." And usually there was something in what he said.

The point was, Castillo lacked the power to impose a new direction on fashion all by himself. He had the ideas and realized them competently, but his timing was bad. When Castillo broadened shoulders dramatically in a season when Balenciaga, Cardin, Dior, and Chanel all held to the narrow shoulder, the buyers would either avoid the Castillo collection like the plague, or else demand that on the suits he delivered to them the shoulders be cut back by a couple of inches. Then, when the most powerful designers, such as Saint Laurent and Givenchy and Dior, would themselves broaden shoulders eighteen months later, and thus put broad shoulders into the mainstream of fashion, poor Castillo would wail and have me up to the flat and pull out more documents proving how prescient he had been and how dull I was not to have noticed, not to have applauded him in my newspaper.

Paris, and the fashion world generally, is full of Castillos, tugging at your sleeve and whispering how they had been the first to drop hems or round bosoms. Fashion is a business where prophets really are without honor, if they indulge in their prophecies without having the power to impose them on the buyers.

A designer who thinks he was first, and sometimes really was first, to take a new fashion line, can become paranoid about the fashion press. I think it is pretty clear that André Courrèges really put contemporary women into pants. From 1961 on, after he quit as master tailor to Balenciaga and opened his own couture house, Courrèges relentlessly and rather courageously pushed the idea that in a modern world of car and jet travel, it was logical for women to wear pants. He developed a pant shape of his own, the legs tubular and uncreased, usually in white, and those pants became the basis of every collection he's done for the past dozen years. André and I used to lunch down the street from his shop, always with his assistant — and later, wife — and he would go on for hours with messianic fervor about the necessity to modernize clothes. It was an impressive vision that he had, and I wrote it that way, beginning with the first stories ever written about Courrèges and following him through his career. When pants began to catch on, and other designers put pants into their collections, I wrote that Courrèges had indeed carried the day and deserved the credit. Then one day I did an interview with Coco Chanel, who remarked that she herself had worn pants in the 1920's and pulled out some snapshots from the Côte d'Azur to prove it. I wrote this too, and next time I dropped in to see Courrèges he was in a rage.

"All this time that I have fought and suffered to establish the idea of pants for women, and now you turn around and give her [Chanel] credit. It is the basest sort of treachery."

There was no reasoning with André. It was weeks before he cooled down. And even then he was never again as amiable as in the days when we used to go out to the Stade Colombes to see the rugby together and drink beer in the best seats, which Courrèges arranged for and into which we slipped without paying.

All the truly great fashion designers work in an evolutionary manner, one design leading to the next, without an abrupt and revolutionary change that suddenly makes everything in the closet, or in a store's inventory, look dated. There have been two exceptions: Dior's New Look in 1947, which worked, and the mini-midi-maxi controversy of four years ago on which I spend a chapter later in this book.

Dior's New Look was a fashion revolution. But it was a logical one. The world had been in uniform since 1939, fabric had been in short supply, austerity and real shortage followed the end of hostilities, and by 1947 people were ready, whether they knew it or not, for a New Look in clothes. Christian Dior, a master of timing, backed by the cotton empire of Marcel Boussac, dropped skirts almost to the ankle, put as much as twenty-five yards of cloth in a single dress, and single-handedly ended the wartime look and the cloth-saving severity of 1939–1947 fashion. And despite masculine guffaws, within a year all the world's fashion had changed and Dior had won the day.

Even as powerful a fashion influence as Yves Saint Laurent can find himself in difficulty trying to impose a style before the world is ready to absorb it. Following the May 1968 student riots in Paris, Saint Laurent confessed that he found himself depressed by politics and the world situation generally. Out of his depression came what were, for their time, some of the ugliest clothes in years. For several seasons Saint Laurent persisted with a look that he himself described as "the happy whore" — all broad shoulders, short skirts, ankle-strap shoes, vivid, streetwalker makeup, frizzy hair. The press ripped into him, the buyers threw up their hands, and Saint Laurent's American backers (the great perfume house of Lanvin–Charles of the Ritz) fell into an attack of nerves. I considered the clothes ugly and ill-advised and said so repeatedly in the pages of WWD. John Fairchild, a more astute fashion analyst, agreed the clothes were ugly but insisted they were also prophetic. He realized, as did Yves, that France's internal difficulties, the American urban riots, Vietnam, made it impossible for a sensitive designer to turn out "pretty" clothes. Saint Laurent was reacting violently to the world he thought he saw around him. His logical means of protest was through his clothes, and he produced the "happy whore" look. Those of us who criticized Saint Laurent were proven wrong within a year when young women began to pick up the "ugly" look, Seventh Avenue started broadening shoulders, cosmetic firms began to produce vivid red lipsticks and rouge after years of pastels, and the footwear industry came out with the lumpy, blocky, built-up-sole shoes that now even men are wearing. There is no question but that Saint Laurent saw something coming that the rest of us were not sufficiently sensitive to see, but he lost money for the time it took for the "ugly" look to catch on, and whether his "happy whore" was a contribution to civilization, or simply an act of supreme despair is still an open question. Fortunately, a year or two ago, "pretty" came back in style and clothes once again made women look better rather than worse. You will discern this cyclical aspect in fashion through the years, short-long, pretty-ugly, tight-loose.

A couturier will try to do several things with a new collection. The average Paris line will contain anywhere from a hundred to a hundred and eighty models (Cardin is known to present as many as three hundred, but then he can't stop talking either). A good Paris collection will contain a half-dozen dramatic numbers for the fashion press, items that are simple to describe and which are rather different from what went before. No need that they sell; their publicity value is what makes them worth doing. Then there are, hopefully, the fashion "Fords," the important and easily copied numbers for Seventh Avenue to buy and knock off by the millions. Then the private client numbers, the clothes rich women will buy and for which they will undergo unspeakable torture in the fitting room, clothes that because of their intricate cut or hand-detailing are not practical buys for the big American stores and manufacturers with their machine techniques of reproduction. The last group of dresses, and for a professional the most interesting, are the five or six prophetic numbers in which the designer tips his hand to the direction he may take six months from now. At *WWD*, and later at *Harper's Bazaar*, these were always the numbers I tried to feature in order to show the professional reader, and the woman who wanted to know where fashion was headed, what the really creative designers were thinking, where clothes were going.

5

The Legend Called Coco

When I first arrived in Paris I wrote a polite little note to all the designers informing them that I was the new man on the beat and asking if I could drop by and pay my respects. Only Balenciaga, who never saw the press, and Coco Chanel made no response. After some weeks Thelma Sweetinburgh, *WWD*'s Paris fashion editor, telephoned Chanel's secretary to ask why I had not been invited to meet her.

"After all," Thelma said, "Mademoiselle Chanel received Mr. Fairchild."

"Ah," came the response, and Thelma was sure Chanel herself was listening in on another extension, "but Monsieur Fairchild waited three years for that honor."

Thelma hung up the phone and told me she had been on the verge of saying that I was a young man, and could wait, but could Chanel? I was glad she hadn't for a few months later I again asked to see Chanel and she agreed. What began as a brief interview turned into a lunch and a four-hour conversation, dominated, of course, by her.

Coco deserves a book of her own, and there have been a few, and will be more. She wanted me to write that book, using a tape recorder and simply talking with her for a couple of hundred hours. But a couple of hundred hours would not have gotten Coco past her opinion of General de Gaulle or her theories about the cinema, to say nothing of fashion or her own fantastic life, and so I said no, that I hadn't the time, and why didn't she simply do it herself?

I don't know that she took my advice on that or on anything. But that didn't matter. What did matter was that for ten years Coco Chanel influenced me, and through me the publications that I ran, and helped more than any other single person to form my notion of elegance, of culture, of style.

Chanel died on a Sunday evening in January 1971. She was eighty-seven. She had worked all that Saturday on the next collection, to be shown in a fortnight's time, and on the Sunday had been driven out into the countryside for lunch with friends. They got her back into Paris about six and Coco went upstairs to her small fifth-floor suite in the Ritz Hotel on the rue Cambon side, overlooking the gardens. She complained to her maid of not feeling well, said she had difficulty breathing, and within an hour was dead, having rather cleverly avoided a lingering illness or incapacity that would have annoyed her terribly.

I had been in the country for the weekend with my wife and the girls, and when we got back to the apartment Sunday evening the office phoned to tell me the UPI had carried a flash that Chanel was dead. I told them to confirm it with Dryansky, our Paris man, and to hold the paper. When I hung up the phone my wife asked what was wrong.

"Chanel's dead."

"Oh, I'm so sorry." She put her arms around me. "I mean I'm sorry for you. I know how you'll miss her."

When I went down to the paper June Weir, the fashion

editor, and Rudy Millendorf, the art director, were there
ahead of me. We went to work making over page one and
the big inside pages. The standing obituary, which I had
written several years before in Paris, could of course not be
found. I went through my ritual cursing and swearing and
then got behind the typewriter. Mort Sheinman, one of the
senior editors, had come in and he played copyboy. We
pulled together a new obit from the clippings, Miss Weir
reading them to me as I typed, and Millendorf selecting the
photos of Chanel and of her clothes. Other reporters called
around to solicit comments from the fashion people and we
got the paper to bed about an hour late. When I got home
that night, toward midnight, my wife said, "Well, of course
you're going to the funeral." I hadn't thought about it but
now I said, why, yes, of course I was. I had to go.

The next day Freddie Brisson phoned me from, I think,
Cleveland. "Dear boy," he said, "it's just too dreadful. We're
opening here this week. And now for this to occur. We're so
upset, all of us."

I sympathized with Mr. Brisson, who had made a good
deal of money that season with his musical comedy *Coco* on
Broadway and now was launching a national company, also
starring Katharine Hepburn. Was he going to Paris for the
funeral of his old friend?

"There's nowhere I'd rather be, dear boy. But with the
opening here I don't dare leave. She'd want me to stay, to
get the show opened."

I said she would more probably want him to be in Paris
for the last farewell. But Brisson would not be moved. He
and Roz would be represented, of course, but they wouldn't
go.

Neither could anyone else from America, I learned. Of all
the Seventh Avenue manufacturers and the great fashion
stores that had been influenced and inspired by Chanel
clothes through the years, who lived off her commercially, no

one bothered to go. Of course, like Freddie Brisson and Roz Russell, they were represented. Their resident buying office chaps were there. And they sent flowers.

Jerry Dryansky met me at Orly. I asked if everything was arranged for our coverage of the funeral. He said that it was, and added that the funeral arrangements were also in the best of form, that Coco had arranged things long ago, just as she wanted them to be.

A little smile played around Dryansky's mouth. "They say there'll be a German sentry at the Cambon door of the Ritz," he said. The story of Coco and the Germans was such old coin even she laughed about it. We got into a taxi and dropped my bags at the San Regis and went up someplace on Montmartre for a steak and some wine. Dryansky was wheezing with silent mirth, waiting to give me the latest dirt. He had this from a reporter in the office who had it from one of the mannequins at Chanel who had it from . . .

It seemed that one in Chanel's long series of paid companions had been there at the deathbed, had stayed until the relatives arrived, a couple of distant nieces and nephews, and then, exhausted, had left the Ritz Hotel to go home while the relatives watched through the night.

The companion awoke at two o'clock in the morning, remembered that Coco had often promised her one of the rings she wore, dressed and went back across town to the Ritz. She went up to Chanel's suite, excused herself to the drowsy relatives, selected the ring Chanel had promised her, slipped it off Chanel's finger and onto her own, bade the mourners goodnight, and went back home.

We talked about Chanel until well after midnight. I recalled another companion, an impressively dignified lady who was, as they all were at the beginning, "going to organize things for me," as Coco put it. And there was, with this lady as with all the others, the inevitable moment of disillusion when Coco flew into a rage and showed her the door. A few days later I lunched with Chanel and, always enjoying it when I could stir her up a bit, asked innocently where her latest companion was.

"Ah," Chanel said, "that bit of filth. I gave her the door, of course. She wasn't my sort at all. Not at all. I know it so clearly now. Ever since I sacked her she drives her car past the house every afternoon and shouts obscenities at me through the open windows."

Dryansky and I reminisced about her old manager, a corpulent man with the Legion d'Honneur in his buttonhole, and a man who had, apparently, been a devoted and loyal employee for many years. Then he too was fired. When asked about it Chanel claimed he had been stealing from her for years.

"I discovered this hole broken through the wall of the house, right into the next building, and in there he had a team of seamstresses at work all the day long. They carried away the cloth I paid for and the buttons and the lining and everything right through the hole into this pirate's den of his and they were sewing up false Chanels, with real labels. He made a fortune, the *salot*."

The funeral was the next morning, in that big barn of a church called the Madeleine, a few hundred yards from the Ritz and from her couture house. It was cold and gray and the reporters and the television cameras were on the steps of the church, stepping aside every so often to let pass a busload of German tourists.

There was a large flower arrangement from Freddie Brisson and Roz Russell. "*Merde*," I thought. A pride of Rothschilds, the discotheque proprietor Régine, Yves Saint Laurent, people from the theater, the dancer Serge Lifar, journalists, writers, and Jacques Chazot, a sort of French Johnny Carson, went inside. Then Dali arrived, moustaches aquiver, his cane brandished at the appropriate angle for that hour of the day. Out of nowhere, across the great steps of the church, came the companion, she who had stripped the ring from Coco's finger the night of her death. She sprinted to Dali's side, slipped an arm through his, and ascended the steps to the church door as the flashbulbs popped. Dali's eyes darted this way and that, but then they always do, and they entered arm in arm. Just before the Mass began Chanel's mannequins arrived, eight or nine tall blondes, very erect, dressed not in black but in the latest Chanel suits. They walked down the center aisle, with great dignity, and took the front pews usually assigned to the family of the deceased. It was a magnificent moment and I am sure Coco arranged it that way. For they were, those tall slim girls in their Chanel suits, the mannequins of her *cabine*, all the close family she really had at the end.

You could not really be sad about Coco's death but there was one's own sense of loss. We would not again see her like, and those few of us who had been close to her during the last years would in future have to imagine what her earlier life had been like. No longer could we ask, and get in return the marvelous anecdotes she told so well, the cutting mimicry she employed, the precise turn of phrase. I remember once she was being critical of Jacqueline Kennedy (she was always formal, calling her "Mrs. Kennedy") and I asked what she had against the woman. "She wears her daughter's clothes," Coco stated flatly. "A woman in her position should be more dignified." And so she dismissed the then First Lady's efforts at being faddish.

One evening there was dinner for three: Coco, Serge Lifar, and myself. The plump waiter, who would later graduate to become her last confidant, served with the white gloves that were de rigueur, we ate well and drank perhaps too much, and Coco got onto the subject of death.

There had been a rumor through Paris that she was dead and the rumor got to the ears of Pierre Cardin. Cardin and Chanel had not gotten on at all well, and in recent seasons Chanel would wait until Cardin selected a time and date for his fashion opening and would immediately riposte by setting her own show at about the same hour so that buyers and press would have an agonizing choice to make between these two ferocious monsters. Chanel would have her press attaché put out the warning that the doors would be closed promptly at 3:30 so that any reporter who tried to catch the first half of the Cardin show and the second half of Chanel would be foiled. When Cardin heard the rumor of Chanel's demise there was of course great excitement. Nicole Alphand was assigned to telephone the House of Chanel for all the regrettable details. Madame Alphand is a formidable blond beauty, the wife of former ambassador to the United States Hervé Alphand, and a woman who ruled Washington diplomatic society during the Kennedy years. When Nicole called she was startled to hear Coco's own voice answer the telephone. Trained in the diplomatic arts, Nicole stammered out a greeting and then asked if she could come over one day to be fitted for some evening dresses. "Although I must be Madame Cardin by day," Nicole said, "I would like to be Madame Chanel by night in my private life."

"You can be Madame Cardin twenty-four hours a day," Chanel snapped, and hung up.

Coco told the story with exquisite delight, mimicking the various characters, and then grabbed my arm.

"But wait," she said, "it is even worse than that." She spoke French, of course, using the French words for "filth" and "piggishness" as she always did, descending every so often to her ultimate insult, *"zéro à gauche."* She went on to relate that the death rumor had been embroidered so as to make it appear she had died in her little suite in the Ritz during a weekend when no embalmer could be found, and the management of the Ritz, not sure how to handle the situation, had put her corpse into the refrigerator of the Espadon Grill to wait until Monday when the undertakers would be back on the job.

"No," announced Chanel, "when I die I'll simply lie here on the couch for six months or so, only close friends are to be notified, and there'll be none of this filth in the papers or *chez* Monsieur Cardin and that lot." She lay down on the oversized suede couch and folded her arms beatifically across her chest.

"How will we be notified?" I asked.

"Oh, you'll be sent a postcard and you can drop in to see me next time you're in Paris."

I said I hoped the postcard would be sent airmail, that I'd want to be among the first informed. But for Lifar, the aging ballet genius, all this talk of death had gone too far. He crossed over to where Chanel was lying "in state" with her eyes closed and dug both hands into her middle to tickle her. Coco sprang up and chased him through the rooms, laughing all the time. She was then eighty-four or eighty-five years of age.

In an afterpiece to this story, the ex-waiter turned paid companion sued the Chanel estate after her death, claiming he had been promised certain bequests. Later he escalated his claim to the astounding statement that he and Coco had planned to marry. I suggest this is tripe of the basest sort. Chanel had had her lovers and one of them, the English Duke of Westminster, perhaps the richest man in London at the time, had proposed marriage. I had heard this story so many times that I once asked Chanel about her reply. "I told him no," she said. "There were many duchesses but only one Coco Chanel." The Duke had had two yachts but, being nervous on the water, Coco would only travel on the larger. It was a converted British destroyer, painted white, and with a crew of a hundred and eighty. For a woman of her caliber to wed the fat, unlettered ex-waiter would have been an obscene rejection of everything that had been before.

Even in her later years Chanel never became a recluse. She ate many of her meals in the Espadon Grill of the Ritz, out in full view of the other patrons, ordering up a particular Russian vodka from the cellars because it went especially well with the season's smoked salmon, nodding to passersby and chatting with anyone who screwed up the courage to come and say hello. But she rarely went out at night, preferring to give small dinner parties in her apartment over the fashion establishment at number 31 rue Cambon or in the Ritz Grill. One summer's evening, it must be seven or eight years ago, John Fairchild and I inveigled her into accompanying us to a party given by Suzanne Luling, who had once been Christian Dior's sales *directrice* and was now a sort of fashion consultant and Paris gadfly. I don't know why Chanel agreed to go — she had turned down so many invitations — but she did, and we drove in her limousine across Paris in the soft summer evening with the wonderful light just fading in the west and the buildings not yet illuminated for the night. The chauffeur delivered us at the Left Bank address and we went through the big wooden doors into one of those murky courtyards, half corridor and half vestibule, that you find in old Paris buildings, lined with garbage cans and scribbled notices from the concierge. Coco was in splendid form. As we got to the marble staircase leading up to the Luling apartment John and I instinctively took her by an arm to assist her up the steps. Chanel leaned heavily against us and proposed playfully that we boost her onto our shoulders. "Then we can really make an entrance," she suggested.

Inside the apartment the party was in full flight: a British rock group, American buyers, the fashion press, pretty girls, a couple of minor Paris designers (the important ones only attend parties given for them), and the bustling, buxom Madame Luling shouting hoarsely from room to room. Everyone was drinking champagne. As we came in, those nearest the door, those who saw Chanel first, fell silent, and the quiet crept across the room until even the rock band stopped playing. Chanel just stood there between her two young Americans until Suzanne Luling recovered from her shock to sprint to Chanel, embrace her, and lead her into the room. Coco was placed on a couch where she held court, this one and that being brought up to greet her, and when the waiter brought a tray of champagne glasses she waved him away.

"What will you have?" Madame Luling inquired, her face glistening with triumph, her party suddenly the season's best.

"*Bière*," Coco announced loudly, and a man was sent off to fetch it from, it turned out, the servants' quarters, which boasted the only bottle of beer in the place.

Another night, as we left the Maison Chanel to walk the hundred yards up the street to the Ritz, Coco complained that she was tired. I picked her up in my arms and staggered across the rue Cambon, John whooping and hollering with delight, and Chanel laughing and clinging tight around my neck.

Chanel knew the value of a good quote. When I asked her what she thought of the mini skirt, when it became popular in the mid-sixties, she sneered. "*C'est un exhibition de viande*," she said. "It's a show of meat." She called Courrèges's clothes "the most ridiculous thing in Paris."

For one season she dressed Brigitte Bardot and BB looked quite fashionable for a time. Then they had a falling out and BB went back to her tight dresses and short skirts. I asked Coco what she thought of Bardot's body. "She has marvelous legs and here it is very nice too [stroking her buttocks]. But up top . . . it is too much."

She had also dressed Romy Schneider and when Romy started to buy clothes somewhere else, Chanel said she was not surprised. "After all, she's just a little Swiss milkmaid."

No matter how polite they may be in public, most designers hate all other designers and will be beastly about them privately. Chanel was no exception. During her final years the coming star was Yves Saint Laurent. Although Saint Laurent has a style of his own, it was clear that Chanel's work had influenced his technique, and there were some super-ficial similarities between his clothes and those designed by the great Chanel. Yves was quite frank about this, saying on one occasion that "Chanel is the godmother of us all." Coco had heard the talk, and seen pictures of the Saint Laurent clothes, and one day she said to me for quotation, "Monsieur Saint Laurent has very good taste. And the more he copies me, the better taste he displays."

Although she was capable of a verbal shaft into the sensitive hide of a Saint Laurent, her really vulnerable targets were Cardin and Antonio del Castillo, the rather pompous but competent designer for the great old House of Lanvin. Castillo, a Spaniard ("My name is a very old one," he would tell you. "It means 'of Castille.' "), had a bad stutter and though he spoke four or five languages, I could rarely understand him in any of them. He had once worked, many years earlier, as an assistant designer under Chanel. I asked her once about his work, whether he had been an important cog in the Chanel design studio. "He held the pins," she answered, thus dismissing Castillo's claim that he had kept the old lady going almost single-handed.

Whatever the origin of their feud — perhaps it was simply that Castillo had once worked for her and was now in competition — the ill-feeling was genuine. Chanel once told me a classic story about the evening of a very social summer party held in the formal gardens of one of the great Paris houses near the Étoile. Coco wore one of her flowing chiffon evening dresses and was startled to see Castillo coming across the garden toward her. He asked her to dance, and not wishing to create a scene, Chanel stepped into his arms. The garden was decorated with tall, lighted candles and as they danced, according to Chanel, "I found him steering me toward the candles. I had visions of my chiffons going up in flames like a moth."

For all her sophistication and wit, Chanel had as many

biases and silly prejudices as any of us. "We went to the cinema last night," she would say, "and a black man came and sat near us. We had to move, he smelled so. They have a distinctive odor, you know." Then at another time, unpredictably, she would tell you of "this great American boxer I knew years ago. He was black. Oh, how we danced, that man and I." Some of her closest friends were Rothschilds and yet Chanel blamed most of France's political troubles, and sometimes the bad weather, on the Jews. "They're behind it, you know."

I am still not quite sure what Chanel's position was during the war and the German occupation. She had shut down her couture house and gone into retirement the year before World War II began, so there was no question, as with so many other French couture houses, of collaborating simply to be able to stay in business. There are stories that she had a German officer as a lover, which is certainly possible, but beyond any doubt she disapproved of de Gaulle and the French Resistance. "It was France that asked for an armistice," she would explain, "and therefore any Frenchman who broke the armistice was a criminal. He was breaking the law of France." You could not convince her that her position, while legalistically correct, was ethically in error.

Although Coco favored the Vichy regime during the occupation, she told me of once having been arrested in the South of France by the Vichy police.

"I went for a stroll from my house to a small village nearby and because the roads were bad and it was winter, I was wearing trousers. The police arrested me and said it was against Marshal Pétain's rules that women should wear pants. I made a protest, *bien sûr*, but they ordered me to change into a dress or go to prison. It seemed that *le maréchal* Pétain believed that women in pants gave a militant image to the conquered France he wanted to become pacifist in every respect."

Coco shrugged, "Well, *we* made the armistice, not the Germans."

Serge Lifar was one of Coco's great *copains* during my time. Later, Pierre Galante would describe a wonderful scene in his book about Chanel. It seemed that when Diaghilev died, Chanel and the Duke of Westminster were sailing nearby and they put into Venice for the funeral. Lifar and several other Russians made up the funeral cortege with Chanel. The Russians decided, as a tribute to the late master, that they would follow the casket on their knees all the way to the graveyard. Weeping and groaning, they slowly and painfully made their way inch by inch to the place of burial. Chanel went along with these excesses for what she thought a seemly time. Then she impatiently snapped her fingers and ordered the grieving Russians to their feet. Stiff-legged and clearly relieved, the men got up and the procession made its way speedily to the grave.

When Brisson and Alan Lerner had their musical version of *Coco* nearly ready for Broadway, there was a good deal of talk about who could play the title role. Various names were tossed about. Chanel told me she favored a European, either Romy Schneider, Julie Christie, or Melina Mercouri. When Brisson proposed his own wife, Rosalind Russell, Chanel vetoed her after one dinner with the couple. "Madame Brisson talks too much," she told me. She was pleased when Katharine Hepburn got the role, especially after Hepburn came to her apartment and spent a day asking questions and listening to Chanel's answers. You did not make points with Coco by talking yourself. She liked Alan Lerner and said her only concern was that she did not want her life to be turned into a "My Fair Coco."

When I was in Paris the summer before *Coco* was to open, Chanel suggested that I write a television special which would be a "real" report on her work and her philosophy and which could run counterpoint to the "musical" version by Lerner.

I thought it a splendid idea and Chanel signed a personal contract with me. I asked what sort of money she wanted for the rights and she said she wanted nothing except my promise that I would handle the story and control the product myself. "I trust you," she said.

I hurried back to New York with her contract and met with the television experts at Capital Cities Broadcasting Corporation which was, by this time, the parent company of Fairchild Publications and so my employer. They liked the idea and assigned a producer to the project and he began recruiting a director and crew. The producer and I trekked around to the various advertising agencies trying to find a sponsor. It was my plan that we would run the hour-long special the night before *Coco* was to open on Broadway. We never got there. No one seemed interested enough to put up the money. A year and a half later, when she was dead, one of the ad agencies called me.

"Say," said the television buyer, "did you people ever do that film of Chanel? We'd like to run it now."

Merde, I say again.

6

Publisher of
WOMEN'S WEAR DAILY

On Columbus Day, 1964, we left Paris. There was a boat train out of Paris that evening and my wife and the two girls and I had a compartment. Mary Alexeieff, our nurse, and Pierre Schildge, a textile company executive, came down to see us off. Pierre brought wine and we all cried a bit. We had lived more than four years in France and were leaving a part of us behind. After six years of Europe, we would again be home.

Having paid my dues to the profession I came back to New York to become publisher of *WWD*. John Fairchild was being groomed to take control of the company from his father. The elder Fairchild, a handsome man who had his own view of how to run newspapers and sometimes acknowledged his distaste for our way, had instituted a mandatory sixty-five-year retirement age. His own father, one of the founders, had refused to retire when it was obvious he should have. Now Louis Fairchild, still in full vigor, was snared by his own regulation and John took over the company.

It wasn't the same company he and I had joined in the fifties. WWD wasn't the same. When I came to the paper its editor was a courtly old gentleman named Earl Elhart. Mr. Elhart was a good newspaperman of the old school, but with no flair. At his morning editorial meetings he would count the number of stories on page one and encourage the makeup editor to get one or two more on page one the next day. It didn't matter if you ran only a paragraph before jumping inside. The more stories on page one, the better the paper looked to Mr. Elhart. He was opposed to pictures.

When John was still in Paris, I think it was in 1957, Balenciaga and Givenchy created the chemise dress, or, as it was first called, the sack. It was a genuinely important fashion development, a radical turn away from the marked waist of the standard shirtwaist dress that had been popular for a decade. Fairchild wheedled and pleaded with Givenchy to let WWD have a sketch, and when Givenchy finally gave in, John raced across town and, for the first time ever, wire-photoed the picture to New York with a long and detailed explanation of its significance. He urged that it be published as large as possible on the front page. "I almost burst into tears when the paper arrived," he told me later. "They'd run it two inches high on an inside page.'"

During the fifties there were bright young women on the staff because it was natural for young women to be attracted to a fashion newspaper. But the men were there because they couldn't get jobs on the *Times* or the *Daily News* or the *Wall Street Journal*. *Women's Wear Daily* was held in such small esteem that there were men on the staff who would tell you they worked somewhere else. This was unfair to the paper even then. It lacked panache but it performed a solid reporting function and kept its advertising and editorial employees on different floors. But such men as Frank Engle, an old Hearst reporter who covered ship news, hated the idea of working for a publication that bore such a pink-tea title. Once when I found myself covering a press conference side by side with Engle, he grabbed my arm and whispered hoarsely from under his waxed moustache, "If you must say anything, tell them you work for the Fairchild News Service. Don't mention the paper."

When Engle went on vacation I filled in for him on the ship news beat, taking the customs lighter out from lower Manhattan at dawn to meet the great steamers as they paused off the Staten Island quarantine. Except for the early rising, it was a pleasant and diverting job. You had two or three hours before docking to hunt down the passengers you wanted to interview. The pursers gave you accurate lists, and incoming travelers, relaxed after five days at sea, were usually amenable to questions. It was on one of these jaunts down the harbor that I first met the Windsors, and on another that I got a marvelous insight into the character of newspaper photographers. It seems that whenever a minor movie star or somewhat traveled glamour girl was aboard, the cameramen competed for the best cheesecake photos — perched on the rail with plenty of leg showing, that sort of thing. But whenever they came across a girl who seemed more than usually cooperative, they descended to her cabin to get some nude and occasionally erotic pictures for their private collection. Goggle-eyed, I asked one of the photographers if women weren't repelled by the idea. "Naw," he assured me. "Most of them love to show it off and anyway, we always promise to get them a good play in tomorrow's paper with the rail shots."

As the North Atlantic steamship trade went into decline and the transatlantic jets took over, Engle spent more time at the airports. He met and interviewed arriving and departing business executives and also tried to be helpful with the customs formalities when one of the Fairchild family or one of the company's publishers was coming in. I learned after painful experience to rely on my own resources. As you struggled manfully toward the customs gates with your luggage, Engle would arrive, raincoat flapping, the *Daily News* stuffed into his pocket (I assume he was still denying any association with *WWD*), hat on the back of his head. "Right this way," he would shout, and promptly direct you to the longest line. Then he'd collar the first customs man who passed, get his first name wrong, and tell him out of the corner of his mouth, "This is my publisher. Got to get him through fast." The customs man would see a young man in a leather jacket and turtleneck sweater lugging a Valpack and looking like an exchange student straight out of steerage class. As he attempted to pull away, Engle would hiss, "I'm a pal of the commish." That was generally enough to drive the customs man into a rage which resulted in a microscopic examination of my goods, almost to the point of squeezing out the last of my toothpaste lest it conceal a fortune in industrial diamonds or enough hashish to satiate Chinatown.

A few years ago I had to spend a Friday in Los Angeles and decided to stretch the one-day trip into a weekend, seeing friends and playing golf. I lugged along the bagful of clubs, was duly waved off at Kennedy by Engle, did my business in Los Angeles, played my golf on Saturday and flew home Sunday. On Monday John Fairchild summoned me. "Your friend Engle came right back and went up to see Edgar. He told him you were playing golf on company time." Since Edgar Fairchild was then chairman of the board I should have been impressed, but by then I was the publisher who was producing the biggest profits in the company and I simply made a mental note to chew out Engle and to use Newark airport next time.

In the sixties, papers proliferated, the company grew past thirty million dollars a year in sales, and *WWD* became the most talked-about little sheet in the country. It used to be that *WWD* would be described as the *Variety* of fashion. In the sixties you would more often hear *Variety* referred to as a sort of WWD of show business. John was put on the cover of *Time*, profits rose, and the Fairchild family decided to sell the company, for more than forty million dollars in cash and stock, to Capital Cities Broadcasting Corporation.

I prospered as well. As publisher of the glamour paper, WWD, and also of *Daily News Record*, the textile and men's wear paper, later as editorial director of the entire chain, as a senior vice-president of Fairchild and as vice-president of Capital Cities, the authority and responsibilities and titles I wanted became mine. There were other perquisites. A willing speaker and more approachable to some interviewers than the shyer John Fairchild, I basked in a certain amount of pleasant and generally favorable publicity. John's father, Louis, made occasional cracks about those who read their own press notices. I smiled indulgently. It was exciting stuff. WWD, as it was now officially known, was twitting the White House. I was sending telegrams to the President's press secretary and releasing the text to the Associated Press as I did so, and along Seventh Avenue the designers trembled. One evening there was a television panel show on which David Susskind asked designer Mollie Parnis if she read WWD in the morning or after she got home at night. "In the morning," Mollie responded quickly. "If I read it at night I can't sleep." It was on the same program that Susskind pointed to me and asked Pauline Trigère, "Is this man really so terrifying to you?'" "Absolutely," Pauline shot back.

I don't recall what it was that terrified poor Pauline, but I remember very well the incident that shook Mollie Parnis. La Grenouille, on New York's East Fifty-second Street, is one of the two or three finest restaurants in the country. Its owner, Charles Masson, is not only a great chef but a diplomatic host. John Fairchild and Mollie were lunching at La Grenouille one day — separate tables, you understand — when the Duchess of Windsor arrived with friends and took her table. The royal party was several tables away from that of Mollie

Parnis. It should be made clear that Mollie has always believed in the divine right of kings. She makes the clothes for any First Lady within reach, and since the White House is the only substitute we have for Buckingham Palace, she will go there at the drop of an invitation. Paul, the Swiss headwaiter, was summoned to Mollie, there was a moment's whispered conversation, and *voilà*, her table was moved so that she was, as John reported in the next day's WWD, within earshot of the Duchess. When the item appeared the Duchess didn't seem at all perturbed, Mollie was indignant in her denials, and headwaiter Paul submitted a resignation of honor to Monsieur Masson. There was a shout of laughter throughout the fashion community as Mollie continued to insist that she had wanted the table moved for logistic, rather than nosy, reasons, and M. Masson, the most sensible man on the scene, declined his headwaiter's resignation with a cautionary rap on the knuckles.

Although both John and I needled the sensitive souls of the fashion business unmercifully, reasoning that there was nothing they preferred reading about more than themselves, we also needled one another. Our relationship was an extraordinary one: we were so alike in age (he was two years older) and so disparate in our backgrounds, but as one in our ambitions for the newspaper. Mrs. Gilbert (Kitty) Miller, often a victim of WWD's acerbic comments, was once quoted as saying that she was sure John Fairchild was quite bright, but "he has no manners." Kitty may have had something there, but I suspect that what really upset women like her, women of a certain age and standing in the social structure, was that they were accustomed to polite young men who would hang around and pass canapés, mix drinks, serve as the "extra man" at dinner parties, and perform the usual court eunuch functions. I don't think they ever understood Fairchild, or myself, because we didn't fit into that comfortable and easily understood, and dominated, category. For one thing, we weren't climbers, had no social ambitions. John, to the manor born, was there already. I, born in Brooklyn, product of an unfashionable college, simply didn't give a damn. This social disinterestedness made us stronger than many of the people with whom we dealt, permitted us to assault the Establishment without having to worry what it would cost us in canceled dinner invitations or lost rungs on the social ladder. As for the fashion world, the newspaper's financial solidity, its profitability, insulated us against the sort of advertising pressure the poor fashion magazines suffered, and submitted to, every day.

As the newspaper grew stronger, made more money, and was more widely quoted by other journalists, the competition between John and myself became more intense, usually leavened by the genuine delight we took in the work. Only Bill Dwyer, a young Notre Dame graduate who had been the company's lawyer and then joined us as an executive and later as a publisher, could trade insults with the joyous verve of Brady versus Fairchild. We mimicked one another, our children got to know one another, and when John published a book he paid me gracious tribute. Of course on Seventh Avenue it was said we were lovers. This simply added to the fun, and I recalled that first lunch in Paris when the press attaché of the French couture warned me to be circumspect in my conduct now that I was to live and work in Paris. "You know," she told a wide-eyed newcomer, "they say John had orgies with animals when he lived here. Mind you, I don't believe it. But it's what they say." I phoned Fairchild in New York. "You never told me about the animals," I complained.

The real differences between John and me frequently created confusion among the staff. There was one splendid incident in early 1968 when I came hustling back from lunch to write a glowing paragraph for the EYE gossip column on how vibrant and confident Bobby Kennedy had appeared to me that day at La Grenouille. Next day John sent through a paragraph describing Bobby as listless and nervy when *he* saw the candidate somewhere else. If this muddled our own reporters and editors, you wondered what the piece-goods buyer of the May Company in Cleveland made of it all as he pored over *WWD* looking for price information on domestic worsteds.

I don't want to give the impression that our work was all fun and games or that Fairchild and I put out the newspaper in a loft building with the part-time aid of palsied retainers running a hand press. The truth was that Fairchild Publications produced serious newspapers in a half-dozen trade fields and that most of these publications were considered dominant in those fields. The company employed more than a thousand people, had some forty news bureaus, including a dozen in Europe and Asia, and spent from seven to eight million dollars a year just on the physical gathering and transmission of news. Our Washington bureau, at the time I worked there, had twenty-one reporters, several of them prize-winning journalists, and was the largest news bureau in the capital after the wire services and the *New York Times*. *WWD* itself, for all of its chichi and gossip and headline hunting, was successful because it told forty thousand retailers every business day what they had to know to make buying and other decisions. While it got a reputation for being the most assiduous Jackie-watcher in the country, its reporters went about the more serious business of reporting advance information on fiber price changes at Du Pont or Monsanto, the plans of one great store group to buy another, and which company president was about to be fired and didn't know it yet. The paper's fashion coverage was unmatched, the fur market would have found it difficult to function without *WWD*'s daily price quotations cabled from the Helsinki and London auctions, reporters filed daily market information from Port Elizabeth, South Africa, and Bradford, England, on the cost of wool, and the Tokyo bureau occasionally scared hell out of American textile mills with accurate estimates of the increasing level of Japanese fabric exports to the United States.

An interview with an irritated Truman Capote as he waited for a plane at a Texas airport might run cheek by jowl with a sophisticated appraisal of the merchandising techniques of Federated Department Stores. Whatever the mix of society chat, fashion predictions, social criticism, and accurate business news, the formula worked. Fairchild insisted on one thing: that the paper stress stories with impact, print news that would influence the decision-makers. "Influence those who influence others," he said. And we did.

The journalism John Fairchild and I peddled in *Women's Wear Daily* wasn't the New Journalism of Tom Wolfe and Gay Talese and Roger Kahn and Frances Fitzgerald. It was instead a pretty old-fashioned variety, a journalism that derived from traditional roots, that smacked more of big-city police reporting, of garter-sleeved deskmen and baggy-pants reporters. But we worked at it very hard, we hired the best people we could get, we refused to knuckle under to advertiser pressure, snubbed the press agents, sweated over deadlines and picture captions and better, clearer ways to inform. We told it as best we could and we never forgot the only person we had to please was the man or the woman who stopped by the newsstand to buy what we were selling.

A couple of years ago Walter Winchell called John at home and proposed that his column run in *WWD*. Winchell was washed up, everyone knew it — except, I suppose, Winchell. The *Mirror* folded under him, the *Journal-American* was gone, there were no more Hearst papers in New York, and no one else wanted him. Winchell was finished when he went down to Washington to cover one of the big Senate hearings, wearing his hat in the committee room, and someone went over to him and told him to take it off. Winchell should have known then he was through. But he was still a name and John was excited about his call. It was clear Winchell desperately wanted a New York outlet. Winchell wanted to go up to Connecticut to see John at home, to convince him. John found it difficult to say no to people even in the sanctity of the office. At home he would be a marshmallow. He stalled Winchell, asked him to call back Monday when I would be there and we could all discuss it.

When Winchell called John picked up one phone and I took the extension.

"I'm a newsboy, Mr. Fairchild," Winchell said. "I stand on the corner and sell newspapers. That's what I do. And I can sell your newspaper. Just a newsboy, that's all I am."

We said no to Winchell, of course, but I never forgot what he said. And when he died a few years later I remembered that familiar, rasping voice: "I'm a newsboy. I stand on the corner and sell newspapers."

There was a period in the mid-sixties when *WWD*'s influence, and John Fairchild's personal authority, had grown so great that even the *New York Times* turned to him for advice. Elizabeth Penrose Hawkins, women's page and fashion editor of the *Times* since the era of the bustle, was to retire. The *Times* was casting about for a successor and its managing editor, Clifton Daniel, called John to ask his opinion. John immediately nominated the *Times*'s own Charlotte Curtis, a diminutive, aggressive, and stylish young feature writer who made no secret of her belief that while women were interested in fashion, they were interested in a great deal more as well. Curtis got the job, because of or despite John's endorsement, and began to turn the *Times*'s women's pages into what they are today: a little fashion, a little food, a little home furnishings, and a great deal of cutting and incisive commentary on the world beyond. It was Charlotte Curtis who broke the story on Leonard and Felicia Bernstein's Park Avenue reception for the Black Panthers, a sociological confrontation so grotesque that it would many months later become the occasion for Tom Wolfe's *Radical Chic*.

The business of promoting your own paper by getting other papers to write about it occupied a good deal of my thinking time both at *WWD* and at *Bazaar*. You wanted to get it done, but you mustn't *seem* to be trying to do it. And you must never, as a journalist, get yourself confused with a public relations man. Fairchild's notorious opposition to public relations people was not based on aesthetic or moral grounds but on the more practical rationale that if public relations departments were really doing their job, independent and aggressive journalists could not do theirs. The role of P.R. is to get good stories in the paper and to keep out the bad. This is simplistic, but you know what I mean. And an effective P.R. campaign could also cut into a newspaper's advertising revenues. More than one Seventh Avenue fashion house refused to advertise in *WWD* because "we get all the free space we want. Our P.R. lady gets us plenty of coverage." Whenever John Fairchild or I heard that, we made sure that particular house was not again mentioned for a considerable period of time.

But though we were opposed to public relations for other people, we had no reluctance to practice the art ourselves. It was our belief the publicity machine was out there to be used, and, if necessary, to be taken. Our little newspaper, with a circulation never larger than eighty-five thousand, had an impact much greater than that of mass circulation papers because we scored impressive news beats and got other publications to talk about them. While both John and I would have rolled our eyes innocently toward heaven were we accused of practicing public relations, we did in fact practice it and rather effectively. Both *Time* and *Newsweek* were important to *WWD*. Douglas Auchincloss, who ran the "People" page at *Time*, and Bill Roeder, his counterpart at *Newsweek*, were regular recipients of calls from Fairchild or me with tips on stories we were about to break and which conceivably, with full credit to *WWD*, might make the deadline in one or both of the newsweeklies. We also worked closely with Barbara

Walters of the NBC-TV "Today" show, with several of the talk show hosts at WOR radio, especially Jack O'Brian, with Barry Gray of WMCA, and others. We fed them and they credited us. It was as efficient and as logical as you could get and cost us nothing. We once thought we'd become even more efficient if we hired a first-rate public relations man, Joseph Hanley, an ad agency vice-president who had done the promotional chores for WCBS radio and, earlier, for Macy's New York. But it was all too much for John Fairchild, it smacked of P.R., and the talented Hanley was switched into Fairchild's syndication operation and later into advertising. At *Harper's Bazaar* I would follow the same "good ole boy" technique, tugging at my forelock and pleading my ignorance of sophisticated public relations, and getting many of our stories and pictures picked up by greater journals, and by television, and getting the name of the magazine out across the country at little cost and minor effort on my part.

If this book is a story about people, it is also a story about power. Power in miniature, to be sure, but power nonetheless. When John Fairchild became publisher of *Women's Wear Daily* in 1960, and I took his place as Paris bureau chief and began writing regularly on fashion for the first time, we decided to avoid strict constructionism in our fashion reportage. We wrote about the clothes but we wrote more about the people. Not just the designers but the fabric and fiber men who supplied their stuff, the store buyers and Seventh Avenue manufacturers who bought the clothes and the reproduction rights, the journalists and publicists who fluttered around the fashion flame, the rich and glamorous women who bought the clothes and set trends, the rich husbands who paid for the clothes, the slim young men who cuckolded those husbands, the restaurants, the galleries, the resorts and the country houses where the clothes were worn. Fashion, we reasoned, was more than clothes. It was the spirit that went into their creation, the money, sometimes very large money, that was involved in their distribution, and the people who wore the clothes, or were worn by them.

Of course, there are different sorts of power. The President and Henry Ford and William Paley and the Pope possess absolute power. Such men may be answerable to the electorate, to God, or to boards of directors, but you understand what I mean. Derivative power, on the other hand, resides with Lee Iaccoca, who runs Ford for Mr. Henry, Dr. Kissinger, a hundred or so cardinals, and various CBS vice-presidents. Few journalists have real power — unless they're Punch Sulzberger whose family owns the *New York Times* or Kay Graham who owns *Newsweek* and the *Washington Post* or the Chandler family in Los Angeles. What the rest of us have is leverage. The theory of judo is to use your opponent's weight and strength and thrust against him — in effect, to arrange that he topples himself. The journalist rarely topples anyone, but through the leverage of his words, using the power of the powerful, he occasionally moves mountains. What we moved in the arena of fashion journalism were more often molehills, but by God, we moved them. And once in a great while, just often enough, it was more than molehills.

Roy Howard once said that the job of a newspaper was to "print the news and raise hell." Journalists are supposed to be at odds with the Establishment, with privilege and with power, to develop and maintain an adversary relationship with government at all levels. Once a publication becomes cozy with those in power, it ceases to influence them, having abandoned its lever for a familiarity it mistakes for a slice of power. Louis Fairchild, John's father and a man of almost ponderous dignity, once heard me out as I related a tale of woe involving the Du Pont company, which then contributed about 5 percent of Fairchild's total revenues. There had been a serious difference of opinion over a story we had carried that Du Pont felt was unfair and damaging. I told Louis that as publisher of *Women's Wear Daily* I was going down to Wilmington to hear out the complaint and to present the newspaper's rationale. "I'm afraid if they don't buy it, they could pull out all their advertising," I told him. He questioned me closely on the merits of the argument, wished me well, and said, "Well, if it comes to it we'll just have to get along without their money." Fortunately the Du Pont people were reasonable and we reached an accommodation without suffering the penultimate publishing blow, a cancelled advertising contract.

Not every newspaper proprietor or executive values editorial integrity over advertiser contentment. A *Cleveland Press* editor a few years ago told me there were rumors that a big local department store, Halle Brothers, would be sold. I said I had heard the reports and *WWD* was following the story. "If you run anything on it," he suggested, "let us know so we can pick it up from you. Then Halle won't blame us." Halle Brothers was, of course, a big advertiser for Cleveland papers. But that year the same editor was serving as a juror on the Pulitzer committee and would be voting to select which were the most courageous and enterprising newspapers in the country.

What the wretched fellow didn't understand is that you don't run an aggressively honest and independent newspaper out of altruism or because you are more moral than the other chap. You do it because independence is essential to the levering of the powerful. Once the advertisers own a paper, the paper ceases to have any influence on them.

The Fairchilds had no corner on virtue. I know for a fact that such men as Ben Bradlee of the *Washington Post*, Mike O'Neill of New York's *Daily News*, and Abe Rosenthal of the *New York Times* simply won't tolerate advertising department influence. And there are surely other newspaper and magazine editors throughout the country equally as fierce in their attitude toward what is legitimate news and what belongs in the paid advertisements. But there are other publications, some of them large and apparently powerful, that will sell out every time and whose reporters might as well be carrying around rate cards along with their notebooks.

You don't learn this sort of thing at journalism school — you learn it by working at your trade. Among publishers it is not considered very good form to have been a working journalist. Publishers are uneasy with journalists. Publishers like to talk among themselves of advertising. And advertising is too serious a matter to be discussed with men whose main concern is printing the truth. Most publishers are men of business, of ledger books and bottom lines, men who've come up on the sales side of things, who have mastered the black art of sales management, survived the intramural feuds, and made their quotas. Serious men. As a publisher, I was a throwback.

When I became publisher of *WWD* I learned that we were feuding, for reasons unclear to anyone, with Jimmy Galanos, a spindly Greek who works in Los Angeles. Reasoning that I would stir up my own feuds, I phoned Galanos in California to make peace. He was terribly stuffy over the phone, giving this reason and that for not coming to terms. Dramatically (I had probably lunched well) I announced, "I'll fly out to see you." "When?" "Tomorrow." And so I did and the feud was ended. Galanos confessed to me that he couldn't recall what had started it either.

In January 1965 there was a subway strike in New York and like many citizens I rented a bicycle to get to work. Norman Norell was riding high then and late one afternoon it was necessary that I see Norell and go over some pictures to publish the next day. Cursing the cold and the traffic I rode my bike up to Seventh Avenue, trundled it into the elevator, and on reaching Norell's floor remounted and rode into the salon. "I'll be goddamned," said Norell, and he approved the pictures without looking at them.

One area in which *Women's Wear Daily* failed, I think, to

do the aggressive job we should have done was in exposing gangster influence in the fashion business and especially in the Seventh Avenue garment district. Looking back on the six years during which I was responsible for the newspaper, I find it indefensible that I did not press for some really sustained investigative reporting on garment industry rackets. We got off occasional shots at Seventh Avenue crime but never really came to grips with the problem in a coherent and sustained manner. And don't think there isn't crime in the garment industry. I remember, during one of my intermittent spurts of enthusiasm for a muckraking series on crime, that Mort Sheinman, one of the paper's most talented young editors, reported back that he had asked several of his Seventh Avenue sources who was still running the garment rackets. "This guy looked around very carefully to see if we were alone," Mort told me, "and when he was sure there was no one close, he held out three fingers. That's all, just the three fingers, no words." The three fingers referred, of course, to Three-Finger Brown, a Mafia chieftain of unimpeachable credentials and a man said to have run, for many years, whatever shadowy enterprises flourished along that colorful stretch of Manhattan Island.

I once tried to hire a special investigative reporter, a man who had functioned in that terrain for the lately deceased *Herald Tribune*, but John Fairchild vetoed the notion. "We can't afford a man who might not produce a story for months," he chided me. It is to my shame that I didn't insist on hiring the chap. It was, after all, a year in which *WWD*'s operating profit was $2,881,906. We were planning to pay the investigative legman some $20,000, as I recall.

Frequently over a meal I would ask a Bill Blass or a Sydney Gittler of Ohrbach's or a Jerry Silverman how deeply the rackets infested Seventh Avenue, who called the shots, where the action was. In his own way, each told me to forget the story, that *WWD* was doing well enough, that I had a wife and children, and so did the reporters who would have to do the job.

If we fell down on the job of exposing Seventh Avenue crime, and we did, we put up a better performance on reporting the more subtle forms of Seventh Avenue chiseling. We wrote about the sweetheart contracts by which workers won union representation but got none of the benefits because the Locals' officers were being paid off by management to maintain labor peace and low wages. Our fur market reporters wrote about the "illegitimate" shops which worked furs with nonunion labor in the most highly unionized city in the country. There were stories about reformed thugs who were now respectable garment moguls and able to operate ex union because the union chiefs owed them favors from head-breaking days long past. I didn't even bother with the hijacking of trucks on the Jersey Turnpike, or pilferage from elevators or loading platforms, or the bribes to cops on the beat to look the other way when trucks double-parked. These matters no longer made news.

A venial sin along Seventh Avenue was the selling of clothes wholesale, especially on Saturdays. The New York stores hate the practice, reasoning that their suppliers should not be in competition with them. But the practice went on throughout the year, peaking on those pleasant Saturdays during the Easter shopping season, when a seemingly endless stream of women, young and old, trekked in and out of the Seventh Avenue skyscrapers, "buying wholesale." WWD sent a crew of photographers out one sunny Saturday and the following Monday published two pages of close-ups of Saks, Bonwit's, and Bergdorf customers saving money on Seventh Avenue. The manufacturers whose cardboard boxes could be identified were furious. The stores were delighted. And not one woman sued for having been held up to ridicule.

It is going out and getting the news, and helping create it when times are slow, that makes good journalism. Sitting back and waiting for releases to rewrite is certain death in this business today. *Vogue* and *Bazaar* used to cover the Paris collections after the fact and get the photos in their issues two months afterwards. When I moved over to the magazine business, I found a way of getting the designers to show us things in advance, before even the buyers got there. I eventually cut the *Bazaar* lead time down from two months to one. One month is still too long and it is why *WWD*, with its daily wirephotos from Paris and Rome, has become such a factor in fashion reporting over the past decade. Television once it learns how to interpret fashion and get it off the traditional and boring runway, will be even faster than *WWD*. I was always appalled when the *New York Times*, with its late deadlines, would permit *WWD* to scoop it by twenty-four hours simply by not filing from the evening collections in Rome until the next morning. Using the six-hour time difference between Italy and New York, *WWD* consistently got photos and sketches and fashion critiques into the next morning's paper. Had I been running the *Times* I would have shaken the fashion people out of that sort of complacency. And I shudder to think what John Fairchild would have done.

Fashion designers and some retailers will complain that the fashion press has too much power. They say that *Vogue* and *Bazaar*, in their prime, could make or break a designer or a new fashion. And that *WWD* today has that same power, that it uses its power capriciously to prop up its favorites and to destroy those who do not cooperate.

That is stuff and nonsense. Of course a good review can help and a bad review can hurt. But I believe that quality endures. A good designer will get to the top regardless of the press and bad designers will go broke no matter how much cheering goes on among the editors. I once wrote a headline about what I felt was an especially poor Givenchy collection: GIVENCHY IS FLOP ART. Hubert not only survived but prospered. Another time, when Marc Bohan did a poor job one season for Dior, I wrote overdramatically that Marc was finished. That was ten years ago and Bohan is today more successful than ever. And we have backed, with extravagant praise, losers who eventually drifted out of the business and into fashion oblivion.

Norman Norell, perhaps the greatest of the American fashion designers, tried to pull the same trick himself once with a protégé from Alice, Texas, named John Moore. Moore was a blond young man who later took to wearing a wig. He had a season or two of promise and Norell began boosting him for the prestigious Coty Award, a kind of fashion Oscar. When a competitor got the prize, instead of young Moore, Norell in a huff sent back his own, earlier Coty Award. Later he announced to several stores that unless they purchased the John Moore line, they would be prohibited from buying the much more salable Norells. The stores held firm, and though Norell continued to be successful until his death in 1972, his prestige was never what it had been. Young Moore drifted back to Texas where he is consoled, at least, by the fact that Mr. Norell's will left him forty thousand dollars a year for life. Norell could make Moore financially secure but he couldn't make him a fashion star. That takes talent.

When a number of young women decided, for reasons of philosophy or comfort, to stop wearing bras, the fact was reported in WWD in both word and picture. The corset and bra industry, which I like to think of as "the underworld," protested and a number of bra manufacturers pulled out their advertising. We continued to report news of the bra-less trend and lost more advertising. The American nipple had become a point of contention between business and the press. Finally there was a meeting between several of the leading manufacturers and myself at which they complained of their very real financial losses. I asked what it was they expected the paper to do. It was inarguable that some women, including many who shouldn't, had shed their bras and were quite obvious about the fact.

"Don't show women without bras," a manufacturer urged me. "In that way we'll get them back."

I told him this was foolishness. Many of the couture and top ready-to-wear designers now had their mannequins going without bras when they showed the collections, and clothes were now being made that complemented or enhanced the bare-breasted look.

"Then don't expect our advertising," a bra man said flatly. "We know who our friends are. And our enemies."

I admitted that they were free not to advertise but suggested that instead of cursing the newspaper they put their technicians to work creating a bra that did the job without seeming to be there. "After all," I pointed out, "there are damn few women past twenty who really look better without one."

Whether they took my advice is in doubt, but within months Rudy Gernreich had his "no-bra" on the market and it was followed by a half-dozen similar items. Gradually the advertising came back into our pages and we had moved on to another skirmish in the continuing struggle between industry and press: whether Hot Pants, as John Fairchild christened them, were a major contribution to society or just another quick fad.

It was never dull.

7

Playing the Fashion Game

The fashion game, as we saw it at *WWD* and later as I tried to organize it at *Harper's Bazaar*, was played on many fields: in the design studios, the salons, in the fashion press, and where the clothes were worn. In Paris no one goes out to lunch. In New York, it seems, no one ever stays home. The restaurants, a handful really, became the New York arena where the fashion game was won, and lost. This was where women wore the clothes we wrote about.

The night of New York's great blackout, in November 1965, Carol Bjorkman, a dynamic and beautiful woman who wrote a column for *WWD*, had planned a dinner party in what was then the city's greatest restaurant, Le Pavillon — owned, managed, and dominated by a plump Frenchman called Henri Soulé. I had stayed late at the office, unable to get home in any event, but wanting to get the paper out if the power should come back on, and my wife and I decided to cancel out. I was sure the dinner would have to be postponed, that not even Carol and the resourceful Soulé would be able to produce a dinner for twenty people under the conditions. But the dinner went on and I will always regret having missed it. Soulé lit the place with candles, closed the restaurant to his other customers, and cooked what was described as a superb meal using Sterno cans to do the trick.

Another evening there was a Pavillon dinner at which only one thing went wrong. Merle Oberon and her husband, the Mexican millionaire Bruno Pagliai, were giving a dinner for Carol Bjorkman who had been ill and who would, a year later, die of leukemia. But that evening Carol was in rare form and so was everyone else. One of the earliest arrivals was a young New York socialite who was chatting with us when suddenly she broke away to greet a dinner-jacketed, swarthy little man.

"Senor Pagliai, how good of you to have us here. And how nice to see you again."

"I am the headwaiter, madam," replied the recipient of her gratitude.

Such dinner parties are obviously a part of the fashion game, but in New York it is at lunch that the real action occurs. A fashionable luncheon is as carefully choreographed as a Covent Garden ballet, with every role precisely defined. The scene is nearly always the same, any one of a half-dozen rather fine restaurants, most of them French, on the East Side (one or two drift slightly west of the social international dateline of Fifth Avenue, but one *thinks* of them as east).

La Grenouille is a really splendid restaurant on Fifty-second Street, just east of Fifth Avenue. At one time its name was being mentioned so often in the pages of WWD that John Fairchild said it sounded as if they either had a very good press agent or the newspaper was on the take. La Grenouille had no press agent at all to my knowledge and we paid for our meals in full, but it was a point well taken and we began referring to it as Restaurant X. La Caravelle, west of Fifth Avenue, on Fifty-fifth Street, became Restaurant Y, and so on. Then readers figured out which restaurant we meant, and simply to maintain the cheerful confusion, we mixed up the code names in a random manner so that La Grenouille might be Restaurant X on Monday and Restaurant Y on Tuesday. There was also a period during which it was known as the Frogpond, or simply the Frog (Grenouille, an almost unpronounceable word, is French for "frog"). The place to sit at La Grenouille is in the front room, preferably on one of the banquettes rather than at one of the two to four tables shoved into the middle of the room — rather greedily, I think — when the place fills up. The back room, which seems just as attractive and pleasant, is known as the Ketchup Room. This is not a code name but a little joke. One day I wrote a brief item about who was lunching at Grenouille and mentioned Mrs. William (Babe) Paley. She was, of course, seated in the front room, and I got off a line to the effect that they would no sooner put Babe Paley in the back room than put ketchup bottles on the tables. Charles Masson, a delightful and dedicated restaurateur, is very quick on the uptake and by the next day was calling the back room by its new name.

There is a small bar up front at La Grenouille, a bit too much in the bustle of the doorway to be relaxed, but it has its devotees. One of them is a very old gentleman who once headed a great store but who now sits feebly sipping his lunch at the southern end of the bar. John Fairchild, Bill Dwyer, and I were lunching there one day when John committed one of his truly memorable lines. He pointed out the old fellow at the bar who was shakily raising what seemed to be a dry martini to his lips. "That poor man," said John sympathetically.

Dwyer said the old chap seemed to be rather content.

"Not at all," John replied. "He comes in here every day and never eats anything and then he totters out into the traffic and a couple of months ago he was killed by a truck."

87

Both Dwyer and I expressed amazement at the ingenuity of the embalmer's craft.

"Well," said John, completely unflustered, "he *could* have been killed. They shouldn't let him cross alone."

Your front room roster on any day at La Grenouille could include such disparate characters as John Wayne, the Duchess of Windsor, any number of Kennedys, Happy Rockefeller, President and Mrs. Nixon, every fashion editor in town, platoons of nubile young things, Bill Blass, a couple of store presidents, and either Valentino, Saint Laurent, or whatever other European couturier is in town. I think they check in at La Grenouille before they drop their bags at the hotel. The current headwaiter, Jean, is an elfin figure of exquisite memory, never placing anyone at the wrong table, and it is an almost sensuous delight to see him greeting, say, a member of some fallen European royal house, bowing him to his place with repeated utterances of fealty to *"mon prince."* (The "prince" is usually employed as a public relations man in Philadelphia.) Jean's right hand, Marcel, a delightful young chap with the profile of a good middleweight boxer, was lured away from Grenouille last summer by a Texas hotel which promised him, I am told, several oil wells in addition to the usual gratuities. (He recently reformed and came back home to Grenouille.) Owner Masson himself is almost always there, checking on everything, carving the day's roast on the trolley, and mixing an occasional salad. Masson spends something like thirty thousand dollars a year on fresh flowers which are the most magnificent in town, and it is something to see him clucking at the busboys when he finds a finger smudge on a wine goblet on his final inspection about noon. Masson is of the school of large glasses for wine, to help the wine breathe, and he has so indoctrinated me that I feel cheated when I am elsewhere and they serve good wine in thimbles.

Although the most elegant people in New York will be seen in La Grenouille or La Caravelle, in those two great restaurants they dress to please themselves, or to impress other clients. There are two other New York restaurants where it seems you must dress to please the proprietor.

La Côte Basque, on Fifty-fifth Street just east of Fifth, was founded by Henri Soulé as a spin-off of his legendary Pavillon. It is a lovely room and the food is quite good and perfumers will often be seen at its best tables. Since M. Soulé's death La Côte Basque has been operated by one of his ex-employees, a plump Frenchwoman named Madame Henriette. She is neurotic on the subject of trousers when they are worn by women. There was the famous incident of the trousered lady with a broken leg whose modest but doomed ambition was simply to dine quietly with her friend, Mrs. Douglas MacArthur. But there are others. Just before Christmas a few years ago John Fairchild and I had some business to transact and we sought out a quiet table at La Côte Basque where, we imagined, it would be possible to talk without half a dozen Seventh Avenue designers listening in, as they have been known to do at La Grenouille. There was a commotion across the room where an attractive couple was being dismissed, without lunch, on the grounds that the young lady was in pants. The man of the pair, who seemed to know Fairchild, made his way to our table to file his complaint.

"Mr. Fairchild, you know Signora So-and-so who works for *Vogue* in Rome. She is beautifully dressed and yet this . . . woman says she can't eat here. Can't you or your paper do something?"

There is nothing that so embarrasses John Fairchild as a public scene. He wasn't quite sure who the man was, he was upset at having been drawn into a controversy he'd not initiated, and he mumbled something about being sorry, but what could he do? After a few more angry exchanges the couple was ejected and John and I went back to our food. But Madame Henriette would have none of it. She arrived at our table, looked toward heaven in her exasperation, and called on both of us to witness the justice of her position. John mumbled something equivocal and Henriette turned to me.

"Since you ask," I said, "I find your rules ridiculous."

She scurried away muttering. "Try to run a decent place and their filthy newspaper holds you to ridicule . . ."

John pushed his plate aside, too upset at this point to continue, while I shoveled up my food, delighted with the more passionate turn an otherwise pedestrian meal had taken. At that juncture, just as everything seemed to have calmed down, another young woman in pants arrived at the door, leading a tall young man in dark glasses who was carrying a white cane. I looked at Madame Henriette, she stared at the new arrivals, then back at me, and bustled off into the kitchen where I am sure she spent the next hour in prayer and meditation. The blind man and his trousered lady were seated without comment.

The other major New York restaurant which bans women wearing pants is Lafayette, located on Fiftieth Street east of Third Avenue. Jean Fayet, the owner and another graduate (as is Masson of La Grenouille) of the Soulé school, is a more multidimensional zealot than the pants-hating Madame Henriette. Monsieur Fayet hates many things, among them: shopping bags, sunglasses, coffee before the meal, raincoats, people who "steal" his menus, and briefcases full of papers. Angela Lansbury, the actress, was lunching at Lafayette one day with her sunglasses perched atop her head when the headwaiter asked her to remove them. Miss Lansbury, reasoning that perhaps light was glinting off the lenses into someone's eyes, did so, and put the glasses on the table. The headwaiter returned. Would she please take them off the table and put them away somewhere? Female clients who attempt to keep their raincoats with them, to be thrown over the shoulders or perhaps over the back of the chair, are told this is forbidden. The raincoat must be checked. And I have seen virtual tugs-of-war between M. Fayet and a woman who attempted to claim her table without first having divested herself of a Bloomingdale's shopping bag. Men of property, serious men with business to discuss and papers to hand around the table, are brusquely informed that their papers must be put away lest they offend. Oskar Werner, the actor, was sent packing one day as he attempted to lunch in a white turtleneck and blue blazer. M. Fayet informed him that a necktie had to be worn. Werner looked at him with that superior gaze with which he had outstared the Gestapo in many a film, but Fayet was unyielding. Then Werner turned on the charm. Smiling out from under his blond hair and those heavy-lidded eyes, he suggested to Fayet that "dressed like zis I can go any-vair in Europe. Any-vair, even ze opera."

"I don't care what you do in Europe," Fayet snapped. "You can't eat here."

Werner and his companions got up to leave. One of the ladies, who looked like a studio flack, asked Fayet if they could use the phone to call and make another reservation for lunch.

"There is a public phone down the street," Fayet announced with the finality of a sideman at a beheading in the Place de la Concorde.

Jacqueline Kennedy Onassis enjoys Lafayette but then she neither carries a shopping bag nor wears trousers downtown. And though she occasionally wears her sunglasses atop her head, it is not within view of Monsieur Jean Fayet. John Fairchild and I were lunching at Lafayette one day, seated on one of the banquettes, while to the left of us sat an older woman, alone. Jackie came in, radiant, wearing whatever was the latest thing, and waved to her luncheon companion, who of course was the woman next to us. When Jackie saw us, her face went flat, whatever conversation John and I were having died, and Fayet looked toward the ceiling as if to implore his patron saint, Soulé, to rescue him from this beastliness. But there were no other tables, Jackie had to stay where she was,

Fairchild and I where we were, and two less stimulating luncheon conversations would be hard to come by. Jackie chain-smoked and looked airily about and made brittle remarks while John and I spoke of matters as substantive as the respective ski lift capacities of Val d'Isere and Gstaad. We finished lunch first and had just time enough to get to the public phone, the one Fayet pointed out to Oskar Werner's friends, and to get a photographer on the job for what turned out to be our front-page picture the next day.

If we got some of our best photos of Jackie arriving at or leaving Lafayette, there was one evening when we staked out the restaurant and got nothing. And one of our photographers nearly got something he hadn't counted on. Frank Sinatra was then wooing Mia Farrow. Somehow we had gotten the word that the two would be dining at Lafayette and we sent up a photographer, Harry Morrison. As Morrison told the story next morning, Sinatra's car had pulled up, the singer and Miss Farrow had disembarked, and when Morrison moved toward them to get a picture, one of Sinatra's gorillas jumped in front of the camera, pushed Morrison up against the brick wall, and held him there until the bashful couple had gone into the restaurant. There was a crying of baptismal vows and several recitations of the First Amendment before Morrison gave it up and came home.

My favorite Lafayette story may be apocryphal but it is so splendid that I hope it is true. It's the sort of story that reflects great credit on the entire cast. It seems that Bette Davis and her young son were lunching at Lafayette and they noticed Yogi Berra eating at a nearby table. The young man was understandably excited to see the great baseball player in the same room and at some point Miss Davis sashayed over to Yogi's table, got his autograph on a menu, and returned triumphant. As Bette and son were leaving, Fayet's eye, as keen as Natty Bumppo's, caught sight of one of his precious menus being "stolen," and launched himself to the door.

There was an exchange of compliments, then a tug of war, and finally a handbag swung with considerable effect by Bette Davis, who emerged on the sidewalk, the story goes, with half a menu. And, presumably, half a Yogi Berra autograph.

Orsini's is the only one of the top fashion hangouts that is Italian, rather than French. This perhaps reflects on the relative strength these days of the French, as opposed to the Italian, school of design. The restaurant is located on Fifty-sixth Street, west of Fifth, and is one of the most handsome rooms in town. Presiding over it is the most handsome restaurateur in New York, Armando Orsini. Armando is no longer in the first blush of youth but his trim figure and carefully arranged salt-and-pepper hair provide a certain air. One day recently I was at one of his tables, with an attractive young woman, and I rose to shake hands with my host. Armando grimaced and pulled his hand away. "Oh," he said with the proper note of drama, "it is my tennis elbow. I played twelve sets of singles yesterday and it is agony." All this with an eye cocked to see if the young woman understood that to play twelve sets one must be very *macho* indeed.

The fashion people love to hang out at Orsini's, to see and be seen. But there is a restaurant further east where they go to eat. It is Le Veau d'Or, close by Bloomingdale's on Fifty-ninth Street between Park and Lexington. It is a bistro, really, with red-and-white checked tablecloths, and the place to sit, if you can get there, is the very front table they call "the garden." The place is full of Frenchmen, serious eaters, men with the rosette of the Legion d'Honneur in their buttonholes and red veins in their noses. These are men who take their food seriously. Le Madrigal, a sunny, pleasant place with a back garden, on Fifty-third Street east of Third Avenue, is a sometime fashion favorite but recently has taken to attracting more serious people, publishers and editors, men and women of the world of books.

Of course there are other establishments, but this is not a

guidebook to New York dining. The point is that the fashionable people, those who make the clothes and those who wear them, will be seen at fairly regular intervals in all these joints, and for a journalist, such gatherings have significance. When I was running *WWD* it was the restaurants that gave us our best photos, the memorable candid of this clotheshorse or that wearing the latest long skirt or short. *WWD*'s photographers took to wearing beeper phones that would enable us to summon them to one restaurant or another to get the front-page picture that would help sell the next day's paper — an off-guard shot of Amanda Burden in her new, tight, faded blue suede pants, or the Duchess of Windsor, still elegant in her fading years, or Ali MacGraw, with or without Steve McQueen, or Tricia Nixon Cox, the world's oldest living teenager, in one of her darling little ceramic milkmaid's costumes.

Of course we received tips from these restaurants, and others, whenever newsworthy persons were in attendance. But, unlike the late Walter Winchell, we didn't pay for our tips. There wasn't a headwaiter in New York on the *WWD* payroll. And for our part, we paid for our lunches. This wasn't mindless altruism; it just made good journalistic sense. How could you rap a restaurant for the deficiencies of its smoked salmon or for lumps in the potage St. Germaine, if you were, as are too many reporters, eating free? Paying your own way was a rule at Fairchild Publications and it was a rule I tried to install at *Bazaar*.

The free load and the junket are still with us and maybe always will be. There are journalists I know who simply never pick up a bill, even when their publications obviously could pay. I have never understood how fashion reporters can spend a week cruising on a yacht off Acapulco and come back and write an objective story about the perfumer or dress designer who had just played "good mine host." But they continue to go cruising and seem to sleep just as soundly of a night. I suppose it's a matter of warping your conscience into shape. I am less intolerant these days, which may be a function of age or just the experience of having run a deficit operation at *Bazaar*, where the editorial budget was constructed in such a way as to take into account a certain number of free trips.

So the next time you page through a fashion magazine and come across a particularly splendid series of color pages on the Dry Tortugas or the upriver regions of the Malagasy Republic, with the new Halstons or Blasses or Calvin Kleins displayed amid the local shrubbery, don't think it's because the editors have suddenly discovered the Tortugas or the Malagasy. No, it is probably because an airline agreed to fly, and a hotel shelter, from six to eight models, editors, and photographers without any charge whatsoever. In return, the magazine will credit, in words and on film, the airline, the hotel, and indeed the whole bloody country if need be. A woman who pays her dollar for the magazine, and consequently becomes passionately attracted to the Dry Tortugas for her next holiday, may eventually enjoy the islands as much as did the magazine's employees. But she will pay full rates.

I always paid full rates myself, or at least I tried. There were those rare instances when it was nearly impossible.

There are two nights spots in Paris. One is Castel's, which is operated like a private club by an ex-rugby player who sits near the entrance, drinking with his pals. The other is New Jimmy's, also known as Régine's, run by a redheaded lady of Polish extraction who also happens to be one of the most successful popular singers in France. Régine is best described as a combination of Barbra Streisand and Toots Shor. To dance with her is a physical experience just short of actual intercourse. On my trips to Paris for the fashion collections, I inevitably headed the first night to Jimmy's, and before I could order it, a bottle of Scotch with my name pasted on would be on display behind the bar. Chez Régine you buy a bottle of Scotch for some extraordinary figure, fifty dollars or so, and your name goes on it. You can dance and drink and pass evening after evening in her place on the strength of that one bottle, so long as it lasts. One is expected to drop ten francs in the waiter's palm but that is all. I know a careful drinker who spent an entire season dancing with all the pretty girls and playing the hell of a fellow on one carefully considered, scrupulously sipped bottle of Johnny Walker Black Label. Since Régine liked me, and thought it her duty to encourage young journalists, I found it difficult ever to pay for the damn Scotch. Finally, one season, I got to the barman my first night before Régine learned I had arrived. I paid for the bottle and when Régine gathered me to her ample bosom, I announced proudly that I had already arranged for my bottle, "and this time I paid for it."

"Ma fortune est faite," said the unimpressed Régine.

Another fashion game that annoyed me, and drove Fairchild into a fury, was the selection of people as the "best dressed" of this or that year.

There is a good deal of otherwise valuable newspaper space and even television time given to the Best Dressed List, which itself is nonsense, and perhaps some sort of press council should investigate this waste of newsprint in a time when ecologists tell us trees are in short supply. Surely the Federal Communications Commission should carefully review the license of any station that includes even a passing reference to the BDL in its eleven o'clock news.

The list is operated by Eleanor Lambert, an able and energetic New York press agent, who sends out ballots to several hundred fashion and women's page editors across the country. Many of these rustics have never laid an eye on the BDL candidates and wouldn't know Babe Paley from her daughter (Amanda Burden), each of whom in past years has been voted number one. To help the benighted heathen in the provinces, Miss Lambert thoughtfully sends along suggestions of the women who *really* should be considered in that particular year.

Miss Lambert's contribution to American letters is not without its value. Her lists of best-dressed women, more recently of best-dressed men, her lists of those who have ascended into her "hall of fame," by dint of having (like Mrs. Paley, Gloria Guinness, Jacqueline Onassis, and so on) been voted in year after year, make amusing copy in a slow news week and fill columns that might otherwise be occupied by recipes for apple pan dowdy or home cures for catarrh.

I have discussed the Best Dressed concept with Miss Lambert and in response to my questions she admitted that she had been offered bribes by insecure women who felt a BDL nomination would help them socially. Though educated in Catholic schools, I suspected that such women exist, and I was not at all surprised by Miss Lambert's disclosure. What was news was that she had once been offered rather substantial monies by a wealthy businessman who wanted his wife kept *off* the list. The man in question felt that having a Best Dressed wife was not at all the sort of figure he wanted to cut in his particularly conservative branch of the world of commerce.

The frenzy the Best Dressed List arouses can be gauged by an incident that involved a famous movie star's wife, a woman who apparently fancies herself quite a fashion plate. It is important to women like her to appear on the BDL. Two or three years ago, Eleanor Lambert's office sent out the usual preliminary list of that year's best-dressed women for the "guidance" of provincial editors who would later be asked to submit their votes. Through a clerical oversight, the lady's name did not appear on this long, preliminary listing. Her designer got on the phone to Lambert's office. The woman had taken to her bed, the designer informed one of Eleanor's staffers. How dare the BDL omit one of the most elegantly clad women in America? Then the designer tried to whip across the high, hard one. If the star's wife was not immediately restored to grace by the BDL, Lambert's girl was told, "You'll lose my account."

The BDL probably reached its low point when Barbra Streisand was elected. Miss Streisand is a magnificent singer and actress and an exotically beautiful woman but she has no taste in clothes. Her appearance at the Academy Awards several years ago in an Arnold Scaasi contraption with the seam running up between her ripe buttocks is proof of this. Her choice of Scaasi, who spells his real name, Isaacs, backwards, should have been the tell. Yet she was elected one of the best-dressed women in the land.

Not content with naming the best-dressed women in the world, Eleanor Lambert broadened the exercise to include men. Such classic dressers as Fred Astaire and Cary Grant were elected without debate. But the BDL shortly ran out of such marvels and was reduced to nominating retailers, saloon proprietors and journalists. Even George Hamilton had his day.

At *WWD* we asked our editors not to participate in the voting and unmercifully ragged the convention with our own joke lists, timed to come out at the same time as the solemn and deadly serious genuine BDL. One year we listed Princess Margaret, whom we called "Her Drear," as a tribute to her courage and resource in appearing in such monstrous clothes at public event after public event. I think that same year we named Golda Meir, Grandma Moses, and the Pope to our own list. Later I got some mail which said that naming the Pope wasn't at all humorous, that his robes and accouterments were really quite marvelous.

During the 1960's and into the seventies it would have been convenient to have a Lytton Strachey to inform us about our more celebrated contemporaries. Instead, as chroniclers of the age, we had to settle for the more superficial assessments of such columnists as Eugenia Sheppard, Aline Mehle (Suzy Knickerbocker), Charlotte Curtis of the *New York Times*, WWD itself, and several books which more or less tried to package those years in a cogent and understandable way. Marylin Bender, a competent professional who has now moved on to better things as a financial page writer for the *Times*, put together a book called *The Beautiful People*. It came out in 1967 and claimed to be "a candid examination of a cultural phenomenon — the marriage of fashion and society in the 60's."

One point Miss Bender seemed to be making was that fashion designers have moved, subtly but very definitely, out of the class of tradesmen and servants into the friend and companion class. It reminded me of the earlier days of professional golf when the golf pro, especially in England and Scotland, was not permitted in the clubhouse, less his coarse and sweaty presence disturb the members. It was Walter Hagen who demolished this golfing caste system single-handedly by driving up to the clubhouse in his Rolls-Royce and demonstrating to the gentlemen amateurs that association with a professional would not necessarily bring on bleeding gums or even a milder form of leprosy. So fashion designers were invited home for tea, and society survived, and was perhaps the better for it. Of course society has now gone too far, as it will, and made hairdressers welcome. But then, there will always be excesses in this less than perfect world.

The "beautiful" people Marylin Bender wrote about were, of course, an updated version of the so-called Jet Set of the decade earlier. It's my impression that *Vogue*'s Diana Vreeland coined the "beautiful people" line which is now used by Arlene Francis on her radio show and which, by 1970, had become so clichéd that at WWD we abbreviated it to BP and later threw it out entirely in favor of the Cat Pack (John Fairchild's invention and one of his less inspired ones, I thought then and now). I tried once to launch another category of celebrity, those who did something more with their lives than attend parties, go to bed with one another, and have their legs waxed. I termed this more meaningful social group the Dutiful People but it never caught on. Apparently the reader preferred keeping up with the activities of fashionable layabouts to those of more earnest folk.

The trick was, as I saw it, and as Curtis and Suzy Knickerbocker and WWD did it best, to report on the Jet Setters or the Beautiful People without being impressed by them. You had to keep tongue firmly in cheek, to tell the reader what they were up to but to make it all seem slightly ridiculous. In this way the reader got his ration of inside gossip but at the same time could indulge his own virtue by smiling benignly at the follies of the "beautiful," by shaking his head in a superior manner whenever they went too far. The reason WWD was especially successful in walking this reportorial razor's edge, writing about the rich and fashionable without idolatry, was that we paid our way. Society reporters can be bought, I sadly inform you, and yachts are awfully appealing places to do the buying.

At WWD we stood back at arm's length and tried to write about the BP without ever becoming snared in velvet. We wrote about them with laughter and occasionally with insight, we tried to make distinctions between those who were simply shallow, but not really such bad guys after all, and those whose entire beings were circumscribed by materialism, their own pleasure, and their indifference to real problems and human distress.

One very clear impression I had of all the Beautiful People, of all the Jet Setters, was their extreme prudence. It may be that they paid for their own airline tickets but they paid for little else. They rarely descended in the great hotels on either side of the Atlantic but instead engaged in house swapping and apartment borrowing that would have seemed presumptuous and demeaning among the middle and lower classes. People "borrowed" town houses and great country estates the way you and I might borrow books. To pay a hotel bill or to rent a flat seemed a betrayal of class. It implied that you didn't know anyone in that country who thought you sufficiently desirable to insist that you occupy his digs and no one else's. And of course next season he, in turn, dropped in on you, and so the benign circle of Jet Set hospitality went.

There were the occasional disadvantages. When Marisa Berensen, the beautiful young model-turned-actress, was with Helmut Burger (that young man having temporarily left his older patron, Luchino Visconti, to dabble in girls), they arrived in Paris and moved into Philippe Guibourge's lovely little flat on the rue Jean Goujon. Guibourge, who works for Dior, was delighted to have them, but after a week or so it began to pall. We were sitting late over dinner one evening at, I think, La Coupole, when Philippe remarked: "When I am getting up to go to work in the morning, they are just coming in. And when I get home at night, they are just getting up. And never, *never*, mind you, do they wear clothes."

And there were times, of course, when the BP were not so beautiful. There was the night in Hollywood, in that season's "in" place, The Daisy, when Laurence Harvey baited George Hamilton. Hamilton had been with the President's daughter earlier that evening and now for some reason had joined our party in the company of his mother, an eccentric named Anne Spaulding who affected a medieval coned cap with trailing veils. Lynda Bird had gone to bed. Harvey was with a couple of hard-looking girls he had found out there somewhere on the empty streets of a Los Angeles midnight and he was drinking red wine.

"Why won't you dance with me, Georgie?" he kept asking Hamilton. "You ought to dance with me. You like to dance with me, don't you, Georgie?"

John Ireland kept telling Harvey to shut up. Someone else

tried to get him off the subject. But Hamilton sat there taking it all with a rather sappy grin on his handsome face. His mother, shaking her veils at Harvey, but not in a maternal rage, merely cooed, "Oh, Larry, you are wicked. Now you leave Georgie alone."

Later on Hamilton invited everybody to go back to his place, a big house he had bought that once belonged to Mary Pickford. He beckoned us all to his Rolls-Royce waiting at the curb but I said no, I had to go somewhere, and I got my rented car and drove back to the Beverly Hills Hotel.

And there was the very rich, very social couple, guests on somebody else's yacht. The husband collected coins and there was some dispute about the coins, his wife had touched them or something had happened to one of the coins and the man beat her up very badly down there in the cabin — they said you could hear the punches landing up on deck — and when she appeared that evening for dinner not even the jewels or the makeup or that season's splendid hostess pajamas could hide all the marks.

And the other couple, complete with titles, who decided against accepting the weekend invitation of a very beautiful woman who worked for *Bazaar*. "She only digs men," the titled lady said, and the invitation was never taken up.

Hubert d'Ornano is a very rich young Frenchman with a very attractive wife. He is also a count, which makes her a countess, but that is not so important these days. What is important is that Hubert and Isobel love to shoot, and own thousands of acres teeming with game birds and animals. One night over dinner in Maxim's Hubert was pressing me to give my appraisal of Jean-Louis Scherrer, a fashion designer whom Hubert had bought up. With my usual tact I suggested that Hubert could do better with his money. The argument went on until he tired of it and snapped, "Listen, I spend more money in a fortnight's shooting than I do on the couture house all year." I was impressed and more than ever sorry for poor Scherrer.

There was the time a splendid young Italian girl came to New York, a young woman of good family and magnificently endowed, an import sure to attract attention in New York without seriously trying. I dispatched one of our more astute young women to do an interview. Surely there would be some novel insights into American society, American life, a fresh young European appraisal of colonials at their ease. Instead our reporter came back agog.

"Any copy there?" I asked.

"Well," she said, "if you think we can print it."

She went on to relate the Italian girl's account of life in America, a round of parties that culminated in her having encountered one of the less inhibited young United States Senators, a man who, directly his wife was engaged in conversation with someone else, pressed his phone number on the Italian visitor.

"She said that when she called him," my reporter recounted, "he said he would phone her back, but that he would say it was 'Mr. Smith of Boston calling,' and then she would know it was the Senator."

How long had this been going on, I wondered.

"Oh, they've been sleeping together ever since," the reporter said. "She told me so and I believe it."

I was still mulling over the story and wondering how it could be laundered sufficiently to run when the reporter got back to me.

"She called me this morning and said perhaps it would be inappropriate to write about 'Mr. Smith of Boston.' She thought perhaps I'd better leave out that part of the story."

Princess Margaret and Tony Armstrong-Jones, elevated by marriage to become Lord Snowdon, were irresistible targets for *WWD*, and later for *Harper's Bazaar*. I had learned from mutual friends that Tony referred to his diminutive wife, out of her hearing naturally, as "the dwarf." And I also learned that the royal couple were among the most assiduous free-loaders on the BP roster. The Aga Khan had taken over some great tracts of undeveloped land in Sardinia and by dint of energy and a great deal of money had made portions of that island into a Mediterranean pleasure dome. I had it that Tony would get on the phone during the danker months of a London winter and inform the Aga Khan that he and "the dwarf" were headed that way and would it be okay for them to drop in. The poor Aga Khan, obliged to be civil, would say of course, and then get right back on the phone to call around his BP neighbors to arrange the requisite dinners, luncheons, and *thé dansants* to keep his royal visitors occupied during their stay. And also, not incidentally, to avoid having to be their constant companion during the fortnight they would surely remain. "They bicker so, you see," someone explained to me. "If Margaret wants to go out dancing then surely Tony will suggest bed. And if he wants to stay at a party, she has migraine."

The journalistic solution to handling the Beautiful People, the merely silly as well as the grotesque, was to pin them like rare butterflies in the specimen boxes of your mind, to observe them closely without becoming involved, and to observe the libel laws and the usual decencies when you wrote about them in the paper. You wanted to convey their materialism, their warp, their occasional charm, their perversity and their tang, and at the same time neither be sued nor send your readers flocking to the bathroom to be sick.

The most ironic aspect of the years during which I reported on the Beautiful People was the relatively few real complaints we ever received from our "victims." It seemed to emphasize again the journalistic truism: just be sure you spell their names correctly.

8

Domesticating the Designers

The relationship of *Women's Wear Daily* and the fashion industry is approximately that of Henry VIII and his latter wives: the wives always hope for the best but expect the worst. This is how the average fashion designer thinks of the fashion editors who pass judgment on his work several times each season. There are exceptions, of course, times when the shoe is on the other foot, when the designer has the muscle and it is the press that becomes petitioner, suitor, waiter for handouts. Yves Saint Laurent is currently the single most important designer in the world. Irritated by what he considered superficial reporting of his fashion collection, Saint Laurent recently banned every American fashion journal, except *Vogue*, *Bazaar*, and *WWD*, from his couture collections. His ban included the *New York Times*, syndicated columnist Eugenia Sheppard, and *Time* magazine. Yet when Saint Laurent next visited the United States, his press coverage was superb, even breathless, as the fashion editors fell over themselves to salute a man who had refused to let them review his line.

It usually works the other way. The bankruptcy rate along Seventh Avenue traditionally runs much higher than that of the business community generally. Frequently undercapitalized, often a family business without professional management, few fashion houses can survive more than two or three poor seasons in succession. And to a great extent it is the reviews of the fashion press, especially of *WWD*, that influence the store buyers to buy, or to stay away. There are retailers who make up their own minds, men like Sydney Gittler of Ohrbach's, but too many read the notices and then decide. To a very substantial degree, it was John Fairchild who shifted the balance of power from the fashion house to the fashion critic.

In *WWD*, and then in *Bazaar*, we reported on the designers as people, including the refreshing aspects of their lives as well as some of the less savory. They liked the positive stories and didn't like the bad. "Write about my clothes," they would complain if you got off a nasty crack about their personal lives. But if you saluted them as really decent chaps or some sort of genius, they would say, "That's the stuff. You can understand my clothes only if you understand me as a person."

Norman Norell was one of the best of men when you wrote a good critique of his collection; a ravening hostile when you didn't. Gloria Emerson of the *New York Times*, a great journalist who would later file a distinguished body of reportage from Vietnam, was banned by Saint Laurent for what he felt was a less-than-serious appraisal of his work. Only Emanuel Ungaro seemed sufficiently balanced, or perhaps phlegmatic, to accept a bad review with equanimity. For a season or two Coco Chanel's favorite fashion newspaper was the Communist daily *L'Humanité*, whose critic had somehow gotten it all wrong and praised Chanel's work in a season when the rest of the press was unanimous in putting Chanel down as a platitudinous rehash of things past. Balenciaga hid away from the press for years and WWD mistakenly once ran a front-page photo of a local druggist we thought was the camera-shy designer. Raymond Barbas, owner of the House of Patou, frightened me one year by claiming my review had brought on a massive heart attack. Barbas is still alive and well, and playing near-scratch golf, ten years after that particular crisis.

It's impertinent, surely, for a journalist to set himself up as a "people watcher." All of us are flawed and none of us likes those flaws exposed in public. I'm no exception and have bridled and snarled when an interview portrayed me as something less than a figure of talent, probity, and good humor. But I am convinced that incisive, informed, and accurate "people watching" was what made WWD a success and was the best feature of the emerging *Harper's Bazaar*. People make good copy.

John Weitz is an American designer who has very much made it on his own. Tall and ruggedly handsome, Weitz began as a women's designer but in the past ten years has become one of the most important men's clothing designers in the world. He lives on a yacht with his wife, Susan Kohner, a beautiful young actress, and is one of the few designers who takes marriage seriously, having tried it three times. Several years ago he wrote a trashy novel about the fashion business, *The Value of Nothing*, which many thought was a fictionalized portrait of his close friend Bill Blass. Blass has been cool to Weitz ever since, an understandable attitude since Weitz's protagonist was a social-climbing homosexual who was murdered by an elevator operator he picked up one lonely night. As the story goes, Weitz phoned Blass just before the book came out, told him the plot, and assured Blass, "He isn't you."

Weitz is really a pleasant chap but he has an explosive temper. When I wrote a brief version of the "Blass book" story in *Harper's Bazaar*, John wrote me a letter saying he had never really understood how much I hated him until then. I wrote back that he was being ridiculous and the next time we met he was once again his charming self.

Weitz will pursue a reporter with the relentlessness of an ambulance chaser. John Fairchild couldn't stand Weitz, termed him a publicity hound, and flew into a rage whenever *WWD* or the men's wear publications, *Daily News Record* or *Men's Wear* magazine, had a good word for him. Several years ago I arranged a lunch with Weitz and Bill Dwyer, who headed both of the men's wear publications but who had never met Weitz. We had a good meal at Le Madrigal, and with Weitz bending his considerable charm to the occasion, all went well until coffee. At that point, John produced a mouth spray and dramatically squirted it into his mouth. Dwyer shook his head and when we were on the street whispered, "Now I know what Fairchild meant." The last time I saw John he dragged me off to Rumpelmeyer's, the ice cream and pastry shop on Central Park South, to announce that he was writing a paper comparing Israeli tank tactics in the Yom Kippur war with those used by Rommel over the same kind of desert terrain thirty years earlier. Weitz will sprint through traffic to impart this sort of information or to regale you, perhaps, with tales of his career in the O.S.S. I do not mean to give the impression that Weitz is simply a self-oriented windbag. He is an intelligent man with good manners, the mouth spray notwithstanding, and since he does not employ a public relations counsel, must of necessity promote himself. This he does with great effectiveness. His clothes sell well in this country and he's among the most important American designers abroad. A substantial chunk of his total income now comes from Japan and from his tie-in with Austin Reed of London. If Weitz didn't know more about everything than anyone, if he weren't such a damned blowhard, I would be even fonder of him than I am.

In New York there's a plump young man who makes hats.

He calls himself "Mister John," and modestly adds the quali-
fying phrase "Emperor of Fashion." He doesn't just toss this
out casually, you understand. His stationery is inscribed with
it. John lives with another young man called Peter Brandon.
They keep birds in their apartment and at one point, during
the ecology craze when everyone was riding bicycles, they had
bikes in their apartment and rode from room to room. Peter
likes to demonstrate how the birds will eat birdseed from his
lips. It is a bit disconcerting to have birds flying about during
dinner, and occasionally sitting on your head, but John and
Peter enjoy it, and it's their apartment.

Oscar de la Renta was one of Antonio del Castillo's little
assistants when I first knew him in Paris. A tall, thin boy from
the Dominican Republic, Oscar had good manners and a
not-unpleasing stutter. He had some money from home, I
assumed, because Castillo was not known to throw money
away on his assistants. (In those days, ten years ago, couture
assistants to major designers might make two hundred dollars
a month.) Over lunch one day at La Truite on the rue St.
Honoré, Oscar Renta (the "de la" would come later) told
me he was fed up with the penury of the couture and wanted
to get to Seventh Avenue where he felt he had the stuff to
make it as a designer. He asked whether I could put him in
contact with any of the Seventh Avenue manufacturers who
might be looking for a young designer with Paris training.
Oscar was a decent fellow and I wrote some letters, John
Fairchild made some phone calls around New York, and
within a few months Oscar had been named the designer for
a mid-sized Seventh Avenue house. I read about it in WWD
and was amused to learn he had become Oscar "de la" Renta
somewhere between Paris and New York. I had to assume the
aristocratic "de la" had been handed out on the Pan Am jet
along with the plastic tray and the Rock Cornish game hen
and fruit cup.

A year or two later, when I had myself returned to New

York to become publisher of *WWD*, I wrote a rather vicious "fashion fable" about Oscar telling how a little Paris assistant named "Peter Milque" had miraculously been translated into a leading light named "Pierre de la Crème," and in the process of becoming a Seventh Avenue star had neglected to thank those who had helped him along, had become a social climber, and so on. It was a bitchy piece, and overdone, but I felt its point was valid. Oscar, I learned later, was very upset and went to Bill Blass with the piece and complained about "what Brady has done to me." Blass handled the situation tactfully by acting incredulous. "Why, I didn't think he meant *you*, Oscar."

Renta later married Françoise de Langlade, the ex-editor of French *Vogue*, a statuesque and cultivated older woman, and it was as good a thing as ever happened to a young designer whose head had begun to swell. He matured, opened his own house under the patronage of the Richton Corporation, and with Françoise's guidance and charm, and his own basic qualities, became a successful designer and a quite decent fellow. Someone once wrote a book called *In Praise of Older Women*, and its title very nicely pays tribute to what Françoise did for Oscar and apparently continues to do today.

Anne Klein, who died early in 1974, was one of the most successful women on Seventh Avenue. She was also a very tough cookie who defended fiercely what she considered to be her fashion territory. When, as publisher of *Bazaar*, I hosted a seminar on the newest European clothes I had just seen in Paris, Anne got to her feet.

"I'm fed up with all this talk of Paris," she announced. "It wasn't Paris that put American women into blazers and plaid skirts. I did it."

There was some chat back and forth with Bill Blass, Kasper, and several of the other designers who had joined us for the seminar, and later, over drinks, one of the big Seventh Avenue names pulled me aside. "Maybe Paris didn't create the blazer and the plaid skirt. But hasn't Anne ever seen an English schoolgirl?"

This is the sort of badinage you always get when two designers are in the same room.

Ralph Lauren and Calvin Klein both come from the same neighborhood in the Bronx. Lauren has changed his name (from Lifschitz) while Klein hasn't. (He is, incidentally, no relation to Anne Klein.) Both young men are very hot at the moment and both won Coty Awards in 1973, Klein for his women's clothes and Lauren for his men's wear. Lauren is now also in women's fashion, and when I asked him once what designers interested him, he mentioned two, Norell and Chanel. They are both dead, of course, which may give you some notion of Lauren's competitiveness. Ralph is a small man with a lisp and, according to one major retailer who buys truckloads of his clothes, "has a monumental ego." Although Lauren has sold well and gotten terrific publicity in the past year or two (his men's designs for the film of *The Great Gatsby* having been particularly well received), his profits have been almost nonexistent. In order to strengthen his operation, make it more businesslike, Lauren brought his two brothers into it with him. "I always stayed away from having family in the business," he told me, "but I started the business and now I'm bringing them in. It isn't as if they were in it with me from the start." It is quite clear when you talk to Ralph which Lauren brother is the most equal.

Calvin Klein is a tall, lanky kid who looks younger than he is (thirty-four). When Mildred Custin gave Calvin his first major order at Bonwit Teller, Calvin and one of his workers hung the dresses on a rolling rack, raced them from Seventh Avenue on foot, went up in the freight elevator, and celebrated by descending in the passenger car. Lauren started by designing ties and also made his first deliveries in person, "wearing a bomber jacket" and being taken for the delivery boy. Both men are talented and are going to be around for a long time, but the stresses of fashion success are already show-ing at the seams: Lauren's ego inflation and Klein's split with his wife, a tall, very good-looking, green-eyed girl called Jane.

I always wanted to do a story entitled "The Happiest Bank-rupts" about Luis Estevez and other designers whose busi-nesses always seem to be fizzling but who live better than any of us. When I mentioned this to Estevez, who at last count had two Rolls-Royces, he was indignant. "Companies I have been associated with may have gone bankrupt, but I, never."

Ferdinando Sarmi, a onetime count known to his friends as "Nando," is a magnificently mustachioed old charmer who is down on his fashion luck at the moment. Sarmi, like Luis Estevez, is one of those designers whose corporate structures always seem to be collapsing but who continue to prosper. Several years ago, after the death of impresario Gilbert Mil-ler, Sarmi was reported to be about to marry Kitty Miller, the wealthy and fashionable "merry widow," as she was dubbed in *WWD*. Sarmi would smile tolerantly at such talk and insist he was but a good friend of Mrs. Miller, and that they enjoyed playing cards together. Now Nando Sarmi's business is on the rocks, good friends are said to be helping him keep body and soul together, and for the first time in decades, no Sarmi label can be found on the racks of the great Fifth Avenue shops. Sarmi is, however, an India-rubber man, and it would be premature to write his professional obituary.

You can feel secure, however, in writing off Mainbocher, the stocky, white-haired little man whose name was for so long synonymous with the most elegant, if not the most pop-ular, of American fashion. Mainbocher went broke two ways: gradually and then all at once. An attempt was made among his richer clients to raise a purse to keep him going, but at last, two years ago, the old man accepted the inevitable and decamped for Europe where he could presumably live more economically. At *WWD* we referred to him as Remember-the-Mainbocher and there was little love between us.

Mollie Parnis, a peppery little woman with a few years on her, is an acerbic old party who styles herself one of New York's smartest hostesses. She enjoys giving parties and will invite people she doesn't even know if their names carry sufficient weight. Mollie loves to design clothes for American First Ladies. The only First Lady in my time not to have fallen into Mollie's hands was Jacqueline Kennedy, who was also the most elegant of the First Ladies in my time. I once wrote a wicked essay about Mollie in which I referred to her as "Polly Harness," and went on at great, and what I thought witty, length, parodying her penchant for social climbing. Although we didn't get along professionally, Mollie has always been gracious in her personal contacts, and as a designer is one of those old pros who knows her seams. Another old pro, Pauline Trigère, talks with a staccato accent that might remind you of a French machine gun, has the charm of most of her countrywomen, makes clothes that always sell, and never once phoned me to complain about her editorial treatment. She had her brother do that.

Jacques Tiffeau, the colorful Frenchman whose self-confessed amorous exploits are more entertaining than any singer I've ever listened to, quit designing two years ago and went to work for Yves Saint Laurent as a liaison and production man. Tiffeau had been in partnership with Beverly Busch, and before that with her father, and though he was successful, he would tell anyone within hearing how he had to escape from his partnership with "La Busch" or lose his sanity. Finally a way was discovered, Tiffeau dropped Beverly Busch, and went into the sprawling fashion conglomerate of Gunther Oppenheim, whose keystone designer was Anne Klein. Tiffeau announced his delight, but within a few months there were reports that "La Klein" was inhibiting his free spirit and before long Tiffeau was grousing louder than he had ever done when commercially linked to Beverly Busch. John Fairchild returned from lunch one day to announce dramatically, "Tiffeau's going to commit suicide."

I asked if his latest love had turned sour.

"No," said John, "he just can't go on this way with Anne Klein second-guessing him on everything. They're driving him mad. He's thinking of killing himself."

I tried to soothe John, who always took these things hard but who immediately dictated to Gertrude Price, his patient secretary, an only slightly expurgated version of the above for inclusion in the next day's EYE column.

I must say that the next few times I saw Tiffeau, he looked pretty bad and admitted his depression. After a couple of seasons in the Gunther Oppenheim stable, the deal was nullified by mutual consent. Saint Laurent, very thoughtfully, I felt, hired Tiffeau and got him back into fashion without the strain of having to produce collections. Tiffeau is now very happy, he assures me, and I would not be at all surprised to see him back on Seventh Avenue as a designer. In the meantime, don't shed any tears for Jacques Tiffeau. He has the first franc he ever earned, owns a large farm in France which his parents operate, and has equipped it with giant yellow Caterpillar tractors and other machinery. The farm is his pride and joy, and has a very good resale value on the French market.

Chester Weinberg is an in-and-outer. Some years he flaunts a beard, in other years he doesn't, and his work seems to follow the same pattern. He's triumphed and flopped in successive seasons and frankly I have no feel for Weinberg's talent, but he's still a young man who could be on top once again. He must have something, since he was taken up by Cristobal Balenciaga in the master's later years and Balenciaga had little time for young men whose only qualifications were their bright blue eyes and smooth complexions. Kasper is the most diffident of men, a spare, quietly elegant chap who used to be married to one of the most famous of all fashion models,

Betsy Pickering Theodorocopulos. For a time it seemed I could never be in Atlanta or Chicago or Denver without running into Kasper, who, like Bill Blass, understands that a designer on Seventh Avenue must spend as much time out in the provinces, seeing the stores, talking to the women who buy the clothes, and sniffing the air, as he spends in the design studio.

Blass is a delightful guy. He is one of the few designers who doesn't retail malicious gossip, and who can carry on a conversation that deals with matters other than fashion or himself. He is also one of the most elegant men I know. Another designer I'd prefer to spend a few hours with is Hardy Amies, the very urbane Britisher who served in military intelligence during the war, helps supply Queen Elizabeth with her dowdy clothes, and has made a fortune with his men's wear. On a television talk show during the mini skirt controversy several years ago, John Fairchild was being thoroughly abused by a young journalist called Daphne Davis. John was sputtering his assurances that he was certain Miss Davis was "a very nice girl" — John's stock response whenever confronted by a "liberated" woman — when the host, I think it was David Frost, waved Hardy Amies onstage to join the increasingly one-sided conversation.

Amies came on, took a bow, fixed Daphne with an avuncular glance, and instead of entering into a discussion of the debate's merits, remarked pleasantly, "My, dear, what's made you so cross?"

Daphne sputtered ineffectually and Amies rolled his eyes expressively. John slumped back in his chair with a sigh of relief.

Giorgio di Sant'Angelo diets on spinach salads and is one of the most bizarrely dressed men in fashion, Betsey Johnson is about the prettiest girl, Luis Estevez the most irrepressible (whenever one of his companies folds, there is always a Merle Oberon out there to finance a new one), Marc Bohan the

115

most underrated, Courrèges the most difficult to understand, Cardin the most erratically brilliant, Simonetta surely the hottest tempered. One day in Paris she stood at the top of the marble staircase of her couture house, shouting at me in Italian, French, and English, while I stood at the bottom hurling reciprocal insults up the stairway past poor Fabiani, her husband and then-partner, whose tranquillity was being disturbed by our mutual billingsgate. "*Minuto, minuto,*" pleaded poor Fabiani as Simonetta and I snarled and cursed.

Unlike John Fairchild, who really dug the business, I could never have been a designer. But I sure as hell enjoyed them. And I suspect that in a weird way, most of them enjoyed me, enjoyed professional contact with a journalist who took them as they were, bright, talented, quirky, and never dull, instead of paying them the traditional court affected by generations of fashion writers cooing "divine . . . *formidable* . . . soooper-chic." It was an adversary relationship as stimulating and constructive as a critic could hope to have with creative people whose work, and whose life-styles, he wrote about day after day for a dozen years.

9

Coping with Jackie & Co.

Headlines sell newspapers and covers sell magazines. The *Enquirer*, a sensationalistic newspaper of no special distinction, once achieved the most grotesque headline in my time, and probably sold out that week's issue as a result. The headline read: MOTHER EATS HER BABY.

I am not quite sure what the fashion magazine equivalent of that might be. Obviously a great photograph is desirable, and the cover lines should be provocative, titillating, and even intriguing. Richard Deems of Hearst always said they must assure the potential woman reader that if she would only buy this particular issue, she would almost immediately be more beautiful, healthier, better loved, and universally admired. Not precisely an appeal to the more intelligent American woman, but in the fashion magazine field it appears Deems is correct.

If I had a single issue of a woman's magazine to get out, and my career and the magazine's future depended on the newsstand sale, I would without any hesitation at all choose Jacqueline Kennedy Onassis as my cover girl. It's not that I'm all that impressed by Mrs. Onassis or that I am not aware she's been overexposed. It is simply that there is a continual and enthusiastic, and even perhaps morbid, interest in Jackie, her life and loves.

At *Women's Wear Daily* we were all fed up with Jackie as subject matter years ago. John Fairchild, roving restlessly through the city room, would inevitably end at my desk with whatever latest photo our people had gotten of Jackie, wave it under my nose, and suggest: "Don't put this on page one, James. I've really had it with her. Bury it in the EYE." June Weir, the fashion editor and one of the shrewdest judges of what will, and will not, sell newspapers, would shake her head, raise an eyebrow, and say, "Well, it's a shot no one else has. And she *is* wearing that new Halston . . ." Sometimes I took Fairchild's advice and buried the photo and sometimes I followed Miss Weir's instincts and spread it out across page one. I was usually happier next morning if Miss Weir's recommendation obtained. John would mumble about it and announce over lunch, "Brady has a thing for Jackie," but that day's paper would sell and readers would write letters. Their letters were curious. One sect held that *WWD* was a publicity organ for Mrs. Onassis and that she paid us to print her picture. "We are thoroughly fed up with your slavish idolatry of this silly woman," they would write. Another group of readers, reacting to precisely the same photograph on page one, would accuse *WWD* of "persecuting this noble woman who has already suffered so much. Leave her alone to her family and her privacy if you have any decency whatever."

Jackie herself is said to have a love-hate relationship with the press. It was my experience as a publisher that she alternated between wanting coverage, provided it was favorable, and desperately wanting privacy. There were occasions when her secretary would telephone and say that Mrs. Kennedy would be at such and such a place at lunch that day and she would be wearing so and so. We would thank the secretary, send a photographer to wait outside the restaurant, and have our front-page shot for the next day's paper. At other times she would flee us as from the plague.

Americans have not had a queen since George III's wife. Martha Washington once came close, but her husband had the good sense to say no when some of his fellow aristocrats, mistrustful of the ordinary citizenry, sought to make him king. I suppose it tells us something about ourselves, about the publicity machine of the twentieth century, and about Jacqueline Bouvier Kennedy Onassis herself, that she came closest of all the American women who ever lived to being a sort of royal personage in this otherwise relentlessly home-spun land.

As journalists we tried to understand Jackie, to understand the hold she had on so many of us for those three bright years, the hypnotic attraction she continues to have eleven years after her husband's assassination, the occasionally violent twists of public opinion concerning her, ranging from massive admiration to fretful annoyance, from a very genuine sympathy to outright hostility.

We christened Jackie "Her Elegance." It seemed to fit her driving need to be in fashion, her seemingly genuine love of clothes, and it suggested, in a less than subtle way, our thesis that America wanted a sort of royalty all its own. Lacking such royalty, lacking an aristocracy even, the country made Jacqueline its own very special Lady Bountiful. Later, after the glamour, after the tears, came disillusion in its varying degrees, and she lost some of the gloss. She never became simply "that woman," as had another overexposed First Lady, but a bit of the shine came off. At *WWD* we raged against her, cursed her soundly, relegated her to perdition, and kept her firmly, persistently, aggravatingly in the headlines whenever and however we could. A fashion newspaper seeks out its inspirations where it finds them and gnaws them to the marrow. Later, there were attempts to characterize other women of fashion. Most of them didn't work. Lady Bird Johnson became "Her Efficiency," Happy Rockefeller "Her Happiness," and Pat Nixon "Her Goodness." Babe Paley was "Goddess" Babe Paley, Gloria Guinness was "Glorissima," and a succession of movie stars, politicians' wives, and millionaires' consorts were dubbed by *WWD*. Some of the titles worked, others didn't. For a time Cristina Ford, that smashing Italian playgirl, was "Ciao, bambino," after her customary greeting to anyone she knew and a few she didn't. But only Jackie's title really stuck.

When I was a young newspaperman covering Capitol Hill in the late fifties, Jack and Jackie lived in Georgetown, on the same street I did. I knew a girl who had been at Vassar with Jackie, in the same class. The single memory she had of Jackie was that "she never shaved her legs." A friend of mine lived next door to the Kennedys in those pre–White House days. To him, she was a pretty young woman who wore a baggy Brooks Brothers raincoat and chewed gum. When my wife and I came back from France, we found an apartment across the street from a small Catholic church on the East Side of Manhattan. It is in this church that Jackie hears Mass. John Fairchild's wife Jill serves on a museum committee with her. My children attend the convent school where her daughter passed the grammar school years. But it was the public Jackie, not the private persona, who intrigued me as a journalist and about whom we wrote.

After her period of mourning was over and she had once again surfaced as a public figure, I wrote Jackie suggesting that she submit to an interview, subject to whatever ground rules she proposed. Nancy Tuckerman, her long-time press contact, phoned with the usual response. "Mrs. Kennedy was very touched by your proposal, but . . ." Though Jackie wouldn't sit still for an interview, we forgave her. And stepped up our coverage.

Rose Kennedy, matriarch of the Kennedy clan, telephoned me from Palm Beach early in 1968 to complain that press coverage of Jackie was having a bad effect on the children, Caroline and John. "We had a family meeting on this," she told me, "and it was agreed that I call you and ask for a moratorium on this sort of publicity."

I asked why she had called *WWD*. Was she also asking for such a moratorium from the other papers? Mrs. Kennedy said that it was impossible to contact everyone but that since *WWD* had been "the most ingenious and the most relentless" in its coverage, she would ask us to give Jackie a respite and she hoped other newspapers and magazines would follow our lead. I was delighted at this vision of the entire Kennedy clan getting together in the Palm Beach house with the sole item on the family agenda the little country newspaper for which I labored.

Jackie was headed west with the children for a ski holiday, at Aspen or Vail, as I recall it, and Rose Kennedy asked if we could forgo coverage of that trip and then see whether the other papers would follow suit or if, as I feared, *WWD* might suffer competitively. We had planned to staff the ski trip with a photographer from the New York office and our Denver bureau chief, Dolores Plested. I told Mrs. Kennedy I would be willing to cancel these plans if Rose herself would do us a favor in return. I wanted an exclusive interview for *WWD* at any time convenient to her in the next few months. She agreed and we dropped the ski trip coverage. Actually we were in one of those periods when I tended to agree with John Fairchild that we were overdoing Jackie and I didn't feel this decision meant any great loss.

Rose was as good as her word. June Weir did the interview, a broad-ranging story of several thousand words that conveyed both the charm and the steel of "Mama Rose," as we christened her in headlines. She talked about the joys and the sorrows of her role as wife and mother and was refreshingly frank in her comments about contemporary politics. At that time Bobby Kennedy was well launched in his pursuit of the Democratic nomination for the presidency and June asked about allegations that Bobby was spending all sorts of money to win the nomination. She asked Rose if it were true that the family fortunes were at Bobby's disposal and whether this sort of mammoth campaign spending were in the right tradition. "Mama Rose" responded sweetly that she didn't see anything wrong with it. "It's our money, after all," she said.

June Weir wrote the story, including the "it's our money" comment in its logical place in the running interview. We knew the line was political dynamite but, feeling that Mrs. Kennedy had played fair with us, did not play it up in a sensationalistic manner. Other newspapers, and some politicians, were not as shy. Bobby Kennedy was accused of "buying" the nomination. Newspapers and newsmagazines began to run stories estimating what the Kennedys were spending. Other Democrats still in the primaries issued their own statements of expenditures, most of them so modest as to beggar the imagination. Republicans tut-tutted and delivered public prayers to their own "cloth coat" campaign frugality. Ted Kennedy finally took a hand in the growing debate and shrewdly turned it to advantage by cracking in a press conference that his mother's role in the coming campaign would not include any responsibility for finance.

In that same spring of 1968, WWD ran a double-page spread on "the women around Bobby." It was an amusing, lighthearted pull-together of Rose and Ethel and Jackie, of a dozen or so of the young women in the Kennedy entourage, the campaign workers, members of his New York or Senate staff, and several socially well-placed volunteers who had roles in his growing drive to the White House. The story was well received and, so I thought, in good taste. Several weeks later I was in Washington to attend a black-tie dinner of some sort and dropped in on a reception given by Katharine Graham, the proprietor of the *Washington Post* and of *Newsweek* magazine. When Kay Graham gives a party in Washington people attend it. Ralph Nader was there and aroused my curiosity by asking me to send him all the back copies of *WWD* for the past year. I assumed he was either going to investigate the newspaper or the fashion business now that he had properly skewered General Motors. Mrs. Graham pulled me away from my cross-examination of the enigmatic Nader to introduce me to Teddy Kennedy. She made the introductions and we shook hands. I explained that I ran *WWD* and Teddy said, "Oh, you're the people who are always writing about Bobby and his women."

It was the first suggestion I had had that the story had any sort of cutting edge. I said yes, we were the people, and added fliply, "We'll be glad to write about you and your women, Senator." (This was pre-Chappaquidick, of course.) We drifted on to other small talk and parted pleasantly, and over the years met on several occasions and passed the time of day. Shortly after I had taken over *Harper's Bazaar* I lunched in Washington with Maxine Cheshire, columnist for the *Washington Post* and other papers, intending to fill her ear with self-serving news of *Bazaar*'s revival. We had a corner table in Sans Souci, John Connally and his wife were at the next table with Perle Mesta — the scene was set for my performance. But Maxine didn't seem to want to know about *Bazaar*. "Tell me," she began, "is it true that Teddy Kennedy threatened to punch you?"

If Greta Garbo were the sort, I suppose she might have considered punching someone connected with *WWD* during my time at the paper. We had a staff of about a dozen photographers who spent their time, when not on specific assignment, roving about New York looking for pictures. During lunch one of them carried a beeper in his pocket which would alert him to a possible shot and send him scurrying to a phone to call the city desk and get the information. One day one of the photographers got a tip that Garbo was shopping on East Fifty-seventh Street. He quickly caught up to her, chased her this way and that as the actress ducked in and out of shops and arcades in a vain attempt to preserve her privacy. Finally she was cornered and the cameraman got his pictures. Back at the office we waited excitedly for the contacts to be developed. When they got to my desk I examined them through my magnifying glass. There she was, that still magnificent face clearly shown in several of the shots. And in one picture you could see how desperately she had tried to shield herself, to maintain that legendary privacy. She had held up a newspaper in front of her, between her face and the camera's lens. The paper was that day's *WWD*.

A less private celebrity was Henry Kissinger, whose work as President Nixon's advisor rated only slightly less newspaper space than his associations with movie stars and other attractive women on several continents. Kandy Stroud, *WWD*'s energetic Washington correspondent, wrote in the EYE her estimate of what Kissinger spent in a year on those little lunches and *intime* dinners. Kandy had put the story together from information supplied her by the headwaiters of a half-dozen Washington restaurants. She took their estimate of the average check for dinner and drinks for two, multiplied it by the number of times Kissinger reputedly was on the town, and came up with a figure.

The day the story appeared, Dr. Kissinger called. He said he had no objection to stories about his private life, but the estimates of his entertainment bills were highly inflated, that he was not a rich man and could never afford such expenditures. More objectionable still, Kissinger said, was the inference that the government might have footed the bill. "I have no government expense account," he told me. "I pay my own bills." I said I would check with the reporter and if indeed we were wrong, a correction would be published. When Kandy Stroud was called she said she stood by the figures, which she admitted were estimates at best, but that the government expense account was only a rumor. "I've tried to get Kissinger to comment on it but he never calls back," she complained. I told her I was afraid we owed Kissinger at least a partial retraction. "Well," Kandy said, "then tell him I want a good interview in return."

When my secretary telephoned the White House and asked for Kissinger, his secretary said, "He's in with the President but he'll get right back to you." Annette McQuestion, who I thought was hardened to such matters after a year working for me, was in a high state of excitement. "He's with the President but he'll call you right back," she said. "Well, tell him to hurry up about it," I said with a straight face.

Kissinger was reasonable about the matter. I agreed to publish a correction about the expense account and asked whether he would give Kandy Stroud the interview. He would. "On anything but on my function as a presidential advisor." I said that was agreeable to us since there was so much other ground to cover. Kissinger laughed. "Skirt lengths and sex and so on," he said. Yes, that was the sort of thing I meant. He kept his word and gave Mrs. Stroud the interview.

Neither John Fairchild nor I put the same construction on gossip that some other journalists did. We both shied away from divorce rumors, pillow talk, who was sleeping with whom and the like. That wasn't the sort of newspaper we wanted to run, and by and large we held to our rule. The only time I broke tradition was to report that Senator Eugene McCarthy and his wife "will go their separate ways." I knew the story to be true, McCarthy was very much in the news, and it was an exclusive. I wrestled with my own disinclination for such items and ended by running it in the EYE. McCarthy telephoned while I was at lunch and I called him back. He said he had been told the rumor had appeared and would I read it to him. I did and he said, "Well, it's not as bad as I thought." He thanked me courteously and hung up. His polite and rather sad reaction made me feel worse than if he had threatened to come up and horsewhip me. That was the last item of that kind we would publish in WWD during my tenure.

Not nearly as gracious was an incident which occurred in Paris while I was bureau chief. It involved the Duchess of Windsor, then considered one of the best-dressed women in the world, and the great fashion house of Dior. After each new fashion collection had come out, WWD would sketch or photograph the clothes ordered by the private clients, those wealthy and elegant women for whom the French couture still hold appeal. One of them was the Duchess. The Maison Dior, punctilious in such matters, refused to let us sketch the clothes until the Duchess gave her permission. A WWD reporter telephoned the Duchess's secretary, got the numbers she had ordered at Dior, and the sketches were done. When they appeared in the paper the Duchess complained to Dior and claimed the house was using her to generate publicity. Dior countered by complaining to me, and I blamed the whole mess on the secretary. At one point the Duchess was refusing to pay for the clothes. WWD was suggesting she was "mistaken," thereby skirting the libel laws, and Dior was calling down a pox on both our houses. Years later I shared a dinner table with the Duchess, in Estée Lauder's New York town house, and found her a delightful and witty southern lady whose eyes could still charm any man within view. By this time she and the Duke were fronting for so many causes, commercial as well as charitable, that WWD snidely remarked that the couple were now known as "Commerce & Industry." Of course I didn't bring that up over dinner. Nor, thankfully, did Her Highness.

10

Sex Can Be Fashionable

In the fashion business the suggestion of homosexuality is never far below the surface. When a promising young couturier, Jean Marie Armand, did a poor collection someone remarked, "Well, what do you expect? He's married." When John Fairchild headed the Paris bureau of *Women's Wear Daily*, he wrote that Balenciaga and Givenchy were "hand in hand" in their approach to fashion. Both designers had been feuding with Fairchild over his refusal to accept their dictation on release dates and they claimed the "hand in hand" phrase was sexually intended. It is not clear whether they really believed this or were just using the incident for an excuse, but both couture houses banned *WWD*. The ban was never lifted by Balenciaga, but after his retirement Givenchy relented.

Jacques Heim, who was not much of a designer but had run a couture house for a long time, said once over lunch that he could recall, in his mother's day, when pederasty was unknown in couture and designers were notorious womanizers. "It was worth a lady's reputation," Heim said, "to go to a fitting without being chaperoned. Then one season an assistant was hired who was a homosexual and we all laughed at him and made sport of the poor fellow. He was the exception then, you see." Heim shook his head sadly and you had the impression he missed the good old days.

Of course it's silly to fret about the fact of homosexuality if you are a heterosexual whose job brings you into frequent contact with homosexuals. Those whom I got to know were for the most part delightful and intelligent companions, witty and sensitive men. They had their own friends and lovers and they went their way and I mine. When I first landed in Paris and began to lunch with designers I was priggishly careful to drop, somewhere during the meal, a line such as, "Well, your ideas are most exciting. My wife will want to meet you and hear about them herself." Later I became more sophisticated about the whole business and never, in fact, had so much as a hand dropped casually on my knee.

But many great fashion designers are homosexuals and it is nonsense to say they are not. Some of them take great delight in recounting their amorous adventures, much as the heterosexual braggart will bore you on a Monday with tales of the weekend's conquests.

I remember one lunch at the Colony with John Fairchild and several designers when the talk turned to sex. The subject was, specifically, the age at which one had lost his virginity. The ages got lower and lower as wine bottle followed wine bottle and as the clock moved toward 3 P.M. I was embarrassed to tell the truth about my own sexual naïveté for fear of being thought retarded. One of the designers finally got the age down to nine years. "That was with a woman, of course," he said. "I was much older when I discovered men."

Another New York designer had a male lover who was a city policeman. When he announced this one day over lunch

I must have raised a skeptical eyebrow. "No, really he is," the designer insisted. "Well, what do you do?" I asked. "Oh, sometimes I wear his uniform and blow his whistle." I had visions of my friend becoming overfond of the uniform and cruising his usual haunts dressed as one of New York's Finest.

Andy Warhol is frequently in the company of homosexuals and yet has a curious attitude toward them. One evening at a dinner party Andy introduced a strapping young man, well over six feet tall, with the shoulders of a defensive tackle and a blue beard to defy the Wilkinson Sword Blade. Yet he was wearing ruby lipstick, a facial veil, a satin dress, high heels, and was introduced by a woman's name. Andy took him around the room to show him off. We all nodded our appreciation.

After lunch one day, Andy and I strolled along Fifty-second Street and something got him on the subject.

"They make me furious," he blurted out. "They think they're women, they claim to be women, and yet they don't menstruate, they don't get all swollen up with water every month. It drives me crazy."

I had an urge to pat Andy soothingly on the arm but instead nodded vigorously and tut-tutted for what I felt was a tactful interval.

In Paris there was a very competent young press agent who represented several of the houses and gave very good parties each summer season in a large garden behind his flat. Once he startled the press and fashion buyers by stationing a young black man, naked except for a coat of oil, to take the wraps. Another time the party had a Mexican motif, and in addition to strolling guitarists in costume, he had somewhere procured a small donkey to wander through the garden party with large wicker baskets of fruit attached to his saddle. The guests were to pick the fruit to eat with their cool drinks in the summer evening. Trouble was, the donkey had somehow become sexually aroused and kept trying to mount the guests, amid loud braying noises and fruit spilling all over the grass, while nervous ladies backed away in apprehension.

This was the same man who sent Christmas cards displaying a photo of himself, garbed as Napoleon, draped over the broken gun carriage of an ancient fieldpiece off by itself in a snowy wasteland. Once over lunch he told me he was engaged to be married. I had assumed he was homosexual but fortunately did not take the remark for the joke I thought it to be. When I made no response he said, yes, he was really being married. I asked who the lucky woman was.

"Well," he said, "she's in public relations. For the cotton industry." That explanation would have sufficed for me but he went on. "She goes about the country pushing the use of cotton. She gets nuns to wear cotton sanitary napkins instead of the synthetic kind."

He had the wedding in London and people flew over for it. It was a smashing wedding, apparently. A British fashion editor had a spat with her husband, and when he stalked out, went into the ladies' room to cry and eventually to attempt suicide. To get out the small window and throw herself into the street, she had to stand on the toilet seat. While so doing, her foot slipped into the bowl, breaking her ankle, and they had to force down the door to rescue her. It was that sort of wedding and the marriage didn't last either.

Two other fashion designers I know found themselves in one of the more obscure provincial towns of interior Tunisia. The one had a large house in the area and employed a staff of locals. Knowing his guest's tastes, he arranged for a young Arab boy to serve the guest and accomplish whatever other wonders might be required. The boy apparently did this, the guest was apparently satisfied. Next day as the two designers sat taking the sun and sipping cool drinks in a café on the local square, the Arab boy in question passed by and was called over to chat. The host-designer asked his guest if appropriate services had been rendered.

"Oh, yes," was the reply.

"What did he charge you?"

The guest mentioned a figure. The host turned angrily on the Arab boy. "You little cheat. You charged him tourist rates. This man isn't a tourist. He's my guest. My guest. Your conduct is outrageous."

The young boy stood with head bowed.

"You won't get away with this," the host thundered. "I'm going to tell your father."

Another rather famous Paris designer recently suffered a severe bite on his genitals during a passionate affair and the rumor went around Paris that the bite had been sufficient to have castrated him. This was not so. But it was enough for one fashion editor to assert, "You know, since it happened he hasn't produced a collection worth reviewing."

The men's fashion editor of one of the country's biggest magazines was fired for importuning the male models while they were changing their elastic stockings or plucking their eyebrows in the photographers' studios. This was gleefully reported in the next day's EYE column (no names were used — EYE readers would *know*). Within a few months the item came back to haunt me. I was in Paris for the couture collections when Barney Leason, the London bureau chief, phoned to alert me to potential scandal. It seemed that an art director of one of the Fairchild publications was recruiting London's male models by the platoon and posing them naked in bathtubs.

"What the hell is he doing that for?" I demanded of Leason. "You can't show men's fashions if the guy's naked in the tub."

"That's what I said," Leason replied. "But he says these are layouts for wristwatches and the guy leaves his watch on the side of the tub." He paused for a moment. "Actually, what the models are complaining about, is that he tries to get into the tub with them."

I agreed with Barney that we had better get the art director back to New York before matters got much stickier. But we were already too late. The art director, a dashing Latin American, had by this time moved his road company orgy on to Paris and had set up camp in a Rive Gauche hotel. I phoned and left messages but our young man was elusive. Finally I called the New York office and talked to the editors. They said they had supplied their exotic traveler with several thousand dollars to buy European men's wear and had otherwise given him carte blanche to come back to New York with some exciting photo spreads. I informed them that from what I had heard, the spreads would be exciting — and unprintable.

Rumor began to drift up to Paris from Rome of some pretty fancy living while our boy was in Italy, and by the time I finally corralled him in Paris, he had met half the homosexuals in the haute couture and was busy filling his bathtub with handsome young men supplied by central casting. I presented him with a bill of particulars, told him I didn't give a damn about his private life, but wouldn't have him trading on his position to procure new friends. He rolled his eyes, told me there must be some mistake, but reluctantly promised to be on the next Pan Am flight to New York. I think it was actually three days later before he left, and in New York he was eventually fired, not for his morals, but because he couldn't account for all the money he'd spent.

Six months later I walked into one of the Paris couture houses to see a new collection and there he was, Nikon in hand, on the payroll of the couturier, shooting pictures and providing, I was sure, other essential services. As I recall, the designer in question that season produced the most decadent line he had ever done and six months later the evil genius was gone, presumably on to someone else's bathtub.

Then there was the ex-paratrooper who was smuggled into the mannequins' *cabine* at Balenciaga and actually modeled a collection before the great man discovered he'd been duped by a transvestite. And the boast by another designer that he had once seduced an American bridegroom on his honeymoon aboard the night train from Nice to Paris while the unsuspecting bride slept in the very next compartment. And the gothic tale of a male secretary to Antonio del Castillo who used the cellar of the designer's Spanish castle to whip young boys who were paid to permit the poor fellow to indulge his little weakness. Castillo flew into a rage, dismissed the secretary, and presumably unchained the penitents.

In one of the early issues I edited for *Bazaar*, I got into difficulties with Pierre Cardin over the hint of sexual impropriety in a profile I had written about that great man. I had known Cardin for years and considered him a talent but someone to whom it was difficult to warm. He was self-oriented, much like myself, I suppose, and though we got on it was at a distance. Cardin's then chief assistant, and later partner, is a brilliant and handsome young man named André Oliver. There are those in the fashion field who believe Oliver to be the single most talented designer still working for another couturier, and have urged Oliver to break away from Cardin and go off on his own. But André stays with Pierre. When he was drafted during the Algerian war, André was probably the only private in the French army to have a uniform custom-tailored by a couturier and, by pulling one string or another, Cardin had André flown home to Paris weekends to help out with the collection. This, mind you, from Algeria while the war was in full stride.

Some years ago when Cardin was in financial difficulties, he fell in with the lovely French actress Jeanne Moreau. Moreau was at the top of her career, having made *Jules et Jim* for Truffaut, and she was a careful businesswoman who invested her money shrewdly. She moved in with Cardin and André Oliver moved out. Moreau had the reputation of being a tigress and Cardin had the reputation of being, well, a fashion designer. No one really knows the truth of what their relationship was, but it was rumored that Moreau put a great deal of money into the Cardin business, got him to organize his work habits, inspired him to branch out into the men's wear business, and generally straightened out his affairs.

André in the meantime was mooning about Paris, separated for the first time from the older gentleman who had brought him into the business and into his life. It was reported that André was threatening suicide and that Cardin, upset at the reports, bought him a fine flat. Then it was said that André, while well-housed, was still depressed and was still talking about death. So Cardin set up charge accounts at some decent restaurants. Now André was well-housed and well-fed but still morose. So Cardin got Bernard Buffet to offer André one of his pictures. André was shown through Buffet's studio and supposedly announced, "There are three I can't choose between," and got them all. Later Cardin heard that André was staying out all night, drinking and dancing with young women at New Jimmy's, and Cardin announced he was deeply shocked. How could André's parents permit a young man to carry on so in wicked Paris?

Madame Moreau eventually went on to other things and André and Pierre were reunited and continue to work closely today, though living in separate apartments. I wrote some of this in the profile I did of Cardin for *Bazaar*, reasoning that fashion magazine stories about fashion designers were milk-toast affairs that told the reader nothing but what the designer wanted to get across about his own genius. I believed that *Bazaar* readers were sophisticated and intellectually curious and would want to know more about the men, and women, who created their clothes and not just the usual press agentry pap. So I wrote about Cardin and Moreau and André and got a blistering letter from Pierre in which he saluted my "still young talent," but warned severely that I was in peril of degrading that talent to the level of a "fashion *Confiden-*

tial." I wrote back that he had lost his sense of humor. The readers liked the piece and it drew a good deal of mail.

The most intelligent man I knew in Paris was Pierre Bergé. Bergé had come to Paris from La Rochelle wanting to be a painter. Being intelligent, he realized early on that he lacked the ability to be first-rate, and he put down his brush to become Bernard Buffet's manager. He made a market in Buffet paintings and for several years in the fifties Buffet was the most successful young painter in the world. Bergé wrote a book about Buffet and once, by my own counting, had some eighty Buffets hung on the walls of his own rather modest apartment. Buffet left Bergé to marry a tall girl called Annabelle, and Bergé fell in with a young assistant designer at the House of Dior. The young designer was Yves Saint Laurent.

Saint Laurent is today the most influential and important fashion designer in the world and I am convinced his success derives in almost equal parts from his own magnificent talent and his friendship and partnership with Pierre Bergé. The two men are complementary; Bergé outgoing, politically astute, a figure in the worlds of art and theater and writing in Paris; Saint Laurent basically shy, introverted, sensitive, and cultured. They are a great team.

Bergé hardly fits anyone's image of a fashion figure. Short, physically tough, not given to catty remarks or the retailing of gossip, Bergé was arrested by American MPs near the Palais de Chaillot while still a teenager for demonstrating on behalf of Gary Davis, the American veteran who became a cause célèbre after World War II by giving up his American passport and becoming "a citizen of the world." Bergé continued in the left wing of French politics and is a keen student of the American and British political systems.

One night there was a charity ballet by Roland Petit and Renée Jeanmaire. Saint Laurent, a close friend of the dancers, had done Zizi's costumes and, I believe, the stage sets. It was sleeting and raining the night of the event and Bergé had a bad case of the flu. He arrived bundled up and feverish, a scarf wrapped around his neck to protect a sore throat. There had been a mix-up in the tickets, as often happens to charity organizers, and a crowd of nearly a thousand people in evening dress was milling around the lobby of the theater and out on the sidewalk in the slop. When it became obvious that the organizers would never get the matter adjudicated, an angry Bergé leaped up on a podium, grabbed a seating plan of the theater, and began reissuing tickets with new seat numbers scribbled on the back. In about forty-five minutes he had solved the problem, and, hoarse from shouting out the new numbers, fell into a seat in the back row to half watch the ballet and spend the rest of the time blowing his nose. It was a bravado performance such as I had never seen.

11

Feuding with the White House— and Just About Everybody Else

WWD was a profitable, respected, and obscure little trade newspaper in 1961 when John F. Kennedy came to the White House. The newspaper was also virtually unknown to the general public. Few persons outside the fashion business had ever heard of it. It was Jacqueline Kennedy who gave us our opening.

Kennedy had been elected by the slimmest of margins the previous November and it was clear that his advisors were urging that he broaden, rather than narrow, his popular base by appealing to the entire spectrum of Americans. This was to be done in any number of ways. One minor tactic was for the beautiful, glamorous and fashionable First Lady to come out strongly on the side of American fashion which was then, as now, having its problems with competing imports from Europe and the Orient. Pat Nixon had campaigned in her "Republican cloth coat" and aides to President Kennedy didn't think Jackie should be flaunting her expensive Paris wardrobe around the White House. Jackie was apparently convinced that this made good sense. She announced in a public statement that although she had long worn European clothes, especially couture designs by the great Paris establishments, she would now and in future be dressed only by Americans. She appointed as "house" designer Oleg Cassini.

Mr. Cassini is the brother of Igor Cassini, the old Hearst gossip columnist (Cholly Knickerbocker), and is a diverting and charming fellow. He is also a second-rate designer and along Seventh Avenue there was a shaking of heads over why Jackie had issued him the royal warrant. But she had.

Within a month or two John Fairchild had somehow sniffed out a report that Jackie was still buying clothes from the Paris couture and was having them "smuggled" into the country in the elegant Vuitton luggage of "Sister Lee" Radziwill. John phoned me in Paris and we got the story. Hubert de Givenchy was making the clothes on Jackie's dummy and Lee was getting them to 1600 Pennsylvania Avenue on her frequent trips. Realizing that WWD had a responsibility to the American people, we duly reported this little cloak-and-dagger game in a front-page story. Pierre Salinger, then the presidential press secretary, issued a statement saying we were mistaken or worse, but newspapers and television and radio stations across the country picked up the story. Salinger fumed, but WWD followed up with a story estimating just how much Jackie, and the other Kennedy women, spent on clothes in a given year. Once again the denials came and once again WWD was quoted everywhere. In the spring of 1961 the Kennedys made their state visit to Paris and we got an inferential confirmation of our story when Jacqueline made her grand entrance at de Gaulle's state dinner wearing a Givenchy dress and looking smashing.

When Lyndon Johnson came to power, his daughters came of age, and, in the way of young women, got married. Luci was first. The White House held an off-the-record briefing on details of her upcoming wedding, including a description of the wedding dress. I was back in New York by this time, as publisher, and I gave instructions to our Washington staff to boycott the off-the-record briefing. Within an hour after it was over I had a Washington friend on the telephone, a local reporter who had attended the briefing, and had a complete and accurate description of the famous dress. We ran a front-page sketch in the next morning's paper.

Liz Carpenter, the White House press secretary for Lady Bird and the girls, exploded. She issued a statement saying that WWD had been guilty of unethical conduct for disclosing information given in an off-the-record briefing. I issued a counterstatement, both in a telegram to Mrs. Carpenter and in a press release to the wire services, saying that we were opposed to off-the-record briefings, had purposely not attended this one, and accused the White House of attempting to manipulate the press. Mrs. Carpenter fired back, to my delight, and we kept the whole thing going another week by having Dick Wightman, our White House man, pose a question to Mr. Johnson at the next nationally televised presidential press conference. Knowing Lyndon Johnson's impressive temper, I am still in awe of Wightman's courage in standing and asking the President to comment on the merits of the case and asking how Mrs. Carpenter's response jibed with the President's attitude on press freedom. The Chief Executive had the good sense to reply in a humorous tone that he thought he'd better leave such matters to the ladies of the family.

I was in Hollywood for the Academy Awards the following year and attended a dinner at the house of Actress Donna Reed. Lynda Bird Johnson was then very much in the company of actor George Hamilton, and the young couple joined us for after-dinner drinks. They came in with their Secret Service men and were introduced around the room. When they came to me, Lynda said, "Why are you so mean to my mother and my sister and me?" and sat down in the next chair to get an answer. This sort of question is easy to handle in a speech to journalism students, but it is quite another thing when you are face to face with a beautiful and angry young woman whose father happens to be the President of the United States.

I stuttered some sort of disclaimer, saying we were only trying to do our job, and then suggested that if Lynda and Luci would submit to an interview, we would be delighted to publish an upbeat story on their true attitudes toward all this publicity, their feeling about living in the White House, and the like. Lynda agreed to try to arrange the interview, and she did, and it was a marvelous and widely quoted WWD exclusive. Later, when she married Chuck Robb, we again got a beat on the wedding dress and ran it on the front page. Her dress was designed by Geoffrey Beene, a first-rate New York designer, and though we eventually got the information from another source, we made life miserable for poor Beene for several days. John Fairchild, fashion editor June Weir, and I haunted Beene's Seventh Avenue office, trying to get the story. Later Beene's partner, meeting me at a party, admitted, "You are the most frightening people I have ever met." Before we got the correct sketch and ran it in the paper, someone, I have never been quite sure who, planted a false sketch and we very nearly published it. Only John Fairchild's instincts prevented my making a damn fool of myself and injuring the paper's reputation for accuracy. If I were not a good Democrat, I might have suspected the Machiavellian hand of Lyndon Baines Johnson in the plot. But of course LBJ would never have been party to such wickedness.

Throughout the Johnson years we feuded on and off with Liz Carpenter, a honey-tongued little slip of a Texas girl who weighs perhaps a hundred and seventy-five pounds and has tonsils to match. Although Liz was an accredited journalist and member of the Washington press corps, she had for years functioned as a press agent for Johnson while he was still in the Senate. This is not considered cricket and there were efforts made by the Standing Committee of Correspondents on Capitol Hill to have Liz's press credentials lifted. When LBJ became President, Liz became a full-time flack, and thus narrowly avoided an ugly confrontation with the press corps. Though she and I continued to bicker in print, she agreed to give WWD a free-swinging interview about her job as a press secretary. We ran the story opposite a full-page photo of Liz, her tongue wagging, under the headline: THE NATIONAL MOUTH.

When the Nixons entered the White House it was anticipated that the new administration would be cool, efficient, computerized, and, for journalists, dull as dust. No one, of course, could have foreseen the rise of Martha Mitchell. Or Watergate. As each of the Nixon girls was married, WWD went through its ritual dance of scooping the competition on details of the wedding dress, where the newlyweds would honeymoon, and the like. Either because they were more efficient or because they simply didn't care, the White House failed to erupt in angry outrage as had the two previous administrations. There was barely a murmur when WWD christened Tricia Nixon "Goody Two-Shoes" and said she was the best-dressed subteen in America. The most delightful reaction to that rather wise-guy crack came from a retail buyer in a midwestern store who took the line seriously and wrote a long critical letter to the editor complaining that there were "lots of subteens" better dressed than Tricia. Tricia was, at the time, in her early twenties.

When Tricia began to be seen frequently in the company of a young New Yorker named Edward Finch Cox, it was Randy Smith, our Harvard correspondent, who discovered through some friends that Cox had a nickname: "Fast Eddie." WWD of course snapped up the "Fast Eddie" line and used it whenever Tricia's beau was mentioned. And the other papers quickly picked it up. Cox finally tired of the pleasantry and phoned me. He asked if we could drop the line. Since it was just before Christmas and I was in an expansive mood, I said we'd be glad to do so if Cox would tell me how he had gotten his nickname.

His reply was disappointingly straight. As a prep school boy he'd been a rather eager little beaver, running errands and hustling off to extracurricular meetings and the like. I thanked Cox, wished him a pleasant holiday, and hung up, depressed that "Fast Eddie" did not derive from racier origins.

All our jousting with the White House had an element of showboating, of course, and John and I got an almost juvenile kick out of being important for a day. But underlying the fun was the very basic journalistic reason for being: find out something and convey it to the person who put down good money for your paper. Tell him something he didn't know before, preferably something about people in power. Everything else in publishing is window dressing. It is the natural lot of the journalist to be at odds with government, at every level, and when politicians are contented with the press then there is something wrong. The press has probably stopped doing its job.

I don't think I could be a full-time muckraker, a Jack Anderson or Drew Pearson. Everyone is angry at them *all* the time, it seems. There has to be a small touch of the masochist in a journalist who spends his waking days fighting with everybody. Even people who liked Pearson disliked him. I am afraid I lack the intestinal fortitude to be constantly at war with the *whole* world. Enemies should be limited to a few at a time. John Fairchild taught me that. If you are trying to get something on Macy's, ask Bruce Gimbel. If you're persona non grata with Bonwit Teller, take Saks Fifth Avenue to lunch.

But you ought to be fighting with someone. You really should. It isn't much fun otherwise and you aren't doing a job for your readers. They expect you to take certain risks, to become unpopular in some quarters, and the more exalted those quarters the better the reader likes it.

If you don't have a royal family to scrutinize, then the White House will have to do. I've often been asked what the hell does it matter how the First Lady dresses, or the children behave, or the President spends his leisure time? And in the essential sense, it matters very little. But it seems as if small things sometimes point to large directions. The fact that Mrs. Nixon's first name is not Pat, but Thelma, that she was not born on Saint Patrick's Day, but a day away, these things tell something about a politician who states, as Mr. Nixon once did, "My wife's name is Pat. She's Irish, you know, and she was born on Saint Patrick's Day . . ."

I don't want to make too much of this, but you can go on. Lies told on behalf of Jacqueline Kennedy — that she was buying only American clothes when in fact she, and others, knew damn well she was still buying French clothes — tell you something about the attitude of those running the White House in the Kennedy years. Kandy Stroud's extraordinary *WWD* interview with John Mitchell in his cups gave a hint of events and attitudes that would not become public for several years. We were not running the *New York Times* or the *Chicago Tribune*. We were running *Women's Wear Daily*, and so we stuck pretty much to minor scandals and side issues, subsidiary aspects of the exercise of power. But in our small way, we reported as best we could how power was being exercised, what sort of people these really were who ran the country.

Our free-swinging manner at *WWD* inevitably resulted in some pretty colorful sparring with many of the country's most important storekeepers. When I was still a reporter covering New York's retail scene, Jack Straus, then the board chairman of Macy's, was once quoted as suggesting that

Macy's hire me back "so he'll leave us alone." Years later, when I was publisher, we did a less-than-complimentary profile of some top Macy executives, including the then-president Wheelock Bingham, a delightful, hard-drinking, roly-poly chap. Straus hit the roof and both John Fairchild and I were summoned to Straus's office in Herald Square. I was on time for the scheduled inquisition but John was unaccountably late. Embarrassed at his failure to appear, I sent a message in to Straus to say I'd be glad to start the meeting without him. Back from the angry Straus came word that he'd wait for Fairchild and that he didn't care whether I attended the session or not. I was about to walk out in a huff when John arrived, smiling but pale.

"What the hell happened? Straus is boiling."

"James, I had diarrhea. All morning. I didn't dare leave the apartment. But don't tell them."

We were ushered into Straus's office. He gave us his grim chief-executive's stare but John bounced over, shook hands, and announced cheerily, "I'm so sorry to be late, Mr. Straus. But my plane was delayed."

We all sat down, no further explanations were given or offered, and thanks to Bingham's graciousness, and Straus's basic decency, the whole mess was cleared up. Toward the close of the meeting, when we agreed that on major news stories we would have an open wire to John Blum, the corporate public relations man, I suggested that there would be occasions on which Straus himself ought to be available for comment. Blum looked superiorly at me.

"I can't conceive of any question that I couldn't answer," he announced.

"Oh, I don't know, Johnny," said Straus, "they might be calling to ask if it were true you were fired."

Bruce Gimbel feuded with *WWD* on such a regular and acrimonious basis that even after I had left the paper, and was running *Harper's Bazaar*, he telephoned me one morning to complain about a critical piece in that day's WWD.

"But I'm not there any longer, Bruce," I said exasperatedly.

"I know that. But I want to know who has it in for us."

At a dinner party one evening I greeted Gimbel and asked after his son, Bob, whom I had known in Paris, and who had then gone to work in Saks Fifth Avenue, part of the Gimbel chain.

"How's he doing?" I asked brightly.

"You damn journalists are always out to make trouble," Bruce exploded.

I protested that I didn't know what he was talking about.

"You're always trying to get something on somebody. I know how you operate."

Gordon Greenfield once headed City Specialty Stores, a fashion retail chain that included Oppenheim Collins and Franklin Simon. Gordon was the son of the great Philadelphia real-estate baron Albert M. Greenfield, and a young man trying to live down his father's achievements. One morning I was strolling through the ground floor of Franklin Simon, then on New York's Thirty-fourth Street, when Greenfield spotted me. I had written something the week before he hadn't liked and now, his voice rising to a shout, he called for the store detectives.

"Throw this man out. Get him out of here."

A store detective approached the two of us and some of the women shoppers stopped what they were doing to witness the scene. The store detective didn't seem quite sure who Gordon was, and had no idea who I was or what crime I'd committed. Gordon's rage increased as the detective hesitated.

"I'm the president of this store and I want this man thrown out of here," he shouted.

There were several dozen women around us now. The store dick approached and I squared off.

"Don't touch me," I said. "I'll leave the store but don't put a hand on me."

I exited with what I hoped was a slow, dignified tread while Gordon, right behind me, kept up his yelling.

Several years later I ran into him in the bar of the Connaught Hotel in London.

"You know," Gordon said pleasantly, "I never really held it against you for that scene you made in my store."

I told him he was most gracious.

Of course, there were lawsuits. The sort of not-to-be-intimidated journalism we practiced at WWD was bound to irritate. And irritated men, and companies, bring suit. Fairchild retained an experienced and competent law firm, Satterlee & Stephens, on Park Avenue, and in my time, and perhaps throughout its history, we never lost a lawsuit. Some suits were of the nuisance variety and some were of substance.

My favorite litigant was the young woman who sued for invasion of privacy over some crowd photos we had taken of the running of the bulls at Pamplona. The photos had run as part of a story on the fiesta of San Fermín, immortalized by Hemingway. Some weeks later the corset and bra page editor chose to pick one of the crowd scenes of Pamplona to pose the question: how many women in this picture no longer wear girdles? The question was intended to be rhetorical. No one could possibly know such intimate details about the hundreds of women, anonymous to us, pictured in that seething, milling crowd. But there was one young woman who claimed that she was easily identifiable in the grainy mass of celebrants, a New Yorker who had attended the fiesta and the bullfights, and who now claimed that she had suffered embarrassment and indignity because of our implied suggestion that she might not be properly corseted. Her suit died of its own weight.

W. Maxey Jarman was and is the head of a great fashion conglomerate known as Genesco. His firm owns Bonwit Teller, Henri Bendel, and manufacturing concerns in the shoe and men's wear and other fashion fields. Several years ago *WWD* did a two-page profile of Mr. Jarman to which he took violent exception. He sued for libel, and one afternoon, in the city room of *WWD*, I was served with the papers. They informed me that not only was *WWD* being sued for six million dollars but that I, as publisher, was being sued personally for another six million. When I got home that evening I showed a Xerox copy of the document to my wife. Her reaction was eminently practical. "If he were suing you for twenty-five thousand dollars you might conceivably have to pay it. But six million? Forget it." She poured us both a drink and we toasted the fact that probably never again would such a price be put upon my head. The suit was settled when *WWD* agreed to publish a statement saying that we had not intended to suggest that Maxey was a rascal and that, to our knowledge, he was a pretty good sort.

Alexander Cohen, the Broadway producer, had put together a musical called *Dear World*. Angela Lansbury was the star, and while the play was still on the road prior to its Broadway opening, there began to be talk that *Dear World* was a turkey. Angela Lansbury told someone in Boston, who told Peter Dibble of *WWD* in New York, that the show was so bad she hoped it would not be brought into town. Dibble dropped a line into the EYE column. Cohen's suit alleged that the advance ticket sale had been hurt by the item. Before formally filing against us, Cohen telephoned and I agreed to go uptown to his office in Shubert Alley. John Fairchild and Bill Dwyer, who ran the business side of the company and who was a lawyer, went with me. Cohen was amiable and the meeting pleasant, but he wanted too much in the way of a retraction. We had the feeling he wanted the newspaper to humiliate itself and to plug *Dear World* at the same time. We told him we believed the item to be in the nature of fair comment. He brought suit, but the bottom dropped out almost immediately when one of his associates in *Dear World* withdrew as a plaintiff, assuring me that Cohen had sued without his approval and that he, the associate, wanted no part of the case.

Another antagonist was the so-called Church of Scientology. On one of my trips to London I had found the British press full of stories about the reported excesses of the cult, statements were being made in Parliament, immigration of Scientologists was curtailed, and letters were written to the *Times*. I sat in the bathtub of my room in the Connaught Hotel, smoking Havana cigars and delighting in the controversy. The British appeared particularly exercised over the fact that Scientology was an American import. As soon as I got back to New York I looked into it and found there was a flourishing Church of Scientology that worked out of a midtown hotel. Denis Sheahan, a reporter who had recently joined *WWD* from the *World-Journal-Tribune*, was sent up to see about it. He came back and wrote a sizzling story, highly critical of the new "religion." We were immediately hit with a libel suit. The Scientologists said we were being beastly and I guess we were. During the pre-trial examination by our lawyers one of the Scientology chaps assured the lawyer that he got his directions from a voice on high, and perhaps he did. That was about five years ago, and the issue has never yet gotten into a courtroom and the whole excitement about Scientology has rather died down. I think the *WWD* story, which we put on the front page, may have had something to do with it.

We were considered hard-nosed (even the ladylike and gentle June Weir was once described by a designer as "a nun with knives in both pockets") and I suppose we were. Yet there were opportunities to play the gentleman, to say no to excess, to resist that "one more" journalistic sensation that would sell another thousand papers.

A convent-educated young woman, one of the first middle-class whites deeply into the drug scene, tried relentlessly to get *WWD* to publish her story. She was the daughter of a very well-known publisher, a man for whom I held no brief; but though I would have enjoyed discomfiting him, there was no way in which my newspaper would touch the story. The girl, pitifully fat, open to any sexual or narcotic adventure, had posed nude for one of the underground papers under an assumed name and now wanted to get her dreadful tale into *WWD*. It was obvious she was striking back at her parents, for reasons unknown to me. She had taped a dialogue between herself and her father when he had written her out of the family, and offered to let us publish the transcript. When we turned this down she had another, brighter thought.

"Then I'll go to confession and tell the priest what I've been doing, in gory detail, and tape record the whole thing."

I suggested she stay with the underground papers and see a psychiatrist. Later when I was running *Bazaar* she became a telephone pest, offering to pose for photos, "any kind you want," or to write her memoirs. Yola Carlough, my secretary and out of the same convent school, was magnificent in fending off the poor creature and (thank God) keeping her away from the office.

There were other occasions when to be hard-nosed was clearly, to me, the only course. Kandy Stroud did a piece in which she mentioned Ellen Stewart, the guiding force behind Café La Mama, the off-Broadway theater hatchery. Kandy didn't know who Stewart was, didn't know she was black, and inserted parenthetically after her name the journalistic wisecrack "who she?" It slipped through, and next day Miss Stewart and her manager arrived at the *WWD* offices as grim-faced and vengeful as an Arizona posse on a hot day.

"That was a racial slur," Miss Stewart announced. Her manager, a white man, nodded.

I said it was no such thing but that I was sorry Miss Stewart was upset. I assured her Kandy hadn't even known she was black (I had checked this when I heard Miss Stewart was en route and raging).

"It was a racial slur," she declared again.

"No," I said. "It's a kind of play on Harold Ross's old technique at the *New Yorker*, querying a writer who hadn't fully identified someone, scribbling 'who he?' in the margin."

Miss Stewart would have none of it. I said for chrissake I was sorry, that our theater pages had often saluted her as a pioneer and as a seminal force, and that she was making something out of nothing.

Miss Stewart demanded an apology in the next day's paper in which *WWD* would admit having slurred her and then apologize for it.

I told Miss Stewart we would run a line saying we were sorry to have slighted an important figure of the theater, that we would say our writer should indeed have known who she was. But I'd be damned if we'd admit to a racial prejudice we didn't feel, and hadn't intended. When the unsatisfactory meeting ended, Miss Stewart and I were glaring at one another. As she strode out, her manager sidled back to me.

"You know, she's touchy. But she'd make a great story for the paper. You ought to have someone interview her one day."

I told him to go to hell.

George Farkas, the peppery little retailer who founded Alexander's Department Stores in New York, and whose wife Ruth was recently named ambassador to Luxembourg on the strength of a three-hundred-thousand-dollar campaign contribution to the Nixon re-election, threatened one day to punch me in the nose. A French television crew had been interviewing the American buyers in Paris for the couture collections. When it was Farkas's turn, he was asked if he preferred the interview in English or in French.

"In French, of course," declared Mr. Farkas.

The interviewer launched into his questions and asked

Farkas, in French, whether it was true that "in New York you have the reputation of a shark?"

Farkas's French wasn't up to the word for shark, *"requin."* All he understood were the words "reputation" and "New York."

Smiling broadly at the camera, he replied, *"Mais oui, certainement."*

The television reporter told me the story and of course I put it in the next day's cable. Farkas learned about it, and when he glimpsed John Fairchild and me lunching in the garden of the Plaza Athenée hotel, he charged up to the table. Fairchild wasn't sure who he was and as the older man reached us, John rose, smiled, and extended his hand.

"If you two don't get off my back I'll sue you for all you're worth," Farkas began.

John slumped back into his seat.

"John," I said, "this is Mr. Farkas. Of Alexander's, you know."

Farkas turned on me. "Another wise remark out of you and I'll punch you in the nose."

John was rapidly slipping lower in his wicker chair and around us buyers and designers stopped eating to watch the exchange.

I stood up, several inches taller and perhaps thirty years younger than the belligerent Mr. Farkas. I told him not to be silly, and after a few additional muttered threats, Mr. Farkas retreated. John pushed his plate away.

"I can't eat a thing," he said. John took these things hard.

That night I told the story to my wife.

"You should both be ashamed of yourself," she said. "Teasing an older man like that." She wouldn't speak to me for a day.

There was another occasion when a WWD story led to a nose actually being punched. The story had suggested, rather nastily, that the wife of Bonwit Teller president William

Smith was "flacking" for the store, getting society women to spend their money at Bonwit's. When the reporter who had written the piece next appeared in Smith's office, Smith punched him. The reporter came back to the city room with a swollen face and vague plans to sue Smith. John rose to the occasion, visited Smith, got him to apologize to the reporter, and agreed we would avoid references to his wife in future. At this distance, I'd say that Smith acted rather gallantly, but that instead of taking it out on the reporter, he should have come down to the office and horsewhipped the lot of us.

12

The Great Skirt-Length Debate

Nothing that little country newspaper *Women's Wear Daily* did since its beginning in 1910 could ever match the excitement, the bitterness, the passionate debate, and the publicity generated by what would come to be called "The Great Skirt-Length Debate."

By its very definition, fashion is change. Clothes become looser or tighter, skirts get longer or shorter, bosoms flatten or protrude, orange is in and purple is out. It is all very simple, quite predictably cyclical, and as each new fashion comes in, women renew their wardrobes, buy clothes, alter or throw out the old, and the fashion industry prospers. Fashion changes because, in general, women like change. They like to see themselves differently every season or every couple of seasons. When a fashion change comes suddenly there is a disposition to throw up one's hands, grouse and delay a bit, then go out and buy the new look, whatever it is.

It is nonsense to point a finger at the fashion business for being in fashion. Detroit accomplishes the same effect year after year as tail fins, wheel covers, fastbacks, and stereo tape-decks become crucial to the look of one's car and then, as suddenly, become obsolete. It is the way Detroit sells cars. It is all rather silly but to call it wicked is a bit much. I have bought a number of automobiles in my time and not even once has a salesman bounded across the street with a revolver to force me to buy. Rudy Gernreich, that self-anointed fashion intellectual, holds that the blue denim boiler suit affected by millions of Chinese is the single perfect garment since it covers the body, never goes out of style, and is relatively durable and cheap. Lest you take Rudy too seriously on this recent passion for uniforms, remember that it was only a few years ago that he created and bestowed on an anxiously waiting world what he called the "monokini," a bathing suit without a top. Women don't want uniforms and I am convinced that people want to look different. It all goes back to the fig leaf. As James Thurber might have said, you could look it up.

Ever since Mr. Dior dropped skirts in 1947 to create the New Look skirt lengths have been rising and falling with the regularity of tides. There was, for a change, a quite valid and logical reason for the New Look in 1947. For years the world had been in uniform, fabric in short supply, and fashion lumped with new cars and other nonessentials. Dior understood this, and when he launched his Maison Dior, he dropped skirt lengths nearly a foot, broadened shoulders, and, in general, made women look startlingly different from the way they had looked since 1939. I was in college in 1947 and found the new clothes ridiculous. So did most of the girls I knew. We all laughed together over such French frivolity. Within a few months the girls were wearing their own, cheaper versions of Dior's "ridiculous" New Look.

In the early sixties skirts began to get shorter. The trend began not in Paris but in London, where a young woman called Mary Quant and a whole flock of talented young ready-to-wear designers, not shackled to tradition, decided it was about time for women to show their legs again. There are those who say that this was simply a surface manifestation of a new morality, that the old rules were phasing out. It's a mistake to read too much sociology into fashion, but there is no denying the two trends began, and flourished, simultaneously. The birth control pill came on the market, skirts in Europe rose above the knee, and men could not recall when things had been as promising.

To someone who had spent six years in Europe, New York in 1964 was startling for many reasons, not the least of which was the length of women's skirts. "They're positively dowdy," my wife said, and it was true. I had always thought of New York as an advanced city where trends began, not ended. But in the mid-sixties when young women right across Europe were showing their knees, it was still "knees up, Mother Brown" in New York. And the rest of the country as well. Of course it didn't last long. The mini skirt, as Mary Quant or someone named it, was coming in. There were sermons and editorials but the mini moved inexorably ahead. One day Jackie Kennedy, as she then was, lunched at Lafayette, and when she came out the ubiquitous *WWD* photographer was there. Jackie's knees were in full view and the photo covered most of the front page next morning. *Time* and *Life* and *Newsweek* and the rest of them picked it up and the mini came of age.

Within a few years skirts had gone as high as they could architecturally go — any higher and they would cease to be skirts and become blouses. It was at that point, in 1969, that a number of the more influential fashion designers began sketching clothes with longer, much longer skirts.

As a professional trade paper it was *WWD*'s job to provide the fashion industry, the textile mills, the fiber producers, the store buyers and store presidents with information they could not get elsewhere and information that hopefully was days or weeks or months in advance of events. Our bureaus in Paris and London and Rome began to file stories and to send along sketches of new designs that covered the knee and that in some cases went to the ankle or the floor. There had been skirts like this around but they were not the creations of men in smoke-filled rooms. They were the clothes being worn by a new breed, flower children, hippies, and they were badly cut in cheap fabrics. But the kids had the idea. They had begun to move into a new look that had nothing to do with professional designers. Chanel used to say that fashion came up from the street into the salon, and most designers argued that she was wrong. But as the 1960's came to a close, it was the professional designers who were copying the young and not the other way around. June Weir, the very astute fashion editor of *WWD*, began to publish sketches of the new lengths, interviews with the most influential designers, and reports that skirts were going longer, dramatically so. In the November 1969 showings of European ready-to-wear for spring there were as many long skirts as short, and *WWD* duly reported the news.

At the start we took the position that what would occur now would be what we called "a wardrobe of length." *WWD* said women would now have a closet full of clothes of varying length, from the crotch to the floor. In January 1970 most of the big couture houses in Paris and Rome dropped skirts well below the knee. I had flown to Europe to see the collections for myself, and we dredged up an obscure word out of the French dictionary to describe the longer look. We called it "the longuette." The word meant "long, rather long, very long, or too long." One of the longer lengths, the skirt that reached mid-calf, we christened "the midi." When I got back to New York we began to run pictures of the new skirt lengths on the front page nearly every day. It was going to be another of those cyclical changes in women's fashion to which we had all become inured. Except that two things happened: the country went into the deepest economic recession in ten years and women proved more stubborn about a new fashion than they ever had before.

When unemployment is up it makes good sense for consumers to postpone purchases not absolutely essential, and certainly the new skirt lengths fell into that category. And women had gotten rather used to showing their legs, men liked it, and there was across most of the land a rather warm and cheerful feeling about the mini skirt. So when designers began to create longer skirts, when European women actually began to wear them in the streets, and when *WWD* started its nearly daily coverage of the new fashion phenomenon, everyone chose up sides. Most startling to me in their opposition to the new lengths were the big-volume manufacturers. I would have thought they'd be delighted to have a new fashion to sell. I was naïve. They had so many mini skirts, mini coats, and mini dresses in the pipeline or already in overstuffed inventory that they launched a counterbarrage of propaganda.

What amused me was the hypocrisy of their message. Instead of coming out with an honest admission that the long skirt was bad for businesses already overstocked with short skirts, the attack on the longuette was couched in terms that suggested they were defending the right of free choice of American women. Ban-the-midi clubs sprang up across the country. Few people seemed willing, or capable, of discriminating between the midi skirt, which was only one of four or five different lengths south of the knee, and the more general term "longuette." And all this time the recession deepened, retail business fell off, manufacturers along Seventh Avenue went out of business at rather more than the normal pathetic rate, and the midi was blamed for it all. And with the midi, *Women's Wear Daily*. The midi was un-American, it was subversive, it was against the best instincts and the finest qualities of this great nation. I remember one abusive letter I got from a lady in Dallas, Texas. "We love the mini skirt," it ended. "And we support Nixon and Agnew too."

I went on the NBC-TV *Today Show* to debate the issue with a young woman from somewhere in upstate New York. Barbara Walters officiated and the whole business was quite pleasant. But I was somewhat appalled when the young woman said she was so incensed about the long skirt she had decided to devote all of her time to securing its defeat, that she now barely saw her husband or their small baby, that she was on a countrywide crusade in defense of the mini skirt. When the camera left us momentarily for a commercial break, I asked the young woman when she had begun wearing mini skirts. "Last year," she told me.

Life magazine did a cover story on the issue including color photos of our *Today Show* debate and got Barbara Walters, who had worn a long skirt for the show, into a high state of excitement by quoting her as saying that once she adopted a new style that was it, America would follow. Barbara denied she ever said it, the *Life* reporter swore she had, and I lapsed into an uncharacteristic but diplomatic silence.

David Susskind found the issue to his liking and we spent an hour and a half on TV arguing the point. He brought in several out-of-town retailers who stoutly defended the mini skirt, and, incidentally, attempted to keep their bulging stocks of same off the markdown racks, and Dick Shapiro, then the head of Filene's in Boston, who said quite calmly that fashion meant change and what the hell was all the shouting about?

Time did a cover story and so did *Newsweek*. At WWD we were delighted. John Fairchild's face, dimpled chin and all, adorned *Time* in the form of a needlework portrait. Sydney Gittler, the great Ohrbach's buyer, announced that he was grateful for the long skirt. "In a recession as bad as this," he said, "we're lucky to have something new to sell. If all we had was the mini skirt, we wouldn't be doing any business at all." Dick Schwartz of Jonathan Logan, the biggest single fashion firm in the country, admitted over lunch that while he agreed that fashion had to change, it was damned awkward to have the massive investments he had in short skirts and suddenly be told they were now obsolete.

I went down to Washington to appear on a television talk show hosted by Barbara Howar. Mrs. Howar is one of those Washington phenomena, a middle-aged woman who parlayed blond hair and brash manners into a semireputation as a hostess. Politicians liked Barbara, Lyndon Johnson especially, and a smart producer came up with the idea of putting this marked-down Madame Pompadour on television. She and I spent twenty-nine minutes debating the issue and as we came to a close, Barbara asked, "Do you have a cigarette lighter?"

I had, and handed it to her. She dangled her copy of WWD in front of the camera, flicked on the lighter, and set the newspaper aflame. "That's what I think of your newspaper," she announced. Off camera I could see the technicians, the director, and the producer go wide-eyed. Flames licked their way up the newspaper and I reached across and took the burning paper from Mrs. Howar as she signed off and the closing credits began to roll. Finally I had to drop the newspaper, and as soon as the camera's red lights blinked off, the cameramen and the director rushed on the set and stamped out the blaze.

"What the hell did you do that for?" I asked Barbara.

She smiled her southern girl's smile. "Why, I thought it would make a great wrap," she said.

I was invited to address an advertising group in Boston but before I arrived a classified ad had run in a Boston newspaper assailing me as "a sexist toad who manipulates" women's minds. It urged liberated women in the area to turn out to picket the visiting "sexist toad." I thought this was good business indeed, never having been picketed, and went up to Boston with an anticipatory shiver of delight. But the affair was anticlimactic. No pickets. A week later I got a call from a friend who said that in the same hall where I had spoken, precisely a week later, a group of New England insurance actuaries were picketed by a half-dozen jeering women. The ladies' hearts were in the right place but they had gotten their dates wrong.

The Fairchild building in Manhattan was the target of bomb threats and over a period of several weeks the entire staff was cleared out into the street several times. But at WWD we felt, on balance, we had not been hurt. The fashion magazines had rather fudged the whole issue from the start, even cropping fashion photos so you could not see where the skirt fell, and advising readers sheepishly that they should simply make up their own minds. The fashion magazines had always taken firm stands and had led the way to new fashion. Now they had abdicated their fashion leadership and it was WWD that filled the vacuum. We lost some angry readers but gained more. The value of the publicity could not be calculated. To get cover stories in *Time, Newsweek,* and *Life* in the same month, to get the national television coverage, the Johnny Carson monologue wisecracks night after night, brought our little newspaper, which never sold more than eighty-five thousand copies in any single day, to its peak. And probably got Richard E. Deems of the Hearst Corporation to thinking about hiring its publisher.

As to the fashion, the point of it all? Why, of course skirts got longer. They had to and they did. The mini skirt is now a hot weather and sportswear classic, American women are again wearing skirts at or just below the knee, and once more the great Republic has come through a crisis.

13

Eccentrics and Other
Splendid People

There is no profession richer in eccentricity than journalism. An argument can be made, I suppose, for politics or the theater, certainly for the church, but lacking documentary evidence on those vocations, I shall stay with publishers and editors as a breed set well apart.

I think it was Mr. James Gordon Bennett who shot at a man in the city room and missed, and I'm certain it was Mr. Bennett who dispatched Stanley to Africa to find a Livingstone who, knowing precisely where he was and how to get back, denied that he was "lost." Mr. Bennett later went mad. Joseph Pulitzer spent most of his later years sitting in a soundproof room set on rubber and ball bearings to soothe his tortured nerves. Henry Luce's partner, Hadden, installed a window shade on the driver's side of his automobile and used to startle other motorists by pulling it down at a red light to disclose the single, accusatory epithet "Babbitt!" printed on the shade. Lord Northcliffe was another who went mad, having inextricably confused in his own mind *The Times* of London and what was good for the British Empire. A sort of early Engine Charlie Wilson, if you will. James Thurber's great book *The Years with Ross* chronicles the peculiarities of the *New Yorker*'s founder. Ross once fired a man who spoke to him while both men were at the urinal. Now A. J. P. Taylor has gotten down on paper the oddities of Lord Beaverbrook, who left Canada under a cloud to become a British peer.

Fashion publications are an anachronism, I suppose, and so are Queen Anne chairs and straw boaters and Bach chorales. But there are those who enjoy them, and certainly fashion journalism need not apologize for the quality and number of its eccentrics.

Carmel Snow, who ran *Bazaar* for years, was always accompanied on her Paris trips by a number of subeditors, one of whom had the sole responsibility of pressing Mrs. Snow's clothes in their suite in the Crillon. Diana Vreeland, once the number two at *Bazaar* and for a dozen years editor of *Vogue*, burned incense in her office and employed a dramatically arch mode of conversation. I remember once asking her for a one-sentence critique of a Saint Laurent show. Madame Vreeland cleared her throat, waved her hands in several delicate directions, and issued her quotation for the day. "Think languor," she intoned, stretching out the word "languor" for what seemed to be eight or ten seconds.

Vreeland was still on the staff when Walter Hoving came up to *Bazaar* to talk with the fashion editors. Hoving, who now controls Tiffany's and is the father of Metropolitan Museum of Art chief Thomas Hoving, was then with Lord & Taylor. He was dissatisfied with Lord & Taylor's fashion performance, he admitted to *Bazaar*'s editors. Business should be better and did they have any recommendations to improve sales in the Lord & Taylor fashion departments?

Diana Vreeland spoke up. Yes, she did have a suggestion.

"It would be ever so much more pleasant to shop at Lord & Taylor, Mr. Hoving, if there weren't so many customers milling about. Can't you do something about that?"

Hoving, who is rarely without a comeback, was silent.

Marie Louise Bousquet, the long-time Paris editor of *Bazaar*, is a tiny woman with a painted face and trembling hand. She also chain-smokes so her shakiness involves a risk of fire. A junior editor of *Bazaar* used to be stationed next to Madame Bousquet at all fashion shows so she would not set herself, or the salon, on fire. China Machado tells of having drawn the fire-marshal assignment some years ago. "Marie Louise was smoking up a storm, and talking all the while, and waving her hands about, and dropping her cane from time to time, all this while the show was on, and finally she dropped the cigarette down the front of her dress and we both leaped up, Marie Louise swearing and I beating at her chest with both hands to extinguish the fire." It was a tribute to the sangfroid of the Maison Dior that the show continued without interruption.

Coco Chanel and Marie Louise were contemporaries but their friendship was a sometime thing. Chanel, in her sweet way, once referred to Marie Louise as having "the face of a monkey, the mouth of a sewer." On another occasion Chanel and Bousquet were discussing Cristobal Balenciaga. One of the two women, it's not clear which, commented that Balenciaga, who was ten years younger than either of them, was "too old to stay in business." Whichever said it, Marie Louise picked up her skirts and hurried across Paris to the Avenue Georges V to announce to Balenciaga that Chanel thought him "too old." Balenciaga flew into a rage and he and Chanel, formerly great chums, stopped speaking.

Last year Dick Avedon, the great *Vogue* photographer, visited Marie Louise in Paris. She was bedridden, and, according to rumor, no longer the witty gadfly who had run one of the most interesting salons in Paris. Avedon and his wife reported later that Marie Louise had been as perky as ever. Dick said, "She grabbed my leg when I bent over to kiss her, stuck her tongue in my mouth, and suggested next time I come back without my wife." Madame Bousquet at this writing is close to ninety.

Nancy White, the ladylike and competent editor of *Bazaar* when I was brought in, seemed a much more conservative sort. She wore white gloves and hats and a quiet dignity, but like all fashion magazine editors she seemed to have that uncommon touch the métier demanded. When she was in Paris to cover the semiannual collections, Nancy went into the motor transport business. It was her modest bow toward eccentricity. She had a chauffeured car, of course, a proper black Cadillac, which she shared with Gwen Randolph, her then number two, and one or two notebook-toting subs. Then there was a car to carry the dresses and a car for the photographer and his entourage. Years ago it was Avedon, more recently Hiro, but in each instance the photographer had a secretary, a husky to manhandle the gear, and usually an assistant photographer. Fashion magazines traditionally shoot their Paris couture photos at night since they can most conveniently borrow the dresses during hours when the buyers are not pawing them. So lights, lenses, cables, and mysterious electronic devices filled out the car. The models had to have a car, *bien sûr*, and on one occasion there was a truck and a crane. The photographer and Miss White had decided to film the models in a transparent plastic bubble suspended over the Seine by moonlight. It was said by some startled residents of the Right Bank that General Leclerc had liberated Paris in August 1944 with less motorized equipment than *Harper's Bazaar* deployed that season.

Eccentricity isn't limited to the magazines, of course. On *Women's Wear Daily* there was an editor who drank bourbon out of a large cologne bottle she kept in the top drawer of her desk. When I first became publisher there was still talk of a copy editor forced into retirement by the expedient of placing his desk in front of the men's room, right in the line of traffic. He had lapsed into a kind of senile anti-Semitism and passed his days fulminating against Jews and refusing to handle the copy of a Jew. The trouble was, in his frenzy, he took everyone for Jews and tossed back all copy unedited. Another staff member of more recent vintage refuses to eat or drink in a sidewalk café "with all that strontium 90 falling into the food." This is the same journalist who was seen in the men's room one day, standing on a toilet seat while the building manager stood on an adjacent seat. The two men were tossing bits of confettilike paper up in the air. The bits of paper were falling down again while the reporter pointed out deficiencies in the exhaust ventilation system. "Noxious fumes," he shouted. "Noxious fumes. And there are men on this staff who've not yet sired children."

There was a financial editor who dabbled in real estate on the side and had built an impressive financial portfolio. He spent much of his day on the telephone with brokers or assailing his tenants for tardiness in paying their rent. He was also known to abuse his own landlord, warning that municipal authority would not permit a defenseless tenant to become the victim of avaricious capitalists. It was said that he was so careful with his money that he suffered a heart attack while moving from one Greenwich Village apartment to another, using the subway to move the smaller bits of furniture and cartons rather than paying for a van.

I am personally acquainted with a French correspondent in New York, a man of considerable social prestige and good manners, who dines in the best houses and escorts rich and famous ladies to the theater. He wears excellent wool socks knit for him by his mother in Paris. When the socks need to be darned, he does them up in a neat package and hands it to the next traveler flying to France. "Be a good fellow and deliver this little gift to my dear mother," he will say, and of course the "gift" is delivered and gets back to him eventually by the same efficient, and inexpensive, system of private courier.

And there is Mary Bubb, who was a correspondent for Fairchild at Cocoa Beach, Florida, and for a time the senior journalist at Cape Kennedy. When I covered the Apollo 11 launch, I learned from Mary that she had a local florist create a special hat for each important space shot. She and the florist laid their plans weeks ahead and Mary would unveil the floral hat at the launch site. At dawn on the day of the great adventure, Mary Bubb arrived at the press site wearing a hat of flowers made up in the shape of an American eagle, the name which the astronauts had given the lunar lander. The hat was a formidable affair with wings and beaks and talons reaching for the Bubb forehead. When the ship had been safely launched and the press briefing began, five thousand journalists would hear the NASA spokesman congratulate Mary Bubb on having outdone herself on this historic day. She seemed quite pleased, smiled briefly, and then barked for a Western Union boy to "come pick up this damned copy."

My first boss at the *New York Daily News*, where I worked as a copyboy at night during college, was a former foreign correspondent who sent me out for pint bottles of whiskey. We worked the 4 P.M. to midnight shift and by midnight the man was usually intoxicated, sitting stiffly at his typewriter, eyes glazed, spittle drooling from his sagging lip, but with his nightly summary of foreign news neatly typed, to be carried by me to the appropriate copy editor. Another older reporter at the *News* took delight in describing to a bug-eyed staff of copyboys the various executions he had witnessed, acting out the neck-breaking jerk of the hangman's rope as well as the galvanic shock of the electric chair.

A talented and creative writer on the New York staff of *WWD* had lost his father, and shortly after the death I shared a cab ride uptown with the young man. I said the usual thing and asked if his father had been ill for a long time. He said yes, he had, that he had prostate troubles which had led to the complications that caused death.

"It really began with his attitude on masturbation," he told me.

There was a moment of silence on my part, I am sure, and the cab driver's head swiveled slightly as he picked up the thread of conversation in the back seat.

"Yes," the young man said, "my father was absolutely hell on whacking off among young boys. He refused to let us have bicycles when we were young. Feared we'd be off in the bushes whacking off, that riding bikes would arouse us."

"Oh," I said.

"The old gentleman was ferocious on the subject. Never whacked off himself, I'm sure. I suspect it was one reason he developed cancer."

This was all said in a very matter-of-fact, almost clinical manner, but both the cab driver and I were riveted to his little monologue. We were on the ramp at Grand Central now, heading toward Park Avenue.

"Whacking off relieves the pressures, you know," he said. "If you don't do it occasionally, well, cancer could result."

How we arrived at our destination without the cab going up on the sidewalk, I don't know. I dropped the reporter and the cabbie turned around. He opened his mouth as if to speak, then shook his head, asked me where I wanted to go, and turned back to the wheel.

There was an opening in the Paris bureau of WWD some years ago and we sent a young American woman, an attractive, bright reporter who could speak passable French and who had an eye for a good story. Dryansky, the Paris bureau chief, got her a hotel room near the office and put her on to agents who could help her find a flat. Two months went by and the young woman was still in the hotel room. I queried Dryansky about it. There was no housing shortage in Paris and surely she should have been able to find a place and relieve the company of the hotel bills.

It turned out that the young woman, so assured and independent in America, had grown suspicious and uneasy in Paris, told stories of men following her in the street, and had sent for her mother to come and stay with her. She also had her pet bird, a parakeet, brought across the Atlantic to keep her company. The manager of the hotel had complained to Dryansky.

"This is a single room with one small bed," he told him, "and we have two grown women, and a bird, living there. Really, monsieur, this is a respectable hotel and such behavior cannot be supported."

Dryansky confronted the young woman, who admitted she had developed this unreasonable fear of living alone in Paris and, in the end, we had to send her home. Dryansky said he was too embarrassed to deal with that particular hotel ever again when it came to quartering Fairchild visitors in the French capital.

In my own rare moments of stark self-appraisal I know I do not belong in such distinguished company. I simply don't qualify as an eccentric. It is a matter of great regret and I have frequently essayed little oddities in hopes that one day people would shake their heads and say of me that I was a journalist to be remembered. But while I find myself falling short, there is one man, though still young and with the truly great years of his publishing life ahead of him, who will one day deserve to be ranked with those memorable giants mentioned here. He is John Burr Fairchild.

Mr. Fairchild is a descendant of Aaron Burr, the chap who shot Alexander Hamilton in a duel, and I don't think John takes a back seat to any publisher or editor when it comes to a question of distinct personal style. An original thinker, a clear and forceful writer, John frequently committed spoken sentences that simply would not parse. He was a master of the misplaced modifier. After a weekend in Bermuda where he and his wife, the blond and gracious Jill Fairchild, had been looked over by the commodore of the yacht club at which they were seeking membership, John reported: "Oh, the commodore was very pleasant. He said he liked us. And his wife."

The Fairchild family (John was the third generation to head the publishing company) did not believe in private offices. The publishers and editors were to sit right out there on the city room floor so as to be, at least theoretically, available to anyone with an idea, even a copyboy. This left them open to some good ideas and any number of bores. When John came to power he maintained the family tradition but had a small conference room built behind his desk where he could hold private talks and confidential phone conversations and the like. This office was always being painted. John had a horror of dirt and a thumbprint on the windowsill was enough for him to send for the painters. They worked at night, when the building was nearly empty, and it was only the lingering scent of paint that would tell you in the morning they had been there, that the conference room had once again been painted. But John would know, even without the paint smell. He had catalogued that thumbprint.

Fairchild's obsession with neatness extends to people. One steamy summer afternoon I was summoned to his office for what I supposed must be a corporate crisis. John guided me to the door of his conference room and pointed out a woman employee, plump and no longer young, typing at a desk across the city room.

"Look at that," John ordered. "What is to be done?"

He was obviously in a high state of distraction but I admitted I had no idea of what concerned him.

"She *will* wear sleeveless dresses on hot days."

He looked appealingly to me for a solution and pleaded: "*Must* I stare at her armpits all summer long?"

His secretary, Gertrude Price, often took the brunt of John's penchant for cleanliness. A glass ashtray had been broken somehow in the conference room and the glass swept up. Several days or weeks later, during an important business meeting with several of the Fairchild publishers, John suddenly fell to his knees and peered under a radiator. He had caught the glint of a sliver of glass from the broken ashtray. Mrs. Price was summoned, joined John on hands and knees so the offending bit of glass could be pointed out where it lurked under the radiator, and went off to call for the cleaning man to retrieve it. John shook his head as he regained his feet. "Gertrude," he said, "I don't think it's very nice that I have to have glass all over the floor."

John Fairchild's business trips around the United States achieved the character of legend. You could imagine the shocked reaction on the part of a bureau chief in, say, Dallas or Charlotte or Denver, when the leased wire from New York announced that Mr. Fairchild was on his way. I remember how Mary Neale, the London fashion editor, had described her reaction years earlier to the regular inspection visits of Fairchild's European director, B. J. Perkins, from Paris. "I'd go down the hall to the ladies room," Mary said, "and cry for an hour." It was not that John Fairchild was a harsh employer who, like Mr. Perkins, reduced younger reporters to tears. It was just that he was hard to please. Imagine, if you will, the difficulties of a bureau chief in Greenville, South Carolina, informed that Mr. Fairchild would like to host a dinner for a dozen textile company executives in Greenville's best hotel, and that he would like a decent Pouilly Fuissé with the fish course and perhaps a Petrus '62 with the rack of lamb. This in a region where fried chicken and a well-chilled Dr Pepper might be considered the ultimate in gracious dining. Gertrude Price would wire back and forth, place and receive phone calls, until the seating list, the menu, the vintage had all been worked out to John Fairchild's satisfaction.

Usually it went well and John left for the next stop on his tour, another bureau chief exhausted but triumphant behind him. On one occasion, in the South, a waitress served a red Bordeaux in an ice bucket and John scolded her. "You never chill a good red Bordeaux," he said. "Never. You always serve it at room temperature." The compliant waitress removed the bottle from the ice bucket and held it over one of the table candles. "Warm it up to room temperature in a jiffy," she assured him.

On another trip John was accompanied by William Ormond Dwyer, the lawyer who'd become a publisher. The two men visited the major cities in Texas, and when they returned John couldn't wait to get me alone. "Well," he said, "your friend Ormond distinguished himself. He was running around the lobby of the best hotel in Dallas in his underwear. The manager had to have me speak to him." As soon as I could get Dwyer aside I told him what John had said and asked for his side of the story. Dwyer laughed. "I went next door from my room to his one evening in my shirtsleeves."

It was no trick at all for John to reason from shirtsleeves in a hotel bedroom to underwear in the lobby. One day two young men in the fashion business gave a small luncheon in an East Side brownstone for John and me. They had some sort of project to discuss and when the meal was finished one of them rolled a joint of marijuana and after taking the first drag, passed it around the table.

Now you should understand that John Fairchild, perhaps in his entire life, has never smoked as much as a single Lucky Strike. He simply does not smoke. Ever. So when the joint arrived at his place, he held it rather daintily several inches under his nose, inhaled once, and passed it on to the next man.

"It doesn't do a thing for me," John announced.

I have the impression that from that day on, whenever the question of drugs of any sort arose, John has called on that limited experience to declare with the certainty that is his trademark, "I've tried it. No reaction. You either dominate drugs or they dominate you."

There was the ad manager at Fairchild who had an accident while pruning his trees and was invalided for several weeks. Afterwards, whenever the man's name came up in connection with any project, John Fairchild would sneer, "Why, he falls out of trees. How could you possibly suggest him capable of doing the job? He'd just fall out of a tree again." The poor chap was eventually hounded out of the company and now presumably falls out of trees on someone else's payroll.

The first face-to-face meeting between the top executives of Capital Cities Broadcasting Corporation and those of us who were running Fairchild took place in a private club in the Wall Street area, a solemn and paneled place where you could talk privately about matters of substance. The luncheon meeting was a pleasant one and would lead eventually to a merger of the two great communications concerns. Tom Murphy and Don Pels (Murphy still heads Capital Cities and Pels has become the chief of LIN Broadcasting) were the hosts and John Fairchild, Bill Dwyer, and I represented Fairchild. As we arrived at the club I was reminded of Norman Lonsdale, a London friend of mine whose father was the head of a great private banking house and was sorely disappointed when Norman chose to go into the phonograph record business instead. Norman lunched with his father dutifully once a year in just such a private club in the City, where London bankers and financiers came together. Norman said he always delighted in these occasions because, as he crossed the room to join his father at table, he could hear the murmurs, "There's a chap with brown shoes . . . a chap with brown shoes."

I guess several of us wore brown shoes that fateful day when the merger began to take shape, but the whole event was informal and instructive and generally upbeat. As we left the building after lunch, Murphy very graciously offered to drive us uptown in his chauffeured limousine. There was plenty of room, he said, and they could drop us at the Fairchild offices on East Twelfth Street.

"No, no," said John Fairchild. "We always take the subway," and he ducked into the IRT entrance at the corner, followed by a crestfallen Dwyer and Brady.

"What was that all about?" asked Dwyer. "It was on their way and they could have dropped us."

John looked at him with infinite patience.

"William," he said, "I don't want them to get the idea we throw money around like that. Subways are much more efficient and economic."

This, of course, was a man who thought nothing of a hundred-dollar lunch with two or three fashion designers.

Edgar W. B. Fairchild, son of one of the founding Fairchild brothers and first cousin to John's father, Louis Fairchild, became a rich man when Fairchild merged with Capital Cities Broadcasting. He chose to take stock rather than cash and after several years, with Cap Cities on the rise, Edgar's stock was worth some fifteen or sixteen million dollars. He had not made the editorial contributions either Louis or son John had made, but instead busied himself with administrative chores difficult to define, was given to drinking great drafts of ice water with his pinkie finger extended, and had the habit of clearing his throat into the telephone before saying hello. This irritated the eardrum in great or lesser degree, depending on one's sensitivity, and one man I knew in the organization took to clearing *his* throat, even louder, whenever called upon to telephone Edgar.

Edgar inevitably referred to men as "lads," regardless of their age. Once there arose a question about an old pensioner, a man called Bartley or something like it, who must have been in his eighties. Edgar summoned one of the personnel men and demanded, "That lad Bartley, is he still alive?" On being informed that that "lad Bartley" was still with us, Edgar expressed some doubt.

"I think the lad passed away and someone else is cashing his retirement check," Edgar declared. The personnel man said he was sure this wasn't so, that the endorsements seemed to be genuine, that he'd heard nothing of Bartley's passing.

"Well," said Edgar, "I think you ought to call the lad up and find out."

The personnel man duly phoned Bartley and was assured that the lad was still among the living.

Although Edgar became chairman of the board on Louis Fairchild's retirement in 1967, John ran the company. People were never quite sure *what* Edgar did, but he spent long hours doing it. Though it was known that he owned a cruiser and had a country house out on eastern Long Island, his standard remark on a summer Friday, if anyone suggested he hoped it would be a pleasant weekend, was along the lines of, "Well, perhaps for you. I'll be in the office as usual tomorrow."

His office at that time was a large one on the eleventh floor of the Fairchild building and it was the only room in the whole structure that was air-conditioned. It also contained, or so I was assured, a private shower.

John was given to grousing about his cousin Edgar (he was also known as "uncle" Edgar, the terms, in John's vocabulary, being interchangeable), especially about Edgar's refusal to credit John with having dramatically increased the company's profits and sales during the sixties and making Edgar, as the biggest stockholder, quite a rich man. "He's never said a word to me about what we've done," John would say. "He's never said thanks."

One evening John, Bill Dwyer, and I dined together at La Caravelle. It was during the difficult period of the negotiations with Capital Cities, which the three of us were handling, and apparently Edgar had been more than customarily surly with John.

"God, you'd think he was contributing something," John said. Dwyer and I heard out his tale of woe and ordered ourselves up a splendid meal with some really good wine. When the bill came John seized it gleefully. "I'll sign Edgar's name," he announced. Apparently Edgar paid the bill when it eventually got to him, since we were often back at Caravelle and were never taken up on it.

Edmund Fairchild, who was Louis's brother and had long been retired in Laguna Beach, California, where he ran a coin and stamp shop ("It gets me out of the house," he once told me), was another of the older generation with whom John took issue. "He never says a word about how well we've done."

On one of the rare occasions that Edmund was in the New York office, he stopped by my desk. This was in the late sixties when *Women's Wear Daily* had become a household name, when our profits were nearing three million dollars a year, and when the Capital Cities merger had enriched the entire Fairchild family. Edmund exchanged a few pleasantries and then gestured around the city room. "Why the hell don't you get the copyboys to cut their damn hair?" he growled. It was his only reference to the remarkable team of young journalists we had put together.

14

Some Stars Are Born...
and Recruited

I believed in the star system. The more stars an editor or publisher developed or recruited, the better he looked, the more successful his newspaper would be. John Fairchild pushed me to a modest stardom and in turn I pushed others. Most of the stars we developed in-house, consciously emulating what Jean Prouvost had done with *Paris Match*.

Prouvost was a French textile millionaire who had bought a broken-down French sports magazine just before the war. In 1945, after clearing up some collaborationist charges against him, Prouvost set out to remake *Match* into the French equivalent of *Life* magazine. Unlike Henry Luce, he didn't go to the Harvards and Yales for his bright young men, or even to the provincial weeklies or the great Paris dailies. He hired the most aggressive staff of reporters any European publication had ever had by seeking out the toughest, fastest, smoothest young men he could find anywhere, regardless of their experience in journalism. He found hard boys from the

Maquis, ex-paratroopers, racing-car drivers, barroom brawlers, playboys down on their luck. Whenever Monsieur Prouvost spied a competent-looking young man who had the best-looking girl on his arm, the fastest car at the curb, and the ability to handle his liquor, he gave him his card and suggested he call round at *Paris Match* for an interview. Anyone who turned out to have brains, and could read and write, was offered a job. *Match* is tamer now, not as adventuresome, but during the fifties and sixties, when I was in Europe, it was an exciting magazine. *Match* smuggled reporters into Mecca, dropped photographers by parachute onto hijacked ocean liners, and got great pictures and exclusive stories. It was magnificent journalism and with John Fairchild's backing, and money, I attempted to create the same sort of staff in miniature at *WWD*.

John realized we needed better-quality people. When he handed over the European reins to me in 1960 he said, "You ought to fire half of them. They're no good and I know they're no good. But I had to get this office [Paris] on its feet and I didn't have time to do it all. But you will." Thus I got the reputation within Fairchild of being a ruthless weeder-out of old-timers and an assiduous seeker after talent. Later on, when *WWD* had developed a reputation, it was fairly simple to find good people in the States. But in the early sixties it was even simpler in Europe. There was a whole new crop of multilingual, sober young Americans with some journalistic experience. They could do the job and they wanted to stay in Europe. I went out to hire them.

Bernard (Barney) Leason had been a *Time* stringer and had worked for Radio Free Europe. After I brought him to Fairchild he worked out of Germany, later in London. He liked working behind the Iron Curtain. I always had a hunch Barney was really with the CIA, but he held his whiskey too well and wrote too gracefully to have been on the federal payroll. G. Y. Dryansky was a plump economics and finance writer on the *Paris Herald Tribune*, and had worked for Mr. Annenberg in Philadelphia. After he joined the Paris bureau he slimmed down, found a decent tailor, and published a novel. In between times he wrote some of the most sensitive prose the Fairchild papers had ever had, all of it touched with the dry Dryansky wit. Someone told Dryansky he looked like a decadent Polish count who would whip his servants. "Never as punishment. Only for pleasure," Dryansky insisted with his little pussycat grin.

When the Russians invaded Czechoslovakia, Leason, who knew the country best, was on holiday with his family in Majorca. There was no phone. I cabled Dryansky from New York to tell him to try to get in. He was already on the way and so was Leason, unasked. They met in Vienna, pooled their languages and their moxie, and talked their way into Czechoslovakia posing as American textile buyers on their way to order cloth for the spring collections. They spent ten days in Prague filing eyewitness stories for the newspaper and doing telephone reports for our radio stations. It was a magnificent performance that rivaled anything the *New York Times* or the wire services got out of Czechoslovakia during the troubles.

Dean Prichard looked like a cowboy, was part Indian, and had worked on newspapers throughout the southwest. Dean covered the Leningrad fur auctions twice a year until the Russian police arrested him, grilled him for several hours, and told him to get out of the country. Thoroughly impressed, Prichard went back to his hotel room to pack and found some papers and books that might be considered subversive planted among his shirts and socks. He opened the window and threw them out into the winter wind. At the airport the police collared him again, went over his luggage with great care, and in a frustrated rage hustled him onto the plane. Prichard said he didn't want to cover the fur auctions anymore and I said I understood.

In Italy we had Bill Raser and two Italian women. Elisa Massai lived in Milan, had six children and red hair, and was the only Italian I ever met who admitted to having supported the fascists during the war. In Rome Adriana Grassi was married to a sculptor, knew Fellini and everyone else, and wrote excellent Italian reportage which Raser translated into English and filed to *WWD*. Peter Head was an ex–British army officer who worked for me in Germany and recruited a series of German space salesmen, all of whom proved incompetent and were fired, except for one who was competent and a crook and whom Peter christened "Hitler." The German salesmen, when they were sacked, felt it was a point of honor to steal the office typewriter and copying machine and whatever furniture could move. We never prosecuted. My lawyers told me that in Germany the courts would side with the salesmen and Peter Head and I, as plaintiffs, would probably be jailed.

One free-lancer we picked up was a Turkish photographer who was reputed to be a spy, possibly for both sides, and who had got the one real scoop when the Pope went to the Holy Land. *Paris Match* had sent a staff of ninety with the papal party; the photographer went alone. He got the color photo of the Pope at prayer in the cave of the nativity that *Match* bought, at outrageous prices, and put on the cover. Several years later, when the Charles Manson family butchered the actress Sharon Tate and five others in Los Angeles, he phoned me from Los Angeles to say he had some "super pinups" of Miss Tate, taken shortly before her "most unfortunate end," and for a price I could have them. He also said he knew the whole story of the murders, that it was a mob killing coming out of the drug traffic, and he would also reveal that for a price. To be blunt, until Manson was arrested, I wondered about the photographer.

In the Paris office there were several reporters. No, that's not correct. They were clerks. I replaced them with two countesses and a young woman who had published a book at nineteen and who would later marry the son of the Comte de Paris. It was an article of office faith that if the French monarchy were ever restored, our young lady would be Empress of France. It didn't seem to impress her but we rather enjoyed the conceit. One of the countesses was Claude de Leusse, who had been a mannequin and later the press attaché for Chanel. Claude was and is a woman of grace and beauty who wrote a moving and lovely book about the death of her teenage daughter.

In New York there was Chauncey Howell who wrote eighteenth-century prose and drove a motorcycle. He was dispatched to the Borscht Belt one weekend to do a column on the "swinging singles" but fell in with a reformed rabbi and passed the two days in theological debate. While most young men in New York were growing sideburns, Chauncey shaved his head and took boxing lessons at a local gym. "One of the hangers-on wants me to turn pro," he told me. "He'll manage me. He says I'm not much of a fighter but I'm white and he likes my faggy name. He says it'll sell tickets." Chauncey told stories of Puerto Rican lightweights named Jesus and of one massive black who advocated sexual abstinence as the only sure road to the heavyweight championship.

Howell would be a successful and sought-after free-lance writer if he had the self-discipline of a titmouse. A publisher was so anxious to get a book out of him that he paid Chauncey an advance. But the book never came to be. When I was still with WWD I wanted to publish a collection of Chauncey's manic columns.

"Look, just go over them with me and pick out the best ones," I proposed. "And you can write an introduction and we'll get it published. You ought to be published, you know."

He nodded his head and then confessed, "But I hate to read the stuff over again once it's done."

So there never was a Chauncey Howell book and eventually he was made assistant accessories editor by the newspaper, reduced to interviewing handbag manufacturers and button-makers. Then WNBC-TV rescued Chauncey and put him on the air.

Rex Reed, known familiarly around the office as Sexy Rexy, was an import. Rex had already established something of a reputation as a shrewd and biting film critic and as a clever interviewer. Liz Smith, a successful free-lance writer herself and a sort of "Aunt Liz" to Reed, suggested that I hire him for *WWD*, that he badly wanted a regular New York outlet and would be perfect for *WWD*. I liked the idea of having the talented Reed in the paper but decided that while there were lots of good film critics, there was very little quality criticism of television. TV was too important to be ignored, and over a boozy lunch at La Grenouille I proposed the idea to Rex. He made a face. "I just *hate* television," he said. Rex has a southern drawl, and when he combines it with a sneer, it is very effective and almost impossible to imitate. I continued to push the television column idea and even framed a money arrangement. Rex continued to make faces.

"Come on, Rex, for God's sake. You want a regular pulpit in New York and this is it. If you don't like it after three months we can forget all about it."

He seemed to agree and we wove our way out into Fifty-second Street. That afternoon Rex's agent called me.

"Mr. Reed certainly won't work for that kind of money," she announced.

"Then he will not work for my newspaper," I informed her, demonstrating that flexibility I reserve for agents. As soon as she hung up I phoned Rex and complained to him about his agent.

"She's inhibiting you," I told him. "You know you want to do this column so why let an agent and a few bucks stand in your way?"

Rex and I made the deal over the phone. I don't think either of us ever really regretted it. Reed was already pretty well established, his talent was obvious, his future as assured as anything was in this business, but *WWD* certainly helped. He did some very fine television criticism. I believed his writing about TV to be as good as any done by anyone since John Crosby a decade earlier, and he wheedled his way into doing some movie writing as well, even when I was trying in vain to get drama critic Martin Gottfried to write film. Then Rex wrote something, I forget what, that should have appeared in *WWD* but ran in the *New York Times* first. I told Rex that this sort of thing didn't wash, that we were a much smaller and less powerful paper in competition with the great *New York Times*, and therefore, to have any validity, any leverage, we had to be first.

"The *Times* is so big it can afford to be second," I said. "We can't. We've got to be first."

Rex argued that the two pieces weren't precisely the same but said he agreed with the principle.

Several months later, when we were about to publish his review of *Midnight Cowboy*, the Sunday *Times* ran a major interview by Rex with Jon Voight, *Cowboy*'s star. The interview contained much of the same material that was to appear in the review we had scheduled to run several days later.

That tore it for me. I fired Rex on the spot. Within a few days he was on the Dick Cavett show and poor Cavett, who wasn't aware of our contretemps, asked Rex for whom he was writing at that point, wasn't it for the *Times* and *WWD* and so on? The next thirty minutes of network time were taken up by a sometimes amusing, sometimes petulant attack on *WWD* and on me.

"I mean," Rex whined, rolling his calf eyes toward the studio ceiling, "nobody reads it. Just eighty-five thousand seamstresses. I mean, they think they're as great as the *New York Times*. I mean, where do they get off?"

I was in ecstasy. We had had the benefit of Reed's talent for a modest sum, some one hundred fifty or two hundred dollars a week, had enjoyed our relationship with a name writer, and now he was giving *WWD* national television exposure we couldn't have bought. Rex repeated the diatribe again and again on other programs, and in print. Then, some six months later, he wrote asking if I would take him back on the paper, that he felt he needed a New York outlet, and if money were the problem, well, he would work for less. I replied that money wasn't the problem, that I felt he had broken his agreement, and that we should forget it. Gradually the rancor subsided. I had written a letter to the management of the Dakota, the apartment building where he wanted to live, attesting that he was a solid and reliable person and that they would not regret selling him a flat. Rex was grateful for that, his "Aunt Liz" Smith kept getting us both together for lunch, and later, when I was running *Harper's Bazaar*, Rex wrote several memorable pieces for me, including a smashing dissection of Hollywood's social structure. It may have cancelled a number of dinner dates for Rex in Hollywood, but the readers loved it. Rex has a wonderful ear for self-destructive remarks and a lovely turn of phrase. He once said of Frank Sinatra's daughter, when she launched a singing career, that she looked like a waitress in a pizza parlor. Reed sells papers but doesn't make many friends.

A lanky young woman from Nebraska was covering the curtain and drapery market for *Home Furnishings Daily* when Rex Reed was fired. I put her on television criticism and she was an overnight sensation. Her name was Gail Rock and she is now writing for *Ms.* and doing memorable television specials about her early life in a small town in Nebraska.

Martin Gottfried was John Fairchild's discovery. The theater critic, Tom Dash, was retiring and a half-dozen people applied for the job. Fairchild sent them all out to see *La Dolce Vita*. "The theater is dead," John announced. "Only movies count." Gottfried did the best review and was hired. He is a difficult man. One morning I sent him a note complimenting him on a review. He dropped the note on my desk an hour later. "Then how about a raise," he snarled.

Julie Baumgold was a young poet just out of college when I hired her. There was no opening on *WWD* so she went to *Daily News Record*, another of the Fairchild papers. She filled in for Chauncey Howell when he was on holiday and did some fine stuff. Later Clay Felker hired her away and she became a star at *New York* magazine.

Kandy Stroud was a convent girl we sent to Washington. One evening she met Attorney General John Mitchell at a party. Mr. Mitchell had been to several earlier parties. He and Kandy talked. And talked. The next day we ran the Mitchell interview as the lead story in *WWD*. In it Mitchell got off such gems as, "If you think this country has gone right, you haven't seen anything yet . . . Henry Kissinger is an egomaniac who likes having his picture taken with movie stars . . ." and so on. The Justice Department issued the ritual statement next day, denying the interview had ever occurred. But Martha Mitchell saved us. She got on the phone to her favorite wire service reporter to announce, "You know all those things John didn't say? Well, I agree with him on every one of them."

When the *New York Times* began its publication of the Pentagon Papers, it was a mystery who had leaked them to the press. Then an ex-*Times* reporter named Sidney Zion announced that it had been Daniel Ellsberg. There was a great outcry, Ellsberg was arrested, and when Zion offered to tell why he had made the disclosure, several newspapers turned him down. I cleared space in *WWD* and we ran his story, a remarkable — and arguable — statement on the role of a free press. The Zion report ran about four thousand words, perhaps the longest story ever run in *WWD*, and one of which I was very proud.

I tried to hire Zion for the paper but John Fairchild vetoed the deal. "I won't have a man like that on the staff," he said.

And the ensuing argument was one of many factors which led to my leaving the company to join Hearst.

There were others who achieved stardom at *WWD*. But because of the paper's structure, because of John's generosity, and because of my own regrettable lack of modesty, I suppose I became the brightest star of all. As far as the reading public and the publicity *apparat* were concerned, I was *WWD* personified. And I must admit, shamefacedly, it was rare that I hid my light under a bushel. I didn't set out to become *WWD*'s star turn but that was what happened.

Job offers came along, of course. There is no one more attractive to a prospective employer than a man who is happy in his present job. When you are on the beach, no one wants you. Although I was happy at Fairchild, I looked into the serious offers. I felt I owed it to myself and family and the offers were flattering. John and I had no secrets. And I enjoyed teasing him about the offers, implying that my marketability was greater than his. Then one day, early in 1971, the teasing had to stop. John himself had been offered an attractive job and was seriously considering it. Bill Dwyer and I went to dinner with him and listened while John spelled out the supposed advantages of the proposal, reasoning that since his family had sold the company there was no reason why he couldn't entertain a good offer. I agreed with him, told him that if the job were as good as he sketched it he should go. Dwyer, a lawyer by training, asked questions and cautioned against haste. A few days later John called us both in and announced that he had decided to reject the offer, that its terms weren't all that good, and suggested huffily that I was disappointed since I would not now succeed him as head of the company. I defended myself, but there was some truth in what he said. I wanted very much to run the Fairchild empire, and if John left voluntarily, I felt I was the logical choice. The session turned rather sour with Dwyer attempting to mediate our differences, and that night I realized that if John Fairchild had been that close to going elsewhere, there was no logical reason for me to reject opportunity. Less than three months later a call came from Richard E. Deems, president of the Hearst magazine division, asking whether I was wed to Fairchild or could we chat about my coming to Hearst? I said of course we could chat, and the next day we held our first meeting.

Deems and I discussed all the Hearst magazines, talked about whether *Town & Country*, a favorite with the wives of retired admirals living in stucco cottages in San Diego, should be merged into *Bazaar*. Deems talked a long time about age, saying that he was no longer all that young, and that a man my age could do well in a corporation run largely by men in their sixties and seventies. Jean Deems came in from time to time to give us coffee and sun streamed in the windows of the Waldorf Towers and it was all very pleasant. Hearst would go public soon, Deems said, and that meant stock windfalls for key men. We met again, and then again.

I said I would leave Fairchild to take on the challenge of *Harper's Bazaar* if Deems understood it was a two-year turnaround situation at least, and if I were given total authority. And I wanted a vice-presidency so I could quietly but officially look into the other magazines, especially Tony Mazzola's limping *Town & Country*, and report my recommendations back to Deems. We haggled a bit over money. Over the weekend of the Fourth of July of 1971, the glorious Fourth, I thought about Deems, about *Bazaar*, about *WWD* and John Fairchild. I thought about money. I even thought about journalism in the abstract. And in the concrete.

There were reasons for leaving Fairchild. I'd been doing the same job, essentially the same, for more than six years now. Oh, there'd been different titles, additional duties as the company's editorial director, publisher of the men's wear and textile paper for several years, a brief stint trying to straighten out the fortune of the pariah called *Home Furnishings Daily*.

There'd been other job offers but the time hadn't been right. There was still the challenge of making *WWD* great.

Now the time was right. In another eight years I'd be fifty and you don't change jobs in your fifties. But that wasn't the operative concern. Fairchild wasn't the same anymore. The people from Capital Cities Broadcasting, the people who'd bought the company, were taking over. They were decent enough about it and there was reason for them to move in, to assign some of their men to "help out" on the business side. Fairchild wasn't known for its complement of Harvard Business School graduates. Surely the firm was now more efficient. But was it as much fun? Some of the lust for the chase, that vicious eagerness of going for the story, that was ebbing too. Not that the Capital Cities people ever said anything, they were better than that, but they were broadcasters, subject to the Federal Communications Commission. They couldn't be overjoyed when one of our bright young men or women twitted the White House for one pretension or another. And there was this frustrating delay in launching "W." John had had the idea first: a consumer weekly spun off by *WWD*, a newspaper for women, drawing on the resources of the Fairchild News Service around the world. I'd been put in charge of the project, had done three dummies, written a budget. But the damn thing had been postponed again and again until you wondered if it would ever be launched.

But this was all taradiddle. How do we rationalize such decisions, the leaving of a vital and growing company to take over a limping old magazine whose pretensions were behind it, working for an organization that was anathema to most journalists? The truth was that I wanted to get out from under John Fairchild's shadow, to make it on my own, to prove something to myself, if not to anyone else. John himself had changed. No longer as keen or as vitally interested, frequently querulous, irritated, knowing the company was no longer his, less exhilarated by its triumphs, feeling less pain at its defeats. John seemed to have declared neutrality and a neutral Fairchild was a contradiction in terms. Deems had made Hearst sound good. Aging management, the chance for a young man to make his mark, going public, stock option windfalls, the cavalry to the rescue, save *Harper's Bazaar*, be a hero, total autonomy, do what you want but change things.

So I went.

15

Taking Over
HARPER'S BAZAAR

When the great Carmel Snow died, Hearst named her niece, Nancy White, editor of *Bazaar*. Nancy, the wife of Ralph Paine, the former publisher of *Fortune* magazine, is a delightful and attractive lady, an indefatigable worker, a woman of taste and loyalty, but not generally considered the most innovative of journalists. Among her rivals for the editorship had been Diana Vreeland, more mercurial, a colorful and imaginative fashion editor with a gift for the right phrase, the crisp word. A few years later the disappointed Vreeland would leave *Bazaar* for *Vogue*, where she was editor until 1972 when Condé Nast shunted her into retirement.

During the negotiations with Dick Deems that led to my coming to *Bazaar*, we had discussed what would happen to both Gordon Morford, then the publisher, and Miss White. Deems and I agreed that it would be more comfortable all around if Morford were transferred to a job in the Hearst headquarters. I said I'd prefer that Nancy leave *Bazaar* as well, and for a time it seemed as if Deems thought so too. But after our deal was made he had second thoughts on Nancy.

"She's got a contract and it runs until the end of the year. Why not see if you can work with her? It might be best all around. She's very well thought of in the industry. People like Nancy."

There was no argument on that. I told Deems I would try it with Nancy, but got him to agree that if it didn't go smoothly she would leave *Bazaar* at the end of the year. What would happen to Miss White then would be Deems's concern, not mine. Looking back now on that rather cavalier approach to personnel management, I am reminded of old sayings about petards.

Morford and White were in Europe for the couture collections when Deems and I shook hands. It was July and in a few days I was scheduled to fly to Rome for *WWD*. I had my plane reservations, the hotels were arranged. Deems proposed that we not say anything about the deal until all hands had returned from Europe the first week of August. That made sense to me and certainly was a more gracious way to break the news to the *Bazaar* executives than transatlantic phone. But the story leaked out. A Madison Avenue gossip sheet called the *Gallagher Report* got hold of it. Since I had told no one but my wife, I assumed there was a leak at Hearst. Inspired or not, the leak reached Fairchild when a Gallagher reporter called John to ask him about it and then phoned me. I stalled the reporter and rode uptown in a taxi with John. We were to lunch that day in the normal run of things. It was a difficult lunch. We talked for two hours. I spelled out my reasons for leaving: John was young and not going to retire; I was not getting along with John Sias, the very efficient management expert now administering the company; Hearst was full of older executives and a younger man would have a great opportunity; Hearst would soon go public and issue valuable stock to key officers; the money was somewhat more; and, perhaps a key issue, I wanted to get out from under John Fairchild's shadow and run a great national publication on my own, salvage a once-magnificent property and restore it to power and influence. John was solemn. He cautioned me about Hearst's reputation, listened carefully, and then said, "Well, you've got to take it. If you believe all these things then you have no choice. You have to take it."

Deems and I met again that afternoon and I signed a contract. We issued a press statement saying that I would join the Hearst Corporation to strengthen their publishing and television activities. No mention was made of *Bazaar* and when the question was asked, I fudged, saying it had not yet been determined precisely what my role would be.

No one was fooled. The editorial staff of *WWD* had gotten the art department to work up a mock issue of *Bazaar* with my caricature on its cover and presented it to me that afternoon. I made a brief speech. The *New York Times* story next morning led off with speculation that I would run *Bazaar*. Next day I got a gracious cable from Nancy White wishing me great good luck and saying she couldn't wait until September to start working with me. John and I agreed it would be silly for me to attend the couture collections for *WWD* and I cancelled my trip, gathered up my wife and daughters, and headed for Long Island where we would spend the next month rusticating at our cottage. My last day at *Women's Wear Daily* was July 14. It was Bastille Day. I hoped at the time it had a favorable significance.

Gordon Morford moved to Hearst on his return and was shortly snapped up by Lanvin–Charles of the Ritz, the great perfume empire. Nancy agreed to stay on and work with me. During the autumn months I realized how wise Deems had been about Nancy. She was a superb collaborator, helpful, honest, and of course had the magazine experience I lacked. She retained her title of editor and I became publisher and editorial director. My name went to the top of the masthead just over hers. I used Nancy much as you use a managing editor, issuing orders through her, consulting with her on stories and personnel, and letting her run the magazine day to day while I planned how we would reshape it over the long pull. I decided there should be daily editorial meetings with the senior editors and art directors. This was a practice I had followed at WWD and had found effective. After the initial shock wore off, the *Bazaar* editors said they liked the idea. It gave them a feeling of participation, of being in on the act. I insisted that problems be brought up during the meeting so they could be settled on a face-to-face basis. This was good practice, I had learned years before, and prevented meetings flowing with milk and honey that gave way later in the day to furtive private interviews where one editor would accuse another of having cut into her pages or stolen one of her story ideas. In those instances, my answer would be, "Gee, that's awful. Bring it up at tomorrow's meeting when she's there and I'll get it straightened out." It was surprising how many insoluble problems solved themselves before the next morning's open session.

The meetings were held at first in Nancy's office, at the end of a long corridor from my own. I felt it was a small courtesy and would stroll down to Nancy's shop each day at ten. In those first weeks I sought out Nancy frequently, and always did it by phone or in her office. Then one day there was some question, I forget what, and I told my secretary to ask Miss White to come down to my office to discuss it. Nancy came, with two or three of the people involved, teetered on one of my chairs, rather distractedly, I thought, and then left. My secretary came in as soon as the room was cleared.

"Did Miss White say anything?" she asked.

"What do you mean?"

"About coming down here?"

I said no, but that she had seemed uneasy.

"Well," my secretary told me, "I've been here a couple of years and as far as I know, that's the first time she's ever come to the publisher's office."

I had begun working at *Bazaar* on August 16, the day the stock market rose thirty-two points following Mr. Nixon's Sunday night announcement of wage and price controls and other monetary and fiscal reforms intended to stabilize the dollar and end inflation. It was, I thought, a good omen. A week or two later, it was a Friday, there was a bad omen. The weather bureau warned that a major hurricane was working its way up the Atlantic coast toward New York and already in the morning it was raining heavily and the wind was getting up. As I left for lunch I sent around a memo saying that all employees should go home early except for a duty person in the editorial and advertising departments. I headed home myself after a business lunch, only to be called that evening by my secretary who said all hell had broken loose.

"You see," she said, "you can't close down the office or send people home early unless Eighth Avenue issues the order. So half the people went home and the other half were afraid to leave and everyone sat around arguing about it all afternoon."

I was furious. The hurricane had turned out to be nothing but a nasty gale. But I was angered by the fact that I was not to be permitted to look out for the welfare of my own people. Two old biddies, one in the advertising department, the other the office manager, had gone clucking through the place directly I departed, informing one and all that I had acted "without authorization." On the following Monday I informed the biddies that I was not running a convent school and when I told people to go home because hurricane or plague threatened, the people should damn well go home and the hurricane or plague present itself. John Miller, the top financial man of the Hearst Corporation, then chided me for having acted rashly. "We have a company union, you know, and if you send people home in one division of the company, then they must all go home."

It was all too much.

During the next few months Nancy White was invaluable in steering me through such rocks and shoals of Hearstian regulations. I was used to the free-swinging attitude of the Fairchild organization where executives, once given responsibility, were expected to use their authority. Initiative had been applauded at Fairchild. Hearst seemed to prefer that one check with someone else before making decisions. Buck-passing was an art. Miss White attempted to drum the survival manual's cautionary notes into my head; she led me by a white-gloved hand through the morass of company regulations. She understood the complicated production schedules and the budgeting of color pages versus black-and-white and which contributors delivered clean copy on time and which, like the splendid Sandra Hochman, had the poet's tendency to forget the magazine appeared each month and the subscriber had a reasonable right to expect Sandy's page to be included.

After a few months I felt that Nancy and I had achieved a good professional working relationship as well as a real affection for one another. Toward the end of November I reminded her that her contract would be up at the end of December and that Deems and I wanted to extend it for two more years. Deems was delighted that Nancy and I were working well together. "You're abrasive and she's a diplomat," he told me. "She's good for us in the fashion community." Nancy said she would think about extending her contract. A week or so later she came to my office and told me she had decided to leave. "I've been editor too long to take second place. I think you're terrific but I don't really want to work under anyone. This isn't a personal thing. It's simply what I feel I have to do." She issued a brief written statement to her staff and flew off to Florida to get away from the calls she knew would come.

I spent an uncomfortable forty-eight hours assuring the press that Nancy had not been fired, that this was her decision, and denying that I was the second coming of Attila the Hun. I don't really think many people believed it. The suggestion was that I had made life so difficult for Nancy that she had taken the gracious way out. In subsequent statements she made it clear that the decision to leave had been hers, and that I truly regretted it. And I did. I was left with a managing editor, Betty Weston, who had not been long on the magazine and who had had several bouts of illness. Nancy's departure slowed the work of revitalizing *Bazaar* because I was forced to tend to housekeeping details instead of plotting the long-range course of the magazine and especially the setting of themes our readers would react to and which our advertising salesmen could use to sell pages.

Both Nancy White and Diana Vreeland, the ex-*Vogue* editor, presided over the fortunes of the two great American high-fashion magazines during a watershed period, ranging from the early sixties when the fiber industry giants, the Du Ponts, Monsantos, and Celaneses, poured all sorts of cooperative money into fashion advertising, to the slump that began with the late sixties and is still in progress. Dramatically different in style, Vreeland and White are a breed of fashion magazine editor I don't think we will see again. Vreeland's successor is a bright, young, organized editor called Grace Mirabella. She will get *Vogue* out on time and the spelling will be correct. Tony Mazzola, now running *Bazaar*, will produce a "How to" guide to clothes and cosmetics and will lift some of his own ideas about social coverage and layout from *Town & Country*, his former territory. Neither magazine will be especially thrilling. Nancy White was not herself a great creator, but she brought in people of talent, such as Barbara Goldsmith and Sandy Hochman and Ila Stanger. She is a woman of taste and intelligence. And despite the rumors, she is still a friend. Just before Christmas each year there is a little ceremony at the Brick Church on Park Avenue, near where both Nancy and I live, and this past Christmas we met there in the evening as the carols were being sung and the trees along the Avenue were being lighted. Nancy was holding open house in her lovely brownstone and she asked us to drop by. We had another party to go to and said no, but it was rather nice to be asked.

Perhaps one of the most fundamental facts about that first year of running *Bazaar* was the sheer joy of the job. It was fun being a publisher. It had been fun too at *WWD*, especially with John Fairchild there as a jousting partner. But there were pleasures in running a national magazine that went beyond those of newspapering.

David Halberstam was one of those. Halberstam is a big lumbering bear of a man I first met at Elaine's. He had won a Pulitzer for his reportage on Vietnam while on the payroll of the *New York Times* and it was quite generally agreed that Halberstam was one of the first to blow the whistle on the war. Lyndon Johnson had tried to silence him and hadn't and now Halberstam was a free-lance writer working on *The Best and the Brightest*. He did the occasional free-lance magazine piece but was sticky about it. When I asked Halberstam to do the lead essay for the February issue, "In Defense of New York," he agreed. It was a marvelous bit of writing, witty and graceful, full of the love-hate New Yorkers have for their city. I did not think there was anything wondrous about Halberstam's having agreed to do it until two other magazine editors, far more successful than I, admitted that Halberstam had refused to write pieces they had wanted.

My first issue was the January *Bazaar*. I had decided to give every issue a theme. The January theme was to be, quite predictably, "The Political Year Begins." In the early fall

I wrote personal letters to a score of men, and Bella Abzug and Shirley Chisholm, asking them for a brief essay on what they thought the major issues would be and whether they believed women would vote en bloc as the feminists were urging. Having been a Washington correspondent, I was not surprised when most of the politicians responded promptly. I told Helen Gurley Brown about it one day over lunch, and, in her wide-eyed way, she marveled that they had agreed to cooperate. "When I asked them," she said, "hardly anyone said yes." It turned out that Helen's little survey had to do with their sex lives, rather than with their politics. Teddy Kennedy's reply was boilerplate and I said so in the introduction I wrote to the lead article; George McGovern's came in slightly late and so McGovern's name was not among those on the cover (which may say something about my political prescience); and at first Spiro Agnew refused to comment. His press man, Victor Gold, had written that the Vice-president would be too busy over the next few months to participate. I wrote back sarcastically that I didn't believe Vice-presidents had all that much to do and found it hard to imagine that Mr. Agnew would be so cavalier as to ignore "those millions of thinking women" who would be voting, for or against his boss, in November. The Agnew reply came in a week later.

For that first issue the art department had discovered a man who looked like Richard Nixon. When it was brought up at a morning editorial meeting, I said it sounded corny. "Harvard Lampoon stuff," I sniffed. But then I saw the photos. The man was an incredible look-alike. We posed him with the models in campaign settings, conferring with Chairman Mao, debating with black militants. Maxine Cheshire of the *Washington Post* learned about the stunt and led off her syndicated column with it. The story ran in papers across the country and I went on television to talk about it. It was a good sign, this sort of stir over the first issue. There was also a bad omen: Richard E. Berlin's friendship for Nixon had surfaced.

Dick Berlin, president of the Hearst Corporation, had long been a Nixon booster. In fact, I first met Berlin in 1969 at a party in Washington following the Gridiron Dinner, where the President, in white tie and tails, had dropped by the Berlin suite with his Secret Service men. A half-dozen other publishing executives were there for a late drink. Nixon, Berlin and I had gotten into a discussion. I knew Nixon from the old Senate days when he had been Vice-president and there was some cheerful badinage about WWD's flip coverage of the new First Family. Nixon asked Berlin if Hearst owned WWD. Berlin said no, and on the strength of several Scotches I said, no, but perhaps one day Fairchild would own Hearst.

When Berlin learned of plans to publish the "Nixon" photos in Bazaar he summoned me to his office on Eighth Avenue. It was the second or third time I had been there, Deems having brought me in during the wooing, and Berlin was at his most avuncular. Punctuating his talk with "don'tcha know"s, he told of his friendship for Nixon (he referred to him as "Dick") and for "Pat" and "the girls," and showed copies of letters he had sent the President and replies he had gotten from him. The letters were warm and personal and it was clear that Berlin really considered the President to be a friend. Berlin said he would "never want any of the Hearst publications to do anything that might hurt the President." When he said that, I had a fleeting glimpse of what it must be like to be an editorial writer on a Hearst newspaper. Then Berlin added, somewhat conspiratorially, that he had hopes Nixon would intervene on the side of the publishers in the current debate over increased second-class postal rates, and that he didn't want to do anything which might prejudice the President against the publishers.

I had not brought proofs of the "Nixon" spread with me. I didn't want to start off this early in a career at Hearst by asking for clearance on anything. But I assured Berlin that the pictures were in good taste, a good-natured spoof rather than ridicule. Berlin insisted he would like to see them. I sent them over the next day and Berlin called to say he thought they were fine, that he enjoyed seeing them.

When the issue came out right after Christmas, the reaction to the "Nixon" photos was generally favorable. One or two readers seemed confused and thought the President had actually posed for *Bazaar*. A handful assailed the magazine for not showing respect for "our President." When Berlin later showed me a letter from Nixon saying he had enjoyed the look-alike spread and noting it would be convenient to have such a "twin" on call during these busy times, I began to use Nixon's own reaction when I replied to readers who found the whole thing in bad taste. "It's too bad," I wrote them, "you lack the President's own sense of humor about it."

I occasionally wondered what would have happened had Berlin not liked the photos. Would my Hearst career have ended even before the first issue came out?

More than a year later, during the Watergate hearings in the Senate, I learned that Nixon's cheerful letter had been for public consumption only, that his aides had been irate about the look-alike, and had actually put the poor fellow under surveillance. The look-alike, an actor who had taken the name "Richard Dixon," was seen in those paranoid times as an "enemy" to be carefully watched.

The second issue, in February, had New York City as its theme. John Lindsay wrote an introductory note and Mary Lindsay sat still for a remarkably free-swinging interview in which she allowed, among other things, that she was occasionally tempted to strangle *New York Times* drama critic Clive Barnes. We picked up the line and ran it as an ad prior to distribution of the February issue. I didn't bother about getting a release from Mrs. Lindsay. It was more important we get the ad out. Lindsay's press secretary, Tom Morgan, phoned to complain, but I told him it was okay, that the whole issue was very upbeat about New York. Morgan seemed mollified.

Margaret Case, a long-time *Vogue* editor and arbiter of what passed for New York society, had killed herself the previous August. I had known Maggie Case, though not well, and had been impressed by her gutsiness and spice at an age when most old ladies were sniffling into the coverlet. There were suggestions her suicide was not unconnected with *Vogue*'s decision to retire Miss Case at the end of the year. I had some of the story from friends and assigned a young reporter called Kate Giles to get the rest of it. We had learned that Miss Case had left an Irish maid who was still in the Park Avenue apartment, who knew the whole story and was bitter about the way her mistress had been treated. I told Giles to go up there with a couple of shopping bags and drink tea with the maid. Kate Giles, who would later be promoted to managing editor of *Bazaar*, got the maid to talk, gathered a little bit here and a little bit there, including a telephone interview with Clare Booth Luce in Hawaii. Mrs. Luce told of trying to get a fund together to help Maggie Case through her retirement years.

I made no secret of our intention to run an in-depth piece on Maggie Case's life and death. Weeks before the story was even written pressures arose both inside and outside the organization to have the story killed. Dick Deems said he heard it was an exposé of *Vogue* and an attack on *Vogue*'s retirement policies. I told him it wasn't, that *Vogue*'s retirement plan was probably better than most, but that it was a serious study of a woman whom time had passed by and a close look at the problem of the aging in America. Deems reminded me that the Newhouse newspapers, owned by the same Samuel I. Newhouse who owned *Vogue*'s parent, Condé Nast, were big customers of Hearst's own King Features Syndicate. Jesus, I thought, I never knew you were supposed to be so solicitous about the competition. Not for the first time I wondered what John Fairchild, that supreme competitor, would have made of it all.

The Margaret Case piece eventually ran, and even those fashion industry figures who had warned that it would damage my reputation and slow our efforts to revive *Bazaar* admitted that the story worked. Giles had done a magnificent job of digging and both Barbara Goldsmith, the news editor, and I had worked to polish the final version. Si Newhouse, whose family owned V*ogue,* told me it was a very fair piece.

There had been complaints from Seventh Avenue about my first two issues. The fashion designers were unused to the new photo technique with clothes shot on location. They missed the familiarity of those studio shots against a white paper background. I had always thought of that white paper as giant rolls of seamless toilet tissue coming down the wall and across the floor while thin young girls capered and simpered for the camera. Some of the criticism was justified. Deems complained too and he was right about some of the shots. It was difficult to see how the clothes really looked. This was new ground we were breaking at *Bazaar* and there were bound to be flubs. Now, with the March issue, my third, we had found the fashion handwriting. Bill Blass told people, "This is simply the best fashion magazine I have ever seen." Yves Saint Laurent, the presiding genius of the Paris couture, cabled his delight. The theme of the issue was "Privacy versus Gossip," which may have had something to do with its success. Everyone loved a little gossip.

It was about this time, in the spring, that Deems offered to tear up my one year contract and extend it to two years. He had come up to my office at 717 Fifth Avenue late in the afternoon, making the stop a sort of way-station in his ritual walk from Eighth Avenue to the Waldorf. He went through proofs on my desk and made his comments, pro and con. Then he said something about the need for change to be gradual, that you had to build a new coterie of readers before you dismissed the old. It was pleasant talk and the two of us smoked our cigars in the late afternoon light of the corner office. Then Deems referred back to my request for a multi-year contract. "I don't want you to feel you've got to be in a hurry," he said. "Why don't we make it two years?" I said no, I had put out only a few issues and we should both give it some more time to develop. What I was really thinking was that by September the book would have shown unmis-takable signs of revival and I could renegotiate the contract at a higher figure.

The April issue, with tennis player Chris Evert on the cover, did not sell but in May the splendid-looking Marisa Berenson posed for the cover with an equally splendid heli-copter and *Bazaar* newsstand sales soared. With that issue we had also achieved a breakthrough on the lead-time problem that plagues magazines. The production editor, a tall, com-petent redhead called Judy Beecher, had gotten the printers to agree to a late closing form of twelve to sixteen pages. If they tightened up the deadlines just slightly on the other pages, this would enable *Bazaar* to run much fresher material on the late-closing pages. They could get copy and black-and-white pictures into print as close as ten working days before first newsstand sale. We christened the late-closing portion of the magazine "Newsform" and immediately began to talk about it in the ads. Even though *Vogue* then was pub-lishing two issues a month to *Bazaar*'s one, *Bazaar* would be able to scoop *Vogue* consistently on both news and fashion. If Oscar de la Renta, say, showed a collection on the fourth or fifth of May, it could be covered in the June issue which would be on sale in New York on May 25.

In one of the meetings with the printers (Cuneo of Phila-delphia), the Eighth Avenue production and circulation ex-perts, and Judy Beecher, I proposed that *Bazaar* eliminate the newsstand release date in Manhattan. Because of theft of new magazines, major publishers in the New York area held back their new issues until a previously agreed date. I thought this enforced warehousing of *Bazaar* for four or five days wasted another potential edge we might have on *Vogue*. We got the distributors to agree, the warehousing stage was eliminated, and *Bazaar* went directly to the Manhattan newsstands nearly a week ahead of its direct competitor.

There were other delights. A newspaperwoman's group in Washington gave me one of its "headliner" awards. Helen Brown of *Cosmopolitan* and Henry Grunwald of *Time* were other recipients. There was a black-tie dinner in the capital and George Romney, then Secretary of Housing and Urban Development, was picked to give me the award. He was fine as long as he stayed with the crib sheet but, as politicians will, Romney began to stray. He said he had long followed "this young man's career," had long known I was destined for great things, and then introduced me as "Edward Brady." I muttered something about there being a private joke between the Secretary and myself and grabbed the plaque.

Time and *Newsweek* had done major pieces in their press sections on our innovations at *Bazaar*. Then Julie Baumgold of *New York* did a profile which I liked immensely despite her assertion that I had "mediocre teeth." In it she had asked various fashion figures what advice they would give natives who had never been exposed to the Brady treatment. John Weitz, often an antagonist, got off the best line: "Don't eff around with bwana Jim." Accompanying the Baumgold story was a David Levine caricature of me complete with cowlick and with a dozen or so nubile young things hanging on, one of them in a martini glass. I liked the sketch and in the midst of wondering how to go about getting the original, it arrived without accompanying letter at my office. I rattled off a letter of fulsome thanks to Levine, how gracious, what a generous gesture, that sort of thing, before learning it was my wife who had bought the picture from Levine and sent it to me as a gift.

But while most of the country's major newspapers, the newsmagazines, and specialists such as Don Grant of *Advertising Age,* wrote about the new era at *Bazaar,* there was silence at *Women's Wear Daily.* Having left John, I had abdicated his favor. John had gone into his tent to sulk.

16

Introducing
BAZAAR
to the Twentieth Century

Harper's Bazaar had had a great tradition of good writing and distinguished contributors (Lady Randolph Churchill only one of them), but in recent years the nonfashion editorial had run toward pious little essays on elegance, saccharine poetry, and fiction that had earlier been rejected at other, higher-paying outlets. I had nothing against elegance, poetry, or fiction, but felt that the magazine could not afford really great fiction and therefore should do without it, that poetry bored most readers, and that one essay on elegance every few years was sufficient. I announced elimination of such material during those early weeks in the job and said that we would substitute timely, provocative journalism by the best newspaper and magazine writers in the country. I knew most journalists were so badly paid we would have little difficulty in getting them to write for our modestly budgeted but ambitious magazine.

One of the first casualties of this decision was Mrs. Loel

(Gloria) Guinness. The splendid Mrs. Guinness, witty, beautiful, traveled, the wife of an exceedingly wealthy man, was considered during the 1960's to be just about the most elegant woman in the world. *Women's Wear Daily* said so. While publisher of *WWD* I was delighted each time Mrs. Guinness made news so that I could indulge my weakness for corny headlines, the operative headline in her case being "Sic Transit Gloria Guinness." *Bazaar's* then-publisher, William Fine, hired Mrs. Guinness in the mid-sixties to do regular columns. Given her unargued reputation for elegance, for knowing everyone one should know, and the rumor, which *Bazaar* carefully cultivated, that it was really her good chum Truman Capote who wrote Gloria's stuff, Bill Fine's move was a good one. But by 1971 I felt that Gloria had written herself out, that the material was by now tired, and that we could survive without it. Instead of simply sacking Gloria, I sent her an assignment I suspected she would have to refuse. I outlined our plans to stress real journalism in *Bazaar*, and asked her to go out and get a story instead of writing another of her elegant little essays at the escritoire one imagined her using. "Please go down to Greece and interview Onassis," I ordered. Gloria wrote back that she did not wish to begin trading on friendships and could not take the assignment. I said I understood her sentiments but that since we were bent on injecting journalism into the magazine it was better, perhaps, that we go our separate ways. A month or two later Mrs. Guinness was interviewed by *WWD* and said she thought *Bazaar* had gone tacky, and, under the suggestive questioning of a delighted *WWD* reporter, said she could find the sort of thing I was peddling in any newsmagazine. A few weeks later Gloria phoned to say that she thought my latest issue a great success and the most intelligent magazine around.

I had never believed the Truman Capote "ghost-writing" story. Both Nancy White and Dick Deems had told me only slightly varying versions of why Truman would never write for *Bazaar*. It seemed that when Capote wrote *Breakfast at Tiffany's* he sold the book to *Bazaar* for serialization. In reading the manuscript, Deems came across the word "shit." He asked that Truman excise the word, Truman refused, and *Breakfast* was never published by *Bazaar*. One version of the story has it that Deems then held on to the rights, refusing to hand them back to the author, so that at a time when Capote needed the money, his work was tied up by a vengeful *Bazaar*. Deems denies this aspect of the tale, but will admit that he pulled a boner in not running the story, as written, and says that if it happened today he would run Capote's original, "shit" and all, without hesitation. Whatever the precise truth of the incident, Capote will tell anyone who asks that he will never write for Hearst. I had had good relations with Capote while at Fairchild but got a blunt refusal when I attempted to patch up the *Bazaar* contretemps.

My experience with Red Smith was happier. Smith is a sportswriter who has taken that largely undistinguished category of journalism into another dimension. He is a master of his craft, a writer of such exquisite delight and a reporter of such acuity that the *Herald Tribune* used to send him to cover political conventions. When the *Tribune* died, to be followed shortly by its bastard, the *World-Journal-Tribune*, I grabbed Smith's column for *Women's Wear Daily*. There was no rational reason for a sports column to run in *WWD*, but my view was that if the stuff was good enough, we would somehow find a way to justify its inclusion in the paper. We sent Smith to the 1968 conventions. Now Red was one of the first men to whom I turned for a contribution to *Bazaar*. I wrote asking for a piece about the national conventions for the January issue. Smith said he'd be glad to do it. "Pay me whatever your rate is," he wrote, and when the piece arrived it was typical Smith: cool, mocking, readable, probably the best bit of writing in that first January issue. It contained the lovely description from 1968 of John Lindsay's seconding the nomination of Spiro Agnew: "Lindsay walked to the platform tall and straight like Sydney Carton en route to the guillotine." He recalled Mayor Dick Daley of Chicago "screaming obscenities at Sen. Abraham Ribicoff of Connecticut," and the fulsome oratory of Tennessee Governor Frank Clement, of whom Smith wrote, "The Democrats smote the Republicans with the jawbone of an ass."

Sandra Hochman was one poet who survived the new regime. Blond, beautiful and plump, Sandy Hochman had written a novel called *Walking Papers* that had been a commercial success but her reputation was in poetry. She lived with her daughter, Ariel, in an East Side penthouse and wrote beautifully, if erratically, of her own very private view of the world. Her poet's vision enabled her to write a brilliant piece on what Nixon's Peking venture would be like and I became fond of her as a contributor and as a person. Nancy White deserves the credit for Hochman, for having brought her to *Bazaar*. I acknowledged my poetic illiteracy, admitting I had never even heard of Hochman before coming to the magazine. Sandy arrived at the office one day to announce that she had been invited to visit Chile ("Neruda arranged it," she told me, and I had to ask someone later who the hell Neruda was) and could she do a piece on Chile? I said sure, please interview Allende because he says the CIA and ITT are trying to start a counterrevolution and either get him out of office or assassinate him. To my amazement Sandra spent two hours with the Marxist Chilean president and got an on-the-record interview. But Sandra Hochman would retain her poetic license to the end. "I'm going to the [1972] Democratic convention as a delegate for Shirley Chisholm," she told me. She was quite pleased about it. "You mean you're going if you win in the primary," I reminded her. No, Sandra replied, she was definitely going to the convention as a Chisholm delegate. She had not yet quite grasped the idea that she had to win a primary vote to do so. I argued the point and then gave up. Sandra lost the primary, of course, but went to Miami anyway, somehow acquired a floor pass, and produced a movie, and a good piece for *Bazaar*, about the convention. I shook my head, much as I did when Sandy would arrive at the office without warning and ask if she could borrow a dollar. "What for?" For a taxi to get home, she would say. "But you need more than a dollar. You need two dollars." She hated to borrow two dollars, she would say, and I would end up giving her five. It was never repaid except in the beautiful prose poetry that I believed no other magazine was offering.

Norman Mailer was one of Sandy Hochman's fans. He had called her work "gold filigree," and had long been a friend. I had had some dealings with Mailer at Fairchild, generally pleasant except for one interview Mailer had submitted to and later felt was harsh. I admired Mailer's work inordinately and, the few times we'd met, liked him as a man. One night another journalist and I were in Elaine's and Mailer was there. We said hello and I introduced my friend, who had covered the Chicago Seven trial and had become quite exercised over the fact that Mailer had written about Apollo 11 instead.

"You copped out, Mailer," he said, poking his finger against Mailer's chest to emphasize his critique.

Mailer turned from the journalist, who had obviously dined well, and said to me, "Tell your friend I don't like having him poke me in the chest with his finger." I remonstrated with my companion, relieved that Mailer, who had the reputation of being a bad drunk, was quite sober. I turned to talk to someone else and when I looked back, my friend was again lecturing Mailer, again with his index finger in a threatening status. I had visions of the two men coming to blows and hurried over to avert trouble.

"Mr. Mailer doesn't like it when you poke him with your

finger," I told my friend. Mailer looked at me. "It's okay," he said gently. "He missed me that time."

Mailer never wrote for *Bazaar*. There was one piece I discussed with Mailer's agent, at a curiously low price, but the origin of the piece was obscure. Frank Crowther had offered it as an interview with Mailer and then it turned out that Mailer considered it a joint effort for which both he and Crowther should be paid. It wasn't a very good piece and I said no. I would have bought pure Mailer if it had cost five times the amount, but bogus Mailer was a luxury we could do without.

On my trips to London, I paid assiduous court to Fleur Cowles and tried to recruit her as *Bazaar*'s London editor. Fleur showed me through her magnificent flat in the Albany, told me the story of some of the pictures, gave me a copy of her *Tiger Flower* book for the children, and promised to write some pieces. We were still discussing who and when and what when I was fired. Fleur told wonderful stores of *Flair* magazine, drew parallels between what she had actually done and what we were now trying to do with *Bazaar*, and tried to tell me about modern art. If there was any region in which I felt more alien than that of poetry, it was modern art, and I tried instead to get Fleur to retail some dirt about the royal family or other of the London grandees.

David Halberstam wrote for *Bazaar* as we attempted to turn its tired pages into a bright and vital "fashion newsmonthly." And so did Tennessee Williams, written off by the critics as a drunk, but turning out two pieces of delicacy and wit and talent. Charlotte Curtis, with her Joey Gallo story "Mafia Chic," was only one of a number of *New York Times* staffers who flocked to our banner. There was a particularly memorable line in the Curtis story, a quote from a society matron asked what people saw in Gallo. I had subtitled the piece "The Last Delicious Days of Joey Gallo," and the matron's quote put a cap on it. "It was like Stravinsky or Yevtushenko. If you didn't know him you weren't in."

I liked the *Times* people. They wrote well and accurately and they delivered on deadline. But there was one embarrassment when a *Times* writer reported that novelist Jacqueline Susann (*Valley of the Dolls*) had had cosmetic thigh surgery and went about town "lifting her skirts" to show off the happy results. Jackie Susann called to complain that her mother had been shocked by the suggestion that daughter Jackie was "lifting her skirts." "I'm not a character in one of my novels," Jackie primly reminded me. She offered to put up a million dollars for my favorite charity if we would match the offer and submit the case to a board of medical examiners. Knowing the current state of the budget, I declined the challenge and said we would take Miss Susann's word for it and run a correction.

I was intrigued by Henry Kissinger, as were most other Americans in 1972, but more intrigued by the fact that Kissinger's ex-wife was a mystery woman. I wasn't sure myself who she was, or where she lived, but I gave out the assignment. A *Boston Globe* reporter, Marion Christy, tracked Anne Kissinger down to a half-brick house in a Boston suburb and wrote a fascinating piece about "the only woman with whom Henry Kissinger's name is never linked."

Rex Reed swallowed his irritation at having been fired by me once before and started writing about film for *Bazaar*. Chuck Mitchelmore, one of my first recruits at *WWD*, was now writing free-lance in Vienna. He must have shaken his head when asked to go into Transylvania and do a story for *Bazaar* on the "real" Count Dracula. Mitchelmore went and did a marvelous piece. Several months later an American travel agent sold out a thousand-dollar-a-head packaged tour "in search of Dracula."

One of the most radical departures I brought about at *Bazaar* was my insistence that the fashion editors actually write their own copy. This may sound strange to someone who has never worked on *Vogue* or *Bazaar* or *Mademoiselle*, but the truth is that any fashion editor who actually wrote about the clothes she saw was in peril of being stripped of her credentials and sent off to work in a massage parlor in the Amish country.

At *Bazaar* the editor who attended a fashion collection came back to the office and wrote up what was called a "blue sheet," a bit of flimsy on which she jotted down the facts, colors, prices, accessories, and her own appraisal of the clothes she had seen. The "blue sheet" was then turned over to a copywriter who had never seen the clothes, who didn't know Mollie Parnis from Chester Weinberg, but whose responsibility it was to write captions, headlines, and occasionally a more lengthy appreciation of that particular designer's fashion message.

This made no sense to me. At *WWD* the same person who attended the show wrote the review. She knew the designer, had presumably talked to him at some length about what he was trying to achieve with this new line, and had been exposed to the showroom atmosphere, had gauged the visceral reaction of those around her to the clothes, had felt the material, and so on.

When I informed my editors that from now on they would write their own copy for *Bazaar*'s fashion pages, there was considerable weeping and rending of garments. China Machado informed me privately that she had never written a line of magazine copy in her life. And she was the top fashion editor. Sanna Lurie, the number two, simply shook her head. Several of the junior editors began preparing résumés and one, Sheila Sullivan, later confessed to me, "I was terrified."

Once the initial shock wore off, most of the editors turned out to be surprisingly literate, to possess a good turn of phrase, and to bring to the writing freshness it had always lacked. In the first few months I went over each line of copy painstakingly, usually with Kate Giles or Barbara Goldsmith, who as news editors were presumed to have the grasp of English that fashion editors lacked. By the time I left, all the editors were writing their own stuff and enjoying it immensely. I understand that Carrie Donovan, trained in the *Vogue* school, went back to the old system when she replaced Machado. Pity.

Not every idea worked. Marion Christy did a profile of Pat Nixon that Dick Berlin vetoed. "I'm so close to Pat and Dick, don'tcha know," he informed me, insisting that Pat must approve the piece in advance. In journalism you never give the subject of a profile an advance look, never mind the right to kill it. But Berlin sent his copy of the story to Mrs. Nixon without my knowing it. Later, he told me, "This is an election year. She prefers that we not run it." It was not the only occasion when Berlin intervened to protect the Nixons from the velvet lash of *Harper's Bazaar*.

Inside Hearst the story went that Nixon's gratitude to Berlin for his support through the years had led to embarrassment on the part of both Berlin and the White House. Early in his term, Mr. Nixon made one of his less distinguished appointments. He nominated Willie Mae Rogers as consumer affairs watchdog for the new administration. Willie Mae was director of the Good Housekeeping Institute, the Hearst invention which grants, or withholds, Good Housekeeping seals of approval to various commercial products. *Good Housekeeping* was and is one of Hearst's more important magazines and Nixon's choice of Miss Rogers would be interpreted, quite naturally, as an endorsement of *Good Housekeeping*, and of its commercially valuable seal. A sort of presidential endorsement of an endorsement.

It didn't quite work out that way. Four days after the President nominated her in February 1969, Willie Mae Rogers resigned, citing a "misunderstanding." What had happened was that Mr. Nixon asked her to sever her ties with *Good Housekeeping* while serving the administration and she refused. A congressional subcommittee on consumer protection asserted that certain products bearing the Good Housekeeping seal had been found defective and alleged that the seal was available to anyone who bought sufficient advertising in the magazine. Hearst and Willie Mae both denied this, but the harm had been done and Mr. Nixon's gracious gesture to old friend and supporter Dick Berlin had done neither of them any good. Still, for all of that, Berlin continued to be a close friend and made it a standing order that any story or photo coverage of Mr. Nixon and his family should be shown to him prior to publication. Later Dick Deems expanded this, quite possibly on Berlin's instructions, to include any "political" story. Nineteen seventy-two was, you will recall, an election year.

Yousuf Karsh, the Armenian portrait photographer who became famous in Ottawa, was another experiment that didn't quite succeed. In the case of Karsh, Dick Berlin was the midwife. He invited me to a black-tie dinner in the "21" Club at which Karsh would be present, and suggested that the photographer might be talked into doing fashion pictures for the first time and *Bazaar* would have an exclusive. You had to like Karsh, a balding gnome with expressive hands and a store of anecdotes. That evening he told, perhaps for the thousandth time, the story of how he secured his greatest photo, the portrait of Churchill-as-bulldog, an effect Karsh achieved by the simple expedient of snatching away the Prime Minister's cigar just before opening the lens. Karsh agreed to do a photo essay for *Bazaar* and we met several times to decide on a list of women. I wanted a broad spectrum, not the usual fashion magazine faces, and we agreed on about eight names. They included Gloria Steinem, Cristina Ford, Buff Chandler, Joan Baez, the Duchess of Windsor, and Ann-Margret. Only Jacqueline Onassis and Pamela Hayward Harriman, who pleaded a trip to Russia with her new husband Averell, turned us down. The photos ran in the July issue and were dreadful. The fault was only partially that of Karsh, whose charming marginal notes did not quite make up for the old-fashioned quality of the sittings. The *Bazaar* art department chose a muted sepia tone which gave the pictures the texture of mud. Since the art directors had opposed the use of Karsh's work in the magazine at all, the suspicion was that the poor reproduction was not an accident.

Another addition to the *Bazaar* staff of contributing editors was Felicia Roosevelt. Felicia was a Warburg who had married a Sarnoff and later Franklin D. Roosevelt, Jr., and among them all she had the sort of contacts *Bazaar* wanted. My first-rate editor, Barbara Goldsmith, had recruited Felicia, nattered with her over expense accounts, edited her copy, and said no when Felicia demanded a secretary to transcribe her notes. One evening Felicia gave us dinner in her Park Avenue apartment, a gracious, old-world sort of meal at which Frank Roosevelt toasted their guests and the ladies left the men to cigars and brandy after dinner. Lou Harris and Joe Lash were there, and with Frank they swapped tales of politics and politicians. Roosevelt talked about how effectively FDR would have used television. He surprised me by claiming that his father was not a "natural" performer but had taken lessons from both voice and film professionals to improve his radio and newsreel appearances.

Harris told a splendid Kennedy story about the 1960 West Virginia primary. "Herbert Hoover was the devil in West Virginia, of course," Harris said. "The Depression had been worst there and had never really ended and we worked up a film for the local West Virginia television stations, attacking Hoover. Hoover was the man to run against down there. Never mind who was on the ballot. Well, Bobby saw the film and he told us we couldn't use it. He said Mr. Hoover was a friend of 'Father' and came to the Kennedy house, and that 'Father' wouldn't want to do anything to hurt Mr. Hoover. Then Jack arrived and we argued the point and Jack asked,

'Is Hoover really the devil in West Virginia?' and we said yes, he was, and Jack said, 'Well, Father loses again.' And we ran the film."

I inherited some stars at *Harper's Bazaar* and we tried to produce others. The big obstacle: the penurious level of pay at the fashion magazines. The old philosophy still obtained, that rich men's daughters worked for a few years on the fashion magazines to while away the time between college and marriage. There were full-time journalists on the *Bazaar* staff who took home a hundred dollars a week or less. My secretary at Fairchild had made twice that amount. I was shocked at the salaries and promised to try to bring them up to a respectable level, but warned the staff it would not be done overnight nor perhaps ever if we didn't get the magazine moving again.

Barbara Goldsmith was a star. Having published short stories in the *New Yorker* at age seventeen, she had worked for several of the major magazines and had been brought in by Nancy White, at Deems's urging, to strengthen the articles section. Barbara knew all the big writers, could get their work for reasonable prices, and edited superbly whatever she got her hands on. During Miss White's time she was listed as an editorial advisor. I made her news editor right away and gave her total authority over the nonfashion aspects of the book. A friend of movie director Frank Perry, Barbara also knew the Hollywood scene and helped us get actresses to pose for cover shots.

China Machado ran the fashion department, aided by Sanna Lurie, and Shirley Lord was the beauty editor. All have since left *Bazaar*. Shirley was not the simplest person in the business to handle. A blooming English beauty, the former wife of British carpet king Cyril Lord, Shirley had worked on the big London dailies and fashion magazines and carped endlessly about changes in her copy. But she was a superlative representative for *Bazaar* in the rich cosmetics field which supplied so much of the news, and most of the ad revenues. She was one of the few persons in New York who could lunch one day with Charles Revson, the next with Estée Lauder, and still maintain an amicable relationship with both of those great arch-rivals.

Kate Giles was a part-time writer and editor, recruited by Barbara Goldsmith. Her first assignment was the controversial Margaret Case suicide story and she handled it brilliantly. I had gone through two managing editors and ended by giving the job to Kate. When I was sacked, Barbara Goldsmith was shifted to managing editor, promptly resigned, and, for all I know, Kate Giles still handles the post today.

Ila Stanger was the travel editor and a good one, and we brought in such promising young people as Wendy Stark, daughter of the movie producer, Dallas Galvin, a lean Texas girl with a master's degree in journalism from Columbia University, and, toward the end, a marvelously named young southerner called Dozier Hasty. I am sorry I was not there long enough to see "Dozier Hasty" achieve stardom.

At *Bazaar* we were constantly in search of new ways to get fashion news and new techniques for showing the clothes and the people we were writing about. Word came to me that Andy Warhol had a bit of leisure and I asked him to lunch. Andy arrived with two or three members of his troupe. Although it was broad daylight, Andy does not usually travel alone, having some years ago been shot by a lady who accused him of one thing or another. The lady was subsequently released from prison and so Andy wisely travels with a little entourage.

It is somewhat difficult to make conversation with Andy Warhol. He speaks very quietly and I found myself leaning toward him on the banquette as we lunched. Knowing nothing of art, especially of modern art, I asked Andy whether he would write a piece for *Bazaar* on where we might expect modern art to go next, in what direction.

"No," Andy said, "I can't write. But I'll take some pictures for you." He reached into a sort of knapsack, pulled out a Polaroid camera, and promptly took a picture of me. We waited the requisite sixty seconds and Andy peeled off the backing from the photo, which was in focus but had little else to recommend it.

"Will you sign it for me?" I asked, thinking, well, this is good business indeed, a signed Warhol. Andy scrawled his initials on the margin of the photo.

"I'll take pictures for you," he repeated.

I asked what sort of pictures, of whom.

"Well," he said, "Like Jackie and Babe Paley and like that."

I perked up a bit. Warhol photos of such grande dames would certainly give circulation a boost. What sort of pictures of Jackie and Babe? I persisted.

When he answered I must have slumped back against the red velvet of the banquette. Andy had raised his normally low voice for the first time, to explain that the pictures of celebrities he wanted to do for *Bazaar* were to be taken at the precise moment of orgasm.

"When they come, you know, like that. Just the face," he assured me. "That wonderful look in the eyes and the face."

I waved the waiter over to pour a bit more wine. I needed it to steady myself.

"Well," I said, "I guess if you can get pictures of those people having orgasms, I guess we can run them."

"Oh," Andy said innocently, "you have to set it up with them. I'll just take the pictures."

It was Charles Masson, the owner and chief mixer of sauces at La Grenouille, whom I inveigled into agreeing to take a camera along on the Newport to Bermuda yacht race to do pictures of the beautiful people and action shots at sea. I envisioned them as the sort of tony stuff we wanted and I knew Masson could handle a camera and knew everybody. He was not actually a yachtsman but had been taken up by Sumner

(Huey) Long, a wealthy ship broker who owned and skippered one of the world's fastest racing vessels, the yacht *Ondine*. Huey Long was a frequent diner at Masson's estimable establishment, inevitably in the company of one smashing-looking girl or another, and Long had come up with the notion that since he and his crew had to eat on those long, oceangoing races, they might as well eat well. Why dine off bully beef and hardtack when you could have La Grenouille's own Charles Masson aboard whipping up Beef Wellington or a subtle soufflé? So Masson went to sea and duly reported later that the crew's favorite was his tray of assorted cold sandwiches.

17

Artists And Models

A color photograph by Hiro Wakabayashi caused the first
substantive breach between Richard Deems and me. I now
believe that Deems was right, and I wrong, but the issue
raised and illuminated the basic question of just what sort
of magazine *Bazaar* was to be. What sort of magazine did
American women really want?

Hiro is *Bazaar*'s contract photographer as Avedon is
V*ogue*'s. Both men are paid very large annual guarantees. I
knew, of course, what Hiro was paid by *Bazaar* and was quite
impressed when he told me offhandedly, "My real income
comes from ads." Hiro had worked for Avedon and years later
succeeded him at *Bazaar* when Avedon leaped over the wall
to join competitor V*ogue*. Deems and Avedon are still a bit
touchy about the negotiations which led to Avedon's break
with *Bazaar*. When I joined the magazine both Deems and
Nancy White emphasized Hiro's talent and energy and his
importance to *Bazaar*. Hiro's guarantee called for a hundred

pages of photos a year, and since he had to be paid extra for anything over the hundred pages, the trick was to budget his output so that you'd have some great Hiro photography in every issue but end up with a total of one hundred pages by the December issue. It was for this reason that I was puzzled to see over twenty pages of fairly routine fashion photographed in black and white in one of the earlier 1971 issues. It seemed to me a waste of Hiro's talent, and of the precious hundred-page budget. We lunched together and he agreed. But the photos had had to be taken, it was a vacation period, and he was available. It was as simple as that. I told Hiro that as far as I was concerned he was our star turn and I wanted to use him only on big stuff, on covers, on photos that would have impact. "Think about that," I urged him. "Think about photos that will get everyone talking about *Bazaar*." I left it at that. When you have a man with Hiro's talent, and you pay him that much money, you're a fool to try to do the job for him. He said he would think about what I said and would have something to show me in a few weeks.

I was summoned to the art department one morning where Hiro was waiting with some color slides. "You understand," he said, "I am not happy with these girls. I think we can get different girls who will be better. But this will give you the idea." He slipped the stack of color slides into the holder and began to show one color photo after another on the white screen. I stood watching, not saying anything. When Hiro had run through the stack the lights came on. "I don't know, Hiro. They're beautiful, but I'm not sure we're ready for it. Let's get Nancy in here." Miss White was brought in. "They're beautiful, Hiro. Where did you think we might use them?"

"On the cover," Hiro said dramatically.

The photos were of two women kissing, their mouths joined and slightly opened, their eyes glazed (or at least I imagined them to be). It was a head shot and one of the women was wearing a hat. Hiro reminded us again that he had two other girls in mind for the final shot, less earthy than these, more ethereal. "It's still a lesbian scene," I said. "Well, you could say that, but there's always an element of doubt. Are they or aren't they?" Hiro responded. "It's pretty damn clear to me," I said. We agreed that he would do another sitting with different girls. I suggested he work on his "element of doubt" thesis. "Maybe they could be almost kissing," I said weakly.

Over the next few weeks "the kiss," as it came to be known, was a matter of frequent conversation. We wanted a dramatic photo for the cover of the January issue, which would be my first, and this was certainly dramatic. Nancy White showed good sense in most things and she did in this.

"If you put that on the cover," she said, "the impression will be that you're changing *Bazaar* into something sensationalistic. I know you don't mean to do it, but putting two women kissing on the cover of *Bazaar* is a tacit endorsement of lesbianism."

The next time Deems came into the office I showed him the photo. He liked it but felt it wasn't for *Bazaar*. "A great shot," he said, "very sexy. But not for us."

Hiro worked with two new girls and the photo was subtler now, but the lesbianism was still pretty explicit. Yet when we tried it with the two women close, but not kissing, it didn't work at all. I scrubbed it as an idea for the January cover and found myself subject to another sort of polemic when we ran a college girl in blue jeans as an exemplar of the new generation of American voters. The girl was a college student and a beauty. But when the issue came out it was said that we had turned *Bazaar* into a teen-age book appealing to the blue jeans crowd.

The theme of the March issue was to be privacy versus gossip, the difficulty of living a private life in the public fish bowl. Hiro resuscitated the "kiss" photo. "What's more private than this?" he suggested slyly. Deems got into the act again and ended very subtly by saying that he was opposed to using the shot but I was the publisher. I must make up my own mind. I ended by pinning the color photo to my bulletin board and not running it in the magazine. As progressive and courageous as I wanted us to be, "the kiss" was a bit much. Even for me.

Art departments and the artists and art directors who staff them are alien ground for the writing or editing journalist. At *Women's Wear Daily* there was, we were fond of saying, the largest publications art department in the country outside of *Life* magazine. As in all art departments there was a great deal of emotion. One young man, I'll call him Alfred, was overheard once telling another artist: "I don't know what he sees in him. I cook better than he does. I keep house better than he does. I sew better than he does."

This same Alfred got into the elevator one morning and was seized upon by Wight Martindale, the personnel director. Martindale, a cheerful type who prided himself on knowing the names of every one of the thousand or more employees, greeted Alfred.

"Good morning, Alfred, how are you?" Martindale boomed cheerfully.

Alfred started at the personnel man.

"I don't know you," he said nervously, and got off the elevator to wait for the next car.

One of the most talented young assistant art directors was named Joaquin Deno, and John Fairchild experienced great difficulty with his name. There was a meeting in John's office, attended by Rudy Millendorf, Bill Dwyer, and myself. There was some question about the layout of a front page.

"Get Rutkeen," John ordered. "He'll explain what I mean."

Rudy Millendorf stood as if transfixed. John waved a hand at him.

"Rudy, Rutkeen will show you what I mean. You know I don't explain these things very clearly."

"Yes, Mr. Fairchild," said the confused Millendorf who, in Dwyer's inelegant but apt words, didn't know whether to shit or wind his watch.

John slumped into one of the sofas and fixed Millendorf with his most tired look.

"Rudy, there's no reason Rutkeen shouldn't simply be asked to come in and explain what I mean about the layout."

"Yes, Mr. Fairchild," Rudy said, his eyes rolling toward the newly painted ceiling.

"I think he wants Joaquin," Dwyer suggested quietly.

"Yes, and he'll explain everything," John said triumphantly.

The artists were simply not like you and me. In Paris one year we used a young American, a southern boy with a pleasant drawl, to sketch the new clothes from descriptions given us by American buyers late at night in their hotel rooms. There would be a good deal of wine as we coaxed the buyers to provide more and more detail. Then a motorcyclist would speed the sketches across town to be radioed to New York for the morning's edition of *WWD* in our frantic drive to beat the *New York Times* by twenty-four hours. The work would be completed at perhaps two in the morning and John Fairchild and the buyer and I would have a last drink before collapsing into our respective beds. Not so the artist, who would announce that he had an appointment and disappear into the dark Paris streets. Next morning, bleary-eyed and rumpled, he would arrive at the office for another day's work and another night's carousal. His stamina, as well as his insatiability, was wonderful to behold.

In another season Kenneth Paul Block would do the sketches. Block was just the opposite, an intelligent, calm and finicky man who never removed his jacket or even unbuttoned it during the long hours and painstaking labor of sketching clothes he had never seen from boozy descriptions by buyers who had been permitted into Balenciaga's show, from which we were banned. Kenneth would do the artwork, go off to bed, and after each season write for the paper a magnificent artist's-eye view of that year's fashion. His assessments were always counter to what the paper had said but were so well done, so astutely critical, that we would run them on two pages as a "minority report." If this confused some readers, it delighted Block, surely the best of the contemporary fashion artists.

Another of the great *WWD* stable of sketchers was lyrical in his praise of Jimmy Galanos's work. He would have paid us to let him sketch the Galanos collections. Several years ago he was so taken by a particular Galanos collection when it was shown in New York that he went backstage after the show and bought one of the dresses, at eight hundred dollars. A week later we were all invited to his house for a cocktail party at which he saluted Galanos's genius, took the dress out of his closet, and tried it on for an admiring roomful of friends.

I am told that even today the artist will bring out his eight-hundred-dollar dress and model it for those who understand that it is the most precious thing he owns.

Art direction of a magazine was an area in which I did not feel at all at home. My experience had been limited to newspaper visuals. *Bazaar* had once been an art director's delight. The legendary Alexey Brodovitch had made it so. Deems told of Brodovitch's demanding perfectionism, of his "deadline be damned" stridency when an engraving or a color failed to meet his standards. Nancy White had wonderful tales of Brodovitch and Carmel Snow, right on deadline, strewing page proofs on the carpet of her office, rejecting and demanding and reducing lesser people to tears of frustration, driving the printers to exasperated rage. These were things I wanted to hear in those early months, hints of a very real respect for quality, of a refusal to compromise.

But what I found at *Harper's Bazaar* was by now quite different. There were two art directors, Bea Feitler and Ruth Ansel. Talented, competitive, each with her own view of what the magazine should look like, the two women worked together on some issues, alternated on others, so that March would have one look and April an entirely different handwriting. I found the dual art directorship a structural abortion and said so. Although I did not yet feel competent to make artistic judgments, I told both art directors in that first month that I would eventually name one of them, or a third party, to the art directorship. I hoped the situation would sort itself out, that either Feitler or Ansel would prove measurably the better or that one of them would resign. None of this happened, and after six months I knew the dilemma could be solved only by dropping one or the other. They were bickering between themselves and the editors complained that their rivalry was making it impossible to get out the magazine.

I had discharged people before but that was a part of the job. Uncharacteristically, I dithered about which of the two art directors would have to go. There was a giddy moment in which I thought of asking them to toss a coin. After an uncomfortable weekend I called the two women to my office, reviewed my unhappiness with the dual direction system, and told Feitler she was fired. A sinewy Brazilian, Feitler had designed the very successful Robert Kimball–Brendan Gill book on Cole Porter. Talented but difficult to handle, was my assessment. I thought Ruth Ansel would function more effectively without the Feitler presence. I was wrong. Within another several months I had concluded that neither of the original art directors was right for the new magazine that was evolving and went outside to hire Rochelle Udell, a Rubenesque young woman who had worked on *New York* magazine and who was married to a young artist. Udell was superb. The editors were in rapture. For the first time you could get a layout from the art department without rendering the Bell Song from Lakmé. Udell was fast, economic, and she seemed to understand. Her first issue came off the presses in late October. It was crisp, clean, and looked like no other publication in the field. But by that time I myself had been fired. I wondered about Udell, whether she would survive. A photographer friend told me, "Don't count on it. Mazzola is an old art director and art directors who become editors hire weak art directors. They really want to do it themselves." The prediction was correct. Rochelle Udell closed the December and the January issues and was dismissed. Goddammit, I thought, the best talent I brought in and they got rid of her right away.

Vogue hired her within a few weeks and Rochelle Udell is today Vogue's art director.

It is not true that I hate models. I am as impressed as the next man by tall, slim young women with long legs, deep-set eyes, and good facial bones. It is simply that I do not believe they convey a very realistic picture of American women, that, being so preternaturally tall and thin and lissome, they are more the ideal than the reality. And when I came to Bazaar, I immediately announced a prejudice in favor of what I called "real clothes on real women."

I was not used to having photographic models about. We never used them at WWD and when the magnificent Jean Shrimpton appeared at the newspaper once to be interviewed, I was as goggle-eyed as the merest copyboy. But at Bazaar the place was sodden with models, striding up and down the corridors, nipping into unused offices to change their clothes, or poking their heads into my office to inquire if they had left their portfolios anywhere around. I was duly cautioned by older and wiser heads to avoid the company of models for they would surely try to use me, feigning affection, admiration, or even passion to get me to force the editors to put their faces on the covers. Sadly, I was never importuned, not once, and I have since relegated to folklore the old saw that models will do anything, anything mind you, to impress a fashion magazine publisher.

When I issued my edict about "real" women and relegated

photographic models to a sort of *Harper's Bazaar* limbo, the leading model agencies immediately struck back. Eileen Ford, who runs one of the best, denounced me as a woman-hater and a fool who knew nothing about fashion and never would. My subsequent difficulties with the Hearst management may have proved Mrs. Ford wise beyond her years.

Most models are disappointing when you meet them in person. And current fashion is of little help. One of the most glamorous of all the cover girls, a young woman whose face has adorned dozens of magazine covers, came by my office one day and was introduced. I was delighted to meet her, knowing her professional reputation. She was wearing an old sweat shirt, Eskimo boots with heavy woolen socks that came up above her knees, and what seemed to be a pair of trousers cut years before for a gentleman of considerable girth. She had a woolen ski cap pulled down to her eyebrows and a college scarf obscured the lower half of her face. Hardly the sex symbol that would send a man screaming for surcease from such overwhelming temptation.

It is an old story that some models read comic books between sittings and I would like to nail it now. Some models I know have not yet progressed to that stage of literacy and instead pass their idle moments chewing gum and coping with the intricacies of record players that produce the loud and monotonous rock music which seems to be their trademark in life. But some of them are, without doubt, interesting and intelligent.

There is one model I know who maintains an apartment in Milan, a small flat in London, and borrows digs in New York whenever she is in town. Gone with the steamer trunk is the notion that young women are less mobile than young men. Not since the Children's Crusade have so many young persons been on the move from country to country and among the most maneuverable of them are the relative handful of photographic models who have really made it in Europe and America.

They travel light. A Vuitton tote bag and a passport, sandals and blue jeans, a silk shirt and a pullover sweater, in winter a duffle coat or long leather coat lined with fur. But traveling light does not mean traveling rough. They live well, these migratory birds, and they do it with panache.

The model I mentioned with the flat in Milan told me of a dinner party she attended in Paris, wearing her blue jeans and sweater, *naturellement*, with singer Andy Williams, a middle-aged jockey, and a half-dozen other people. The dinner terminated at six o'clock in the morning when the group chartered a plane to fly to St. Tropez for a day's sun and swimming. "I borrowed five francs to buy a toothbrush," she recalled, "and we had a super time."

Another of the migratory birds was invited to the theater in London one evening and arrived to announce that her jeans were still damp, and did her escort mind if they stood for the first act? She wore the jeans every day, washed them every night, and when they wore out, threw them away and bought another pair. This model makes six hundred dollars a day when she is working and is the girl you see in all the ads done by one of the country's largest and most successful cosmetics companies.

In the current crackdown on smuggling, and the stricter airport and customs searches in the era of hijacking, these girls seem exempt. Most of them smoke pot, and some are into heavier drugs, and yet they sweep through airport barriers as if they were not there. I asked one girl how she got away with it. "I just smile and ask the man his name and I tell him how helpful he's been and that I'm going to write his boss and say so."

A girl with that sort of *chutzpah* would have made a truly great courtesan.

Fashion modeling has provided a springboard to an acting

career for Miss Shrimpton, for Suzy Parker, for Lauren Hutton and Cybill Shepard, for Jennifer O'Neill, and, most dramatically, for Ali MacGraw. But for every star there are a thousand attractive young women employed in the daily drudgery of modeling clothes in the showrooms of Seventh Avenue or Paris or London or Rome who will never get any further professionally. And there are hundreds of even more attractive photographic models who will make more money but never achieve stardom.

When I first came to Paris as a journalist the top model was Chanel's favorite, Marie-Hélène Arnaud. A beautiful and clever young woman, she was often spoken of as Chanel's successor, the one who had the spark and the intelligence to inherit the business, Chanel's chosen one. Then there was some sort of falling out, Marie-Hélène left the Maison Chanel, tried her hand at designing, and when last I saw her was the extra girl at dinner parties.

Dorian Leigh, Suzy Parker's older sister, enjoyed a vogue as a top model and then ran her own agency. She still lives in Paris and recently was asking friends to invest a hundred or two hundred dollars in a little restaurant she hoped to open. It was to be called Chez Dorian.

Tony Trabert's wife, a beautiful young American beauty-contest winner who fell into the modeling game when Trabert began playing tennis regularly on the European professional tour, was for a time Chanel's star, and later became so diet-conscious she shrank away to almost nothing. "I worry about her," Chanel told me one day. "She won't eat. She's afraid of gaining weight." Mrs. Trabert broke with her husband, and she too, like Mlle. Arnaud, drifted out of the Chanel *cabine* and into obscurity.

One day when I was running *Bazaar* I lunched with my art director and one of our photographers. There was some chat about a girl who had been found dead in her New York apartment the day before, a young model.

"I don't believe I know her," I said.

"Sure you do. She was in the magazine just a few issues ago. She was that girl who . . ." and from the description of her pictures I remembered a beautiful girl, very young, almost ethereal.

"What happened?"

"The usual," the photographer said. "An overdose. She was nineteen."

There are models who do not end badly or become stars but who meet a man and settle down to home and children. There are models who act in pornographic movies as much to satisfy their own exhibitionism as for the money. There is the celebrated model who pays a dirty old man to teach her new sexual tricks, there is a girl who lives on fruit and carrots and milk, and another who swears that honey is not only the perfect food but the ideal skin treatment, especially for the breasts and genitals.

I used to think of Faye Dunaway as playing Bonnie to Warren Beatty's Clyde. But now, when I think of Miss Dunaway, I am inevitably drawn to her underarms. In one of my first issues of *Bazaar* our photographer Hiro was sent up to do a photo essay of Miss Dunaway as one of the first examples of the "real" people I intended to feature instead of using paid mannequins. It was not that I wanted to save money, you understand, since it is cheaper in the long run to use a girl you pay rather than indulge in the negotiations, temperament, and undependability of your usual celebrity. But Dunaway was a fine actress, a beautiful woman, and an interesting interview. When Hiro came back to show us the pictures we were all delighted. They were just fine. Then one of the art directors pointed out to me something I'd missed in my cursory glance at the contact sheets. Miss Dunaway had been posed in bed, a sheet properly tucked up under her chin, one arm raised to support her head, and the armpit of that arm clearly in evidence.

"She doesn't shave her underarms," the art director announced dramatically.

Sure enough. There were these little wisps of hair adorning Miss Dunaway. "Very European," I said with what I hoped was the air of a traveled sophisticate.

"Yes," the art director agreed, "but do we airbrush the damn thing out?"

Miss Dunaway's underarms thus became one of our first causes célèbres. Hiro testified that she had made a point of telling him she didn't shave because she felt no reason to do so, as a liberated woman with her own life-style she could shave or not shave, and she chose not to. Since this was to be an essay in words and pictures on the "real" Faye Dunaway, and not a publicity flack's homogenized version, I decided the hair should stay in. There was a good deal of clucking over that in the corridors of *Harper's Bazaar*, you can be sure. When Dick Deems saw the proofs of the issue he shook his head. "Dames," he said wistfully. "You should have airbrushed it out."

I assured him with a certain delight that it was far too late, that I didn't want to run up overtime costs by holding the issue, and Deems went back to his work wondering, probably not for the first time and surely not the last, what he had gotten himself into. When the issue appeared on the newsstands the mail flooded in: half our audience was outraged, others were confused, and the remainder saluted Miss Dunaway for her courage. Later, when an advertising agency was pitching the *Bazaar* account, they wanted us to run a full-page ad in the *New York Times* with the photo of Miss Dunaway, and her armpit, blown up to mammoth proportions.

"It will immediately set *Bazaar* apart as a different sort of high-fashion magazine," the agency president assured me.

I am certain he was correct.

18

Madison Avenue Always Pays

It is not the fifty cents or the dollar that you put down on a newsstand that keeps a magazine going. It is the advertising. I liked pretending to be innocent about advertising but even my naïveté didn't extend quite that far. I knew that *Bazaar* would live or die on its ad revenue — as would *WWD* or the *Times* or any other publication — and that finding the right sales managers and salesmen would to a great extent determine whether I would succeed as publisher.

My first shock was to learn that, despite its dwindling revenues, *Bazaar* had been consistently and stubbornly rejecting the advertisements from Sears, Roebuck and from J. C. Penney, who had become, by 1971, the biggest spenders in the fashion business. Fred Renz, the ad director I inherited, told me both Sears and Penney had actually tried to buy space in *Bazaar* but had been refused. "We were afraid we'd lose Saks and Bergdorf if we accepted them." There was simply no way to compare the ad purchasing power of the two catalogue giants with the elegantly modest budgets of such shops as Bergdorf. I told Renz to set up meetings with Penney and Sears and we would take our chances with the old-line specialty stores. Not surprisingly, Sears and Penney recalled earlier snubs and said they would have to be convinced their ads belonged in *Bazaar*.

Dan Burke, the president of Capital Cities Broadcasting Corporation, is fond of calling sales management a black art. I have never been entirely comfortable with space salesmen. There are some of them I know and like, others who bore me, others who are repellent, awesome, venal, frightening, pitiable. There was a man who had worked for Burke and later for me of whom Burke said, "The only way to handle that guy is to punch him in the face every morning as he gets off the elevator."

There was a space salesman at Fairchild who snatched the phone from another man who was accepting an obituary notice. "That's my account," the salesman snarled. "I've worked on that account for years." He took the call and in the most oleaginous tones began to commiserate with the bereaved family.

I once had a superb space salesman in Italy who was also a minor official of the Italian government in the department responsible for pushing Italian exports to America. This marvel would shove his rate card across the desk, make a short speech about the pulling power of our publications with American buyers, and go around to the other side of his desk to sign the ad contract on behalf of his government. Then there was an Englishman who set up a dummy company in Spain — owned by his wife — that occasionally bought small ads to justify his making frequent trips, usually during the six months of London winter, to service the account in sunnier Spain.

The first salesman I ever sacked was also an Englishman. He was a poor salesman but that wasn't what bothered me.

He was a slim man in his thirties whose father had been a rather famous British general, and apparently a man of tremendous girth. Among the other bequests, the general had left his entire wardrobe to his only son and heir. The salesman apparently lacked a tailor and wore the clothes without having had them altered. One day when I caught him without his jacket, I noted that his father's voluminous trousers were held up with a bit of rope. I somewhat embarrassedly suggested that his appearance didn't quite fit the image we were trying to create for our newspapers in England and that he might do something about sprucing himself up. He told me that, like most Americans, I was obsessed with materialism.

There was a salesman at WWD who year in and year out had had a bigger income than the publisher. And a sales executive at *Harper's Bazaar* who arrived one Monday with a black eye and a swollen jaw and the explanation that he had fallen down coming out of church the previous day. There was a salesman who would go silent for hours, refusing to answer questions or in any way acknowledge your existence, then suddenly come out of his apparent trance to announce, "I've been in a bad chamber." There are sales managers who lose their confidence without notice and others who will reject as laughable the most obvious signs their publication is a loser that has no conceivable chance of becoming a money-maker.

William Fine, later the president of Bonwit Teller, was the best sales executive *Bazaar* had during the last ten years. He told me once that the reason the cosmetics giants such as Revlon and Lauder didn't sell even more was that American bathrooms lacked enough shelf space to hold the products. "Women have been doing their faces for years. But the face is only ten percent, maybe, of the total body. There are creams and lotions and treatments for the entire body that are out there, that could be sold, if only bathroom shelves were adequate. The way we've got to sell more cosmetics advertising," he told me fervently, "is to get American home builders to redesign the American bathroom." I was then an innocent young publisher at *WWD* and I could only shake my head in admiration for this brilliantly obvious bit of creative salesmanship.

Charles Revson, the tough, self-made genius who created and who runs the Revlon organization, is the biggest single advertiser in a half-dozen of the major fashion magazines. These magazines will go to some length to mollify Mr. Revson and to retain his custom. It is understandable that the advertising manager and his staff do this, and quite right. But when you set the editorial staff to the task of keeping Mr. Revson happy, rather than to the job of acquiring and printing information about his products, then you have prostituted the magazine and not done right by its readers. The ironic aspect is that Charles Revson sees through the charade. Talking with Revson shortly after I had taken on the *Bazaar* job, I confessed my confusion as to why magazines would give perfume credits in the photo captions. "After all, the reader can't smell the perfume and you certainly can't see it. Why mention it? The model usually isn't even wearing any when we do the picture."

Revson shook his head. "A lot of crap. A numbers game. They count the editorial mentions to make sure the other guy doesn't get one more than they do." The "they," in Revson's view, are all the other cosmetics and beauty companies. And the magazines that play the "numbers game," although they get his business, also get his lightly disguised contempt.

Nevertheless, the great cosmetics companies were, and are, the advertising mainstay of the fashion magazines. Of the top ten advertisers in *Bazaar*, six of them were cosmetics firms. Revlon spent the most and had been the first cosmetics company to go into fashion magazine advertising in a substantial and consistent manner. Revson demanded that his ads run further forward in the magazine than those of any other cosmetics house. Estée Lauder, the second-ranking advertiser in the cosmetics field, was a fiery competitor of Revson but had accepted being number two in the page order.

Then, in the first month I was on the job, Estée's son, Leonard, reopened the question of positioning and said he felt that Lauder was not being treated fairly. I consulted with Deems, who told me that Bill Fine, then *Bazaar*'s publisher, had some years before notified Revlon that its ads would no longer always be positioned first, that they would alternate position with those of Lauder. In response, Deems said, Charles Revson pulled out all of his advertising not only from *Bazaar* but from all the other Hearst magazines for a year.

We consulted back and forth, Leonard Lauder set, and then relaxed, deadlines, and Deems fretted nervously. A year later, when I was sacked, the issue was still unresolved, and for all I know, Revlon and Lauder are still feuding, and *Bazaar* and the other fashion magazines are still in the middle.

When a woman buys a fashion magazine she assumes, reasonably enough, that the clothes she sees featured are those selected by the editors as the most beautiful, ingenious, or in other ways the best of that month's crop. But it is a fact of fashion journalism that the dress shown on the cover in full color is usually produced by a manufacturer who is a major advertiser in the magazine. The biggest of the Seventh Avenue manufacturers "buy" magazine covers as they buy advertising pages. The only difference is that the advertising is honest and the reporting isn't. Magazines are understandably reluctant to discuss this trading off of fashion pages for pages of advertising. But early in 1971 Richard Shortway, the publisher of *Vogue* and a man less subtle than some of his competitors, admitted in a Honolulu newspaper story that David Crystal, a giant dress manufacturer, was regularly given a *Vogue* cover not because its dresses were very exciting, but because Crystal was a loyal and generous supporter of *Vogue* through its advertising expenditures. "It's a fact of magazine publishing," Shortway confessed, "that the magazine tends to favor those who advertise regularly."

The educational television channel in New York, WNET, got hold of Shortway's remarks and built a thirty-minute talk show around them. Given the opportunity to comment on Shortway's girlish indiscretions, I made the most of it, acknowledging that I was "shocked" and that at *Harper's Bazaar* we had decreed a separation of church and state which ensured that only the editors made decisions on what merchandise was featured. *Bazaar's* advertising people were under orders to stay out of the editorial department. Such had not always been the case at *Bazaar*. At one of the first editorial meetings I held I asked how many fashion pages we had to work within an upcoming issue. "Sixty pages," said China Machado, the fashion editor, "but advertising has taken forty-five of them."

My church and state memorandum, issued one week after I took the publisher's chair, put an end to that. From that day on *Bazaar's* editors made the editorial decisions, and when they were bad decisions, as sometimes happened, they were at least honest.

This was the *Women's Wear Daily* training, the insistence that the reader be given full value for his money, that a subscriber or newsstand purchaser deserved to know that he was seeing what the editors believed to be news, not what some advertiser had used his purchasing power to disguise as news. Of course, *WWD's* hard-nosed attitudes caused us to lose some advertising. It was inevitable. But for every disgruntled advertiser who went off to pout over the newspaper's independent stance, another would arrive, more than anxious to spend his money in a paper people trusted and cited as "the bible." From 1965 through 1970, the full years of my stewardship at the paper, revenues rose from about eight million dollars to eleven million dollars, paid circulation went up from fifty-two thousand to eighty-five thousand, and the subscription price was increased 100 percent.

During those years at WWD, I had three advertising directors and learned something from all three of them about sales management. But nothing they taught me prepared me for the situation at Harper's Bazaar. One of the ranking men greeted me with the complaint that the company had reneged on some sort of bonus two years before and would I get the money for him? Another senior man resigned immediately, assuring me it was nothing personal but that he had been working on a deal for six months and it had finally come through. An attractive and competent young saleswoman, Claudia McGeary, scored several of the few advertising coups we enjoyed in those early days and was promptly hired away by the New York Times at a 50 percent increase in salary. A senior salesman was sent to Florida on a selling trip and turned in an expense account showing that he had, against the company rules, flown first class. I asked him about it, curious as to why he had done something about which he would so obviously be questioned, and he said disarmingly, "I thought I could get away with it." Another salesman confessed that he was too nervous to make calls and we sent him on his way with a handshake. Another left to become ad manager of a new magazine that immediately collapsed. He called me to suggest that he should come back to us, but as my assistant. A tall, lissome and beautiful young woman called Virginia Regan, who had worked for the Lindsay administration, came seeking an editor's job and I turned her into a saleswoman. After three months she quit, explaining quite logically that she disliked asking people for money. Fred Renz, the associate publisher, transferred to a corporate job and I had to look for a new ad chief.

Interviewing executives in New York so that their current employers will not know they are considering other opportunities is an art form with all its own nuances. Dick Deems produced a list of names, I had a few ideas of my own, and men from other magazines called independently. I spent hour after hour over drinks in the St. Regis Hotel, the bar of the University Club, and one memorable evening in Elaine's, listening to sales executives who assured me they held the secret of *Bazaar*'s, and my, salvation. One or two turned me down, citing Hearst's reputation or the salary or their wish to get a publisher's title before tackling the challenge.

William Lucano, the star salesman at *McCall's* magazine, got the job. He was an attractive and competent ex-Marine officer who came to our first meeting armed with questions and facts. He had been happy at *McCall's*, was making a good salary and bonuses, but was ambitious to take on the job, to manage men, to build a staff and develop *Bazaar*'s potential, or what he and I believed to be its potential. Lucano built that staff, worked sixty hours a week, directed the first market research material in several years, and commissioned the first reader profile study since the mid-1960's. He took the job while the April issue was on deadline and by September *Bazaar* was meeting its budget predictions of pages sold. By year's end it was surpassing them. The magazine was still in the red but it had begun to move. But by then Mr. Deems had sent his "Dear Jim" letter and I was gone and Lucano was reporting to several other people.

I once asked Deems what he thought of Lucano. "He hasn't a lazy bone in his body," Deems said. Two months after my departure Lucano was informed that his contract would not be renewed.

Whenever Hearst executives became depressed, they tended to cheer themselves up by talking about *Cosmopolitan*. The magazine had been close to extinction in the mid-sixties, a tired, old-ladies' book that had no clearly defined position in the marketplace, a magazine whose great days were behind it and whose circulation had almost disappeared. Helen Gurley Brown, looking like a little girl lost but with a shrewd appreciation of a changing morality and a more open interest in sex on the part of American women, had just written a book called *Sex and the Single Girl*. Suddenly it was "okay" for women to talk the way men had talked for centuries. She approached Hearst with the notion of a continuing dialogue along the same lines pioneered in her book, and its sequel, and drew up a rather imposing prospectus for a new monthly magazine for the sexually aware female population. In the course of negotiating with Mrs. Brown, someone at Hearst, no one seems to remember who, suggested that instead of assuming the substantial start-up costs of an entirely new magazine, they turn over to Helen the fly-specked invalid *Cosmopolitan*. "Hell," Deems would later tell me, "nothing she could do would make it worse. It was dying anyway and we figured, why not give her a shot?"

So Helen Gurley Brown was given *Cosmopolitan*. In her first issue she ran a serious and informational piece on the birth control pill and how she believed it could liberate women from sexual hangups and permit single women, or married women not wishing to become pregnant, to enjoy as much sex as they wanted, much as so many men had been doing for years. Newsstand sales boomed, several big advertisers wrung their hands and abandoned *Cosmo*, but many more began to look seriously at the magazine for the first time in its modern history. Today *Cosmo* is nearing two million issues sold each month, sells at an extraordinary 90 percent plus on the newsstands (less than 10 percent of all copies distributed are returned) and is chockablock with advertising aimed at liberated, but not militant, women throughout the country.

Naturally there are others at Hearst who believe they should share the credit with Helen Brown. Deems told me, in one of our talks about the need for a strong editorial product, "Frank Dupuy [the publisher of *Cosmo*] thinks he's a genius now because *Cosmo* is so successful. He was the same guy who couldn't sell it worth a damn before Helen came on board." One night I took Helen and her husband, David Brown, to dinner at Elaine's. David is a motion picture executive and an urbane man who still writes Helen's ad copy ("I guess you could say I'm . . . that *Cosmopolitan* girl"). They swiveled this way and that as writers and fashion designers and actors and pretty girls passed by the table. "Who's she . . . who's that . . . which one is he?" they asked. "You two amaze me," I said. "Here you're the editor of what's supposed to be a sophisticated women's magazine and David's a big Hollywood type and you act like a couple of tourists just off the Greyhound bus from Des Moines." They laughed and agreed it was so.

Which may just happen to be the secret of Helen Brown's success. Despite her triumphs, she's as wide-eyed and ready to be impressed as the merest shopgirl who buys her magazine in hopes of a richer, more acrobatic, happier sex life. Success hasn't spoiled Helen Brown nor has her editorial interest in sex flagged one bit. When last I heard, she had assigned a top *New York Times* women's page reporter to write, pseudonymously, about how a woman should use a vaginal vibrator to get the biggest kicks and the most frequent auto-orgasms. It'll drive the moralists and women's libbers mad. And it will sell like crazy.

At *Women's Wear Daily* there had been a curious disinclination to advertise our own wares. For a company that derived the bulk of its revenues from advertising sales, this was an exotic policy to defend, but John Fairchild believed that the newspapers he put out spoke for themselves, without any help, and since he was successful no one could say he was wrong. *Harper's Bazaar* had an advertising budget but was not successful. There was an advertising agency — Trahey, Wolf — and an advertising campaign. It was aimed at defining the typical *Bazaar* reader as a woman on the "go." Buttons had been issued to the salesmen. They said, "Go." Nobody went. Norman Sunshine was a painter who worked for the Jane Trahey agency. He was assigned the *Bazaar* account and between the two of us we worked up a campaign we thought would tell something about the kind of magazine I would be putting out. Sunshine carried out the concept in his layouts, worked with me to polish the copy I wrote, and suggested changes that improved the joint effort. *Bazaar's* major advertisers were, in this order, the great cosmetic companies, the high-fashion retail stores, the fiber and fabric giants, and the fashion houses themselves, the so-called cutters of Seventh Avenue and other centers. They all read *WWD*. So that was where we placed our advertising, buying the full page opposite the carefully read EYE column once a week for twenty-six weeks.

Adam Gimbel, a great merchant who ran Saks Fifth Avenue for donkey's years, once told me over a meal that he couldn't prove that advertising sold a single piece of merchandise in all his time. But he advertised nevertheless. In that spirit I don't know that our *WWD* ads drew much business, but they told the world that *Bazaar* was alive, that there were people running it who cared about the quality of its editorial, and that we had not abdicated in favor of *Vogue* or, dammit all, anyone else. "Brady's Green Eyeshade Gang Has Taken Over," the first ad announced, less humbly than it should have perhaps, but with a certain verve. The copy announced that editors at *Bazaar* had put away their white gloves and their flowered hats and their afternoon tea to don the green eyeshades of the newspaper city room, that journalists had taken over, and that a new breed of fashion magazine was about to emerge. "No one has yet shouted 'tear out the front page,'" my copy read, "but the other day someone whispered, 'could we perhaps stop the presses.'"

Deems was good about the advertising. He gave me the seventy-five thousand dollars I needed for the *WWD* campaign. After the fact he said he thought the approach was wrong, that we should have stressed the demographic qualities of our readership, and he may have been right. But he didn't interfere. He let me go my own way, talking about *Bazaar* and its journalists. There was one moment when the *WWD* campaign focused on the reader. I had gotten a form letter from the commander of the President's plane, Air Force One, asking that we be certain always to have the current issue of *Bazaar* on board. It turned out that Air Force One carried a half-dozen copies of *Bazaar* for the presidential party to thumb through while in flight. I realized the plane probably carried a hundred other periodicals, but didn't feel conscience-bound to mention that fact in my next ad.

The Nixons were about to leave on their historic voyage to Peking and *Bazaar*'s next ad suggested they would be well-equipped for it. "Their" issue of *Bazaar* would tell them all about travel, and would provide them with articles of interest, an up-to-date horoscope, and other divertissements. I was so fond of that particular ad we did a reprise the following week, finding somewhere a photo of a little Chinese newsboy whom Norman Sunshine armed with a copy of *Bazaar*, carefully pasted up. In that ad we implied that the Nixons had left their copies of *Harper's Bazaar* behind them in Peking and that by this time, Madame Mao Tsetung was probably wearing one of the more attractive Bill Blass numbers featured in that issue.

After that campaign ran out, I took Deems's advice and began to plug the quality of *Bazaar*'s readership. I wanted to say that our reader was a "thinking woman." People wiser than I warned that you never wanted to attribute "thought" to readers of your magazine on the grounds that thinking women do not purchase products as indiscriminately as those who do not stop to ponder. So we called our reader "The *Bazaar* Woman," and said she was affluent, intelligent, and interested in fashion. Norman Sunshine selected photos of attractive women from the pages of the magazine and I wrote the copy and we ran the campaign in *New York* magazine on the theory that Madison Avenue read *New York*. And we needed the advertising agencies to make the breakthrough to success.

I had found the big advertising agencies extraordinarily helpful and willing to listen. *Bazaar* had been such an advertising sad sack for so many years that I wouldn't have been surprised if the agencies had simply written us off. On small accounts, with limited budgets, it was logical that the money be spent in *Vogue* alone, rather than diluting it over both *Bazaar* and *Vogue*. Our demographics and those of Condé Nast's *Vogue* were approximately the same. The larger advertisers, the ones with substantial budgets, tended to spread their money across both high-fashion magazines, with a bias toward *Vogue*. The big ad spenders do not, you understand, support both *Vogue* and *Bazaar* because they are philanthropic by nature. They realize that if one of the two magazines goes under, the survivor automatically achieves a monopoly position in the high-fashion field, and that advertising rates just might go up as a result.

Magazine salesmen usually call on media buyers at agencies but I found it surprisingly easy to get to top management. I had something of a reputation from the *WWD* days, I had the publisher-editor title, and perhaps they were just curious. With Bill Lucano's help, and Norman Sunshine's guidance, I took what I called a "dog and pony show" on the road. Usually I had China Machado, the fashion editor, Barbara Goldsmith, the articles editor, and Shirley Lord, the beauty editor, along with me. All of them were articulate and attractive and though I did most of the talking, as is my wont, the presentations we made seemed to work.

You understand that a magazine makes money by selling advertising, not by selling magazines. The trouble was, *Harper's Bazaar* was not selling enough of either. The paid advertising pages for twelve issues had run to about seventeen hundred during the early 1960's but had dwindled to an annual average of about seven hundred pages by the time I took over. At six thousand dollars a page this meant a decrease in revenues of some six million dollars a year. Bill Fine had been publisher when the slippage began until, in his wisdom, he went off to run Bonwit Teller. Al Traina had briefly succeeded him and then gravitated to the Downe Publishing empire. Gordon Morford had lasted just under two years. And the advertising sales continued to go down.

Less vital to the revenues but perhaps more essential to the magazine's vigor, the circulation analyses put out by the Audit Bureau of Circulation revealed an equally dismal decline in copies sold. From a peak of some 485,000 in the early sixties the slide had gone on for about ten years so that when I took over, the audited circulation stood at 417,000. It would go still lower, to 409,000, in the first ABC report of my regime, until, for the first time in more than a decade, it would level off at 409,000 in the next six-month ABC report. Vogue's advertising and circulation had also slipped steadily during the ten years, but not quite so drastically. Still, I knew that Vogue's overheads were higher. Bazaar had done a good job on trimming costs. Morford had been especially good at this, and I trimmed another hundred thousand dollars out of each of the several budgets I prepared. No, costs were not the problem. It was the damn revenue, eroding all the time. There had to be some way of turning the corner.

It was hard to know what sold a magazine. Why should a woman, faced with perhaps sixty titles on her neighborhood newsstand, at least ten of which were directly pitched to her needs and desires, select one over all the rest? Loyalty came into it, I supposed, but more experienced magazine people told me, and I came to believe it, that the cover photograph and the cover lines, those words that went with the music, made the difference between a good-selling issue and a bad.

I was not terribly good at selecting covers that sold. It was surely one of the major flaws in my performance at *Bazaar*. Clay Felker, who runs *New York* magazine and presumably should know, had told me that you had to sell 70 percent of your total newsstand distribution to be successful and that an 80 percent sale was really good. I touched the 80 percent figure only once during the year. (Neither was I under 70 percent very often.) It was difficult to graph. A March cover of Rex Reed and Suzy Knickerbocker sold well. An April cover of tennis prodigy Chris Evert was a disaster. An Ali McGraw cover sold adequately, a Barbra Streisand cover, the next to last I chose, sold much better than had the one for the same month a year earlier. Yet a September cover with Lauren Hutton and pianist Billy Taylor did not sell. I wondered if it was because Taylor was black.

Deems wanted more active cover lines. "Tell them how to be more beautiful, more elegant, happier. Those are the cover lines that sell magazines." I was opposed to the "how to" cover line, and the "how to" approach in general, for that matter. I assumed intelligence on the part of the readers, a degree of sophistication. I reasoned that "how to" journalism was patronizing, offensive to the contemporary women who bought *Bazaar*. *Vogue* went its own way, always the same girl, or her sister, set in the right-hand side of the cover, her eyes fixed precisely on the camera lens, the cover lines marching predictably down the left of the page, informing the reader "how to" be more elegant, more interesting, more witty and desirable.

Yet *Vogue*'s newsstand sales were steady, almost always near 80 percent, while *Bazaar*'s went up and down like a Yo-Yo. Was it that more readers thought of *Vogue* as a newsstand item? *Bazaar*'s mailed subscriptions were substantially higher than *Vogue*'s and under me they began to rise dramatically. So despite the irregularities of newsstand sales, I felt that *Bazaar* really had turned the circulation corner. After a ten-year slide, the total readership had leveled off. In 1973, I was sure, it would begin to rise. I never had the opportunity to prove it.

After my departure, the November and December news-stand sales skyrocketed. Those were issues I had planned, had edited, that still bore my name. It was nice to go out with a bang.

What none of us really came to grips with in that first year was the precise sort of magazine we wanted to produce. And our understanding of the kind of woman we wanted to buy it was, at best, rather fuzzy. I wanted the magazine to appeal to liberated women in their late twenties through their forties, women of education, of taste, and obviously with a decent income. "Our readers have brains," I announced rather dramatically. I had no wish to get down into the trenches with the "girl" magazines like *Mademoiselle, Glamour,* and *Seventeen.* They had their own market and the competition was fierce. Gloria Steinem and Pat Carbine had successfully launched *Ms.* and though I did not at first like the magazine, I had to admit it carried out its expressed function, to provide a pulpit for American feminists and their causes. *Vogue* was clearly a "how to" book, packed with information women would want. I was shooting for something a cut above that, packaging fashion and beauty news with reading of some substance. By late fall of 1972 I felt we had reached that balance, and the newsstand figures had begun to show results, but by then Tony Mazzola had taken the editor's chair and announced that *Bazaar* would, in the future, tell American women "how to" be more beautiful, sexier, happier, and in all ways the epitome of virtue and grace.

19

President Nixon's Good Friend

Distance helps in the appreciation of great men. While I would later come to think of Richard E. Berlin as a garrulous, name-dropping old gaffer, I was really quite impressed at our first meetings. Ruddy, erect despite his great age, he had been president and chief executive of the Hearst Corporation since 1941. At the time he took over, Hearst was a company badly in need of a savior. Old W.R. and the Depression had combined to run Hearst's once-great empire a reported two hundred fifty million dollars into debt. Berlin is credited, and credits himself, with having saved the company from bankruptcy. Founder Hearst's free-spending and erratic management, especially during the last years of his life, became the stuff of legend. A man who once worked for the Hearst paper in Los Angeles, the *Examiner*, told me that in the 1930's a corner of the warehouse had been set aside for several thousand rolls of lavender, scented toilet paper, monogrammed M. D., that had been made up in Japan especially for Marion

Davies, the old gentleman's companion. At the same time, said my source, the staff of the *Examiner* had no toilet paper at all in their stalls, but a large hook from which hung sheets of newsprint waste. "It was like wiping your ass with tin," said the old *Examiner* man with a certain rugged pride.

Despite such admirable cost controls, Hearst was broke when Berlin was given full authority to rescue the company. He promptly did so, performing prodigies of cost cutting, kiting checks, selling off losers or simply closing them down, and charming creditors, especially the big paper suppliers, into waiting — in some cases years — for payment.

The first time we met as employer and new employee, Berlin told me that one of the first big businessmen who tried to "help" him salvage the company was the late Joseph P. Kennedy. Berlin said Joe Kennedy phoned after W. R. Hearst's death to say he'd like to help the firm in its hour of need. Kennedy mentioned that he'd been looking for a country house in northern California, someplace to go with the children in the heat of summer. He knew that Hearst had such a place, and he wondered whether he could assist Berlin by taking the property off his hands. He offered several million dollars for the house and land, according to Berlin, who thanked the elder Kennedy and said he'd get back to him. As Berlin told me the story, "I knew if that son-of-a-bitch Joe Kennedy offered that much, it must be worth a good deal more." He consulted with his experts and authorized a timber cruise of the thousands of acres in the northern California property and six weeks later had the information that the timber alone was worth four or five times what the shrewd Kennedy had offered "to help out, as a friend."

My assessment of old man Berlin is probably cruel and essentially unfair, since I knew him for only a year and that toward the end of his life, rather than in his prime. During my time with Hearst it often seemed to me that his wife, Honey, who resembles one or several of the Gabor sisters, was calling many of the shots and Dick Berlin simply went along to maintain whatever shred of domestic peace he could. Nor do I have any idea what the real relationship is between Richard Berlin and Richard Nixon.

"I was one of his earliest supporters," Berlin will tell you. "When he was still a young Congressman from California I was in his corner." And when he plunges into the drawers of that big desk in his Eighth Avenue office to bring forth sheaves of letters from Nixon, there is no doubt that now the two men have at least a lively, and friendly, correspondence. A typical Nixon-to-Berlin letter will carry such sentiments as, "Pat joins me in sending our very best wishes to Honey and to you."

Berlin is so vain about his age that when he resigned the presidency in February 1973 and moved up to chair the several trusts that control the company, he refused to permit his age to be contained in the press release, though the ages of other executives involved, including the new president, Frank Massi, were set down. The *New York Times* questioned the release and asked for his age, but was turned down. This may reflect Honey Berlin's influence, since I suspect the old fellow is rather proud of his vigor at seventy-nine or whatever age he may indeed be.

Early in 1972 he underwent major surgery and was hospitalized for a long period. When Berlin's convalescence was well along I decided that *Bazaar* might as well make use of his intimate relationship with the President and I wrote him asking if he would intercede to get a *Bazaar* reporter aboard the press plane going to China with Mr. Nixon. There was a tremendous crush of journalists trying to get in on the historic Nixon trip and I thought it would be a coup if *Bazaar* were represented. And of course I fully intended that I would be the *Bazaar* representative. I suggested in my note to Berlin that my background as a Washington correspondent and as a foreign correspondent additionally qualified me to back up or to complement whatever other Hearst newsmen were going along. I was curious about the Chinese, anxious to go to Peking, and sure that Dick Berlin could arrange it. But though his influence with the President obtained on such matters as postal rates, he either had no influence, or no interest in exercising influence, when it came to the gathering of news. There was no room on the plane for *Harper's Bazaar* or its curious editor.

I may have seen Berlin once or twice after that, briefly, but my next extended exposure to the great man was in June. I had learned more about him by this time, but there were still aspects of Berlin that impressed me, not the least of which was his reputed annual salary of five hundred thousand dollars. The occasion when we again came together was an extraordinary day's outing of the sort I had thought went out of fashion during the paternalistic era of the elder Tom Watson of IBM or perhaps the reign of John Jacob Astor.

Toward the middle of each year, senior executives of Hearst magazines are invited to what is called "Mr. Berlin's party" at the Deepdale Golf Club in Manhasset, Long Island. On a rainy Monday morning in late June some sixty Hearst men, publishers, editors, advertising managers, circulation managers, teed off. It was typical business golf, made more interesting by the testing nature of the course itself and the soft summer rain. On one of the short par threes my iron shot was seven feet from the pin, which later that evening would win for me the hole-in-one contest and a voluminous green-and-white golf bag. After the golf there was the usual locker room badinage. As a new man I found it difficult enough during office hours to distinguish the publisher of, say, *American Druggist* from the ad manager of *House Beautiful*. In a crowd of sixty middle-aged men wearing towels it was impossible.

The Deepdale Club is a fine place. They say that at the end of the year someone simply tots up the deficit and they apportion it among the members and it gets paid that way.

After the golf and the showers there were drinks in the wood-paneled bar and out on the patio under a great awning that held off the last of the day's rain. Most of the Hearst people were in suits, a few quite rakish fellows in blazers. I wore a blazer and suede pants I had bought in Paris the summer before. But it was all right. No one seemed to mind. The club servants hustled the drinks around. No one was ever dry for more than a moment. Berlin was there now, pink-cheeked, his face shining like that of the tomato-faced character on the covers of the old *Esquire*. Too old now for golf, he had arrived for the cocktail hour. With him was a priest, one of those ruddy Irishmen who hang around important people. Sort of a house chaplain, like in the old days. I supposed it didn't do any harm, but I thought of my brother over in Bedford-Stuyvesant, working with the kids and filling in for the prison chaplain, living in the ghetto, working there, and still having his car ripped off from time to time, almost as a reflex action.

During cocktails and later over dinner it was clear that there was really no Hearst stereotype. Some of these men, especially some of the younger ones, were competent professionals with that dash of irreverence that said they could make it elsewhere if not at Hearst. Others, generally the older men, were very much of the old retainer variety, sweating out their perquisites and their pensions, laughing just a bit too heartily at adequately told jokes, pressing closer in on the circles surrounding Berlin and Deems and John Miller. The dinner was steak, good steak, and some very decent French wine. I was at one of the lesser tables, no Berlin there, no Deems, no chaplain even. But it was a cheerful group. One old chap enthralled us with baseball trivia. He said he could remember having been to the Polo Grounds even before McGraw's time. We tried him on obscure outfielders, on the name of the Cardinal shortstop in ought eleven, that sort of thing. He was phenomenal. Then he asked if any of us had ever heard of Jigger Stats. No, none of us had. The old-timer rattled off some facts about Jigger Stats and sat back satisfied. We tried to stump him but couldn't. He had stopped us with Jigger Stats and there was no one who could top it. "Jigger Stats," one of the harder drinkers at the table kept saying. "Jigger goddamn Stats."

After dinner there were more drinks and Marvin Sleeper, the corporation P.R. man, said that, following tradition, there would be a little show. Another of the older men got up and introduced the acts. There was a barbershop quartet, a passable violinist, and a man who whistled. He didn't do birdcalls, you understand, he whistled tunes. I stood in the back of the room, wedged against the bar with some of the younger men. I couldn't believe it. A whistler. They had everything but a musical saw. Dick Berlin loved it. You could see it in his face. He was beaming, turning this way and that, poking the corporate chaplain with his elbow, winking at Sleeper or one of the other old-timers. The bartender worked steadily to fill the glasses of the men up against the bar, the generally younger types who weren't yet in the more inner circles around Berlin and Deems. It took a good deal of Scotch or bourbon to get through the whistler.

Amateur hour. It was difficult to imagine their doing this at the *Times* or at Time Inc. John Fairchild would have succumbed to the vapors. Golf was bad enough, of course. When he was a Princeton undergraduate working in the Paris office during summer vacation, John had been forced to caddy for B. J. Perkins, the autocratic bureau chief who claimed, after thirty years in Paris, "I never spoke a word of French and never will." Young Fairchild insisted that Perkins cheated. "I'd find the ball in the rough and call to him and he'd say, 'Well, throw it out here.'" If there was anything Fairchild hated worse than golf it was this sort of fraternity house camaraderie. I asked the barman for another Scotch.

When the musicians had moved off to the wings there

were a few speeches. One gent noted that since Berlin's name was Richard E. Berlin and Deems's name was Richard E. Deems, he was going to change his front name and middle initial. There was some knee-slapping over that, you can be sure. Several of the men would be retiring before the next annual party and they were duly cited. The speeches were mercifully brief. I thought the worst had passed when Sleeper, the ubiquitous P.R. man, began to pass out mimeographed sheets. There was to be a community sing.

"I'll be goddamned," someone at the bar said softly. I looked at my sheet. There were song lyrics printed on it, a set of lyrics for each of the twelve magazines in the Hearst group, with a notation of the tune. The *Harper's Bazaar* song was to the tune of "Santa Lucia." The lyric had a great deal to do with milady's elegance. My eye went down the sheet. The *Cosmopolitan* song contained a number of references to sex. The barbershop quartet came back onstage to lead the community sing. They began with *American Druggist*. Everyone in the room seemed to be singing. Someone nudged me and I raised my rather reedy voice. Some of the men at the bar were fairly well along now, what with the drinks before dinner, the wine, and the heavy-handed barmen filling the glasses even before they were empty. To my left I heard one of the men from the dinner table murmur, "Eff Jigger Stats."

An hour later I was leaving the club, the golf-bag trophy under my arm. Dick Deems met me in the lobby. Preternaturally erect, Deems looked down on his latest star.

"Why, Jim, it's early yet. This bunch won't be going for hours. There won't be a man at his desk until Thursday."

I made my excuses and the boy brought up my car. The golf bag just fit into the trunk of the Mercedes. Barely.

The next morning, slightly hung over, I got to the office at about 9:30. My secretary had left a note on the desk. "Call Mr. Deems," it said. The time noted on the slip of paper was 9:00 A.M.

20

The Hearst Gang Rides Again

It is one thing to be considered a skeptic. Journalists don't mind that, they rather like the tough-mindedness it suggests. Cynicism — well now, that's something else again. Perhaps Mencken admitted to it, but he died and you cannot check with him. A cynic? I prefer not. But what else to call someone who when still quite young understood that hotels put shoe-shine cloths in the rooms, not to accommodate their guests, but to save the towels? Given such potential for cynicism, the years as a working journalist to develop it, and the *Harper's Bazaar* episode to put a hard edge on it, I suppose it's inevitable that I question motives, test the sincerity of handshakes, and peer dubiously into a man's eyes when he is telling me wonderful things about himself, his works and pomps. I doubt that this makes me a better person, but a little cynicism is powerfully handy when you are writing about some of the people I know best.

In the grand tradition of certain publishing empires, news

of my dismissal came not from my employers but from an outsider to whom it had been leaked. It was a reporter from my former newspaper, *Women's Wear Daily,* who phoned me on that Friday morning in October.

"I hear you're out," he informed me, with a certain glee.

Since the reporter had once worked for me, had indeed been hired by me, I summoned up what I hoped was a measure of dignity to say that the report was news to me. I suggested he call my boss, Richard E. Deems. When I hung up I considered telephoning Deems myself but decided against it. It was now ten o'clock and my secretary had made coffee and there were the newspapers and the mail to go through and the daily meeting with the editors and besides, when you ran a deficit operation like *Bazaar,* there would always be rumors. You couldn't always be running to management about them. You'd never get any work done.

Dick Deems, president of the Hearst magazine division, is a sixty-year-old former salesman who would perhaps remind you of the late Estes Kefauver, another tall man who moved with his head thrust forward after the manner of a dignified and upright turtle. Deems's curious posture derives, he will tell you, from a bad back. An hour after the phone call which alerted me that I was "out," a nervous messenger arrived bearing a letter from Deems's office across town on Eighth Avenue.

"Dear Jim," it read. "*Harper's Bazaar* is just not making progress. Therefore I have decided to appoint a new editor and a new publisher, effective on Tuesday of next week. I shall call a meeting of the staff on Monday at 4:30 to make an announcement of your resignation [sic] and the new appointments. I would assume that you would not wish to be a part of that meeting." The letter ended with assurances of his personal regard and a pledge to assist "in whatever new career" I might take up.

I telephoned my wife and then my parents to give them

the news, and then called in the editors. I was very calm, calmer than I would have imagined possible. Probably it was a reaction to the lack of style, the indirection of Deems, his inability to perform an unpleasant task in person. I told the editors, using such arch circumlocutions as "the corporation in its wisdom." Several of the editors cried. One of them, who would herself be sacked a few weeks later, said, "I think it stinks." Down the long hall to the Fifth Avenue end of the office I went to meet with the advertising staff. I made a quiet little speech and thanked them for their efforts. Advertising men do not cry except when they themselves are fired, and I noted with relief not a wet eye in the room. I don't think I could have taken that, if a space salesman had wept. Back in my own office I typed a little press release of my own, dismissing curtly Deems's transparent tactic of a "resignation." He could call it what he would but I had been fired and intended to be quite open about it.

"It is always painful to leave a job half-done," I wrote. "We had, in a year's time, gone a long way toward creating a new breed of magazine with very real journalistic distinction. The long circulation slide had been ended and the advertising forecast for 1973 looked promising." I credited the staff and the contributors for the progress made and ended with the regret that "I will not be here to complete the work I began just ten issues ago."

Yola Carlough, my secretary and one of the beautiful young women who would make leaving *Bazaar* even more painful, retyped the release and sent it out to the *Times*, *Newsweek* and *Time*, to *Advertising Age* and the wire services. I phoned the reporter who had broken the news and confirmed it to him. Jack Cleland, Washington correspondent for the *Houston Chronicle* and an old friend, had called several times during the morning. He was in New York with George McGovern's campaign and he wanted to get together for a drink. I told him I couldn't make it, that I'd been fired. "Now you tell me," Cleland snarled, "and I could have been over in Newark going through the ghetto with McGovern, enjoying myself." It took some time to convince Cleland that I wasn't jesting, that I'd lost my job. Charlotte Curtis of the *New York Times* interviewed me over the phone. "I want to know all about it," she said. Charlotte had played a role in the revamping of *Bazaar*. She had written one of the first important pieces I had commissioned, the story of the so-called beautiful people who'd made asses of themselves fawning over Crazy Joe Gallo before the gangster's assassination.

My wife and I had planned to take the children to Westhampton Beach for the weekend and there was no reason to cancel the trip. The Yardarm Hotel (I thought the name appropriate) is a big rambling barn of a place nestled just behind the great sand dunes that separate the beach from the Atlantic Ocean. Over dinner our daughters learned that I would no longer be publisher, that Mr. Deems had decided to hire someone else in my place. "I think Mr. Deems is mean," Fiona said angrily. Susan, a year younger at ten, said flatly, "I think he's stupid." Old enough to recall the Depression, I assured the children that my contract would be paid off, that I would have no difficulty finding another job, and that they would continue to receive their allowances. Thus relieved, the girls asked if they could ride horseback along the beach next day.

There was no telephone in our rooms and all that evening I went back and forth to the house phone in the bar. *Time* called, and *Newsweek*, and someone from the Associated Press. I had learned by this time that Hearst would name five executives to share my former responsibilities and remarked wryly to a caller that I was flattered. The Channel 5 news at ten o'clock showed a still photo of me in my office and quoted the *Newsweek* interview I'd given when taking the job. "I've never failed at anything," I'd said with more spirit than wisdom, and the television commentator quoted the line and added, "Today, Mr. Brady was fired." I had to admit it was good television, the sort of thing I would have done myself. I made a note to drop a line to the chap to congratulate him. Next day we sunned ourselves in beach chairs while the girls rode hacks along the beach, and in the evening John Veronis and his wife gave us drinks in their great turn-of-the-century house behind the dunes. Veronis, who then ran the *Saturday Review*, thought it shameful this was the first time I'd been fired. We dined with friends and before bed stopped in the Yardarm's bar for a last drink. There was a small band and dancing and it was pleasant sitting near the big windows that gave on the ocean, listening to the music and the chat. A party of people came in and with them was the reporter who had called to tell me I'd been discharged. There was no reason not to be polite and we had a drink together and I danced with the reporter's wife. It was all very civilized.

Next morning, Sunday, a reaction set in. For the first time I felt depressed. Where had it gone wrong, was it my fault really and not just panic on the part of Deems? I had the good sense not to brood about it but to talk it out with my wife, who listened well and said the right things. That afternoon we drove back to the city while over the car radio the Oakland A's were winning the World Series. There was one more call Sunday night. It was from Ed Fitzgerald, octogenarian host of a WOR radio talk show, half of the team of Ed and Pegeen Fitzgerald. Fitz liked me, had had me on the show several times, and enjoyed what I was doing to bring *Bazaar* into the twentieth century. He had also worked for Hearst years before. He launched into his sermon without preliminaries.

"Better men than you, better than myself even, have been sacked by Hearst. I was sacked once. It was before your time. I worked for the Old Man. He was a caution. There's one thing at Hearst, whatever your title, whether it's publisher or editor or whatever, you have but one role: to sell advertising. That was what you were there to do. Remember that and call me in a few weeks when I'm feeling better. We'll go to a decent French restaurant," Fitz promised, "and I'll tell you about Hearst. It'll cheer you up."

But by this time I knew something about Hearst myself. That year-and-a-little of running *Harper's Bazaar* would have made a pretty fair musical comedy book. Given a score you could whistle, it might have reached Broadway. When you realize the executives I was dealing with were the supposedly responsible officers of a gigantic and influential communications empire, a billion-dollar company, they come off as an oddly assorted and curious crew. Consider what a splendid cast of characters they would have supplied for a writer of contemporary farce:

An aging (seventy-nine) publishing czar, Hearst's president Richard E. Berlin, who resembled Guy Kibbee and who boasted of his friendship with the President of the United States. On occasion he would send me Xerox copies of the latest missive from the White House. His critics insist that there is a little string at Mr. Berlin's back and you pull it to set him in motion. But this is a canard. I have looked, and there is no string.

Several senior executives, Dick Deems and John Miller, jousting for Berlin's job once he was gone, or perhaps before. Miller, the financial man, was named executor of Berlin's estate and seemed to have moved into the lead. But four months after my dismissal Berlin himself resigned, took on mysterious duties with the Hearst foundations, and a bland accountant, Frank Massi, succeeded him. The little-known Massi promptly demonstrated fidelity to the company's tradition of nepotism by naming his brother-in-law to head the King Features Syndicate. At sixty-three Massi was likely to be an interim pope and Miller may yet make the grade. He will be seen of an evening commuting on the Long Island railroad to his Garden City home with a briefcase bulging under his arm.

There is nothing suburban about Deems. He and his gracious wife, Jean, have a thirty-fourth-floor suite in the Waldorf Towers, a weekend house in Waccabuc, New York, and a Palm Beach apartment. Neither Miller nor Deems seems to take much notice of the Hearst family. When William Randolph Hearst, Jr., was quoted as saying a merger between two Hearst magazines, *Town & Country* and *Bazaar*, had been discussed, Deems phoned Bill Hearst in the presence of a reporter, chewed Hearst out for having made the statement, and issued denials all around that such a merger had ever been contemplated or indeed discussed. I knew that was untrue, of course, since Deems and I had discussed it many times, but it certainly silenced poor Hearst, Jr.

Tony Mazzola, who had been editor of *Town & Country* and was now to run *Bazaar*, signaled his arrival at my desk directly after my departure by ordering that the radiators be turned up full blast and announcing, "I'm arthritic." Although we worked in the same building, at 717 Fifth Avenue, Mazzola and I had met only occasionally. Since one of my first recommendations to Deems, on being hired, was that *Town & Country* be merged into *Bazaar*, I had no great desire to get to know Mazzola, a man I was urging be eliminated. A horsey friend once told me about a piece Mazzola had commissioned on one of the tonier hunts and claimed that Tony "couldn't tell the grooms from the gentry." I said it probably hadn't mattered and my friend sniffed into his hacking jacket and changed the subject.

China Machado, fashion editor, was a slender and graceful woman, half Portuguese, half Thai, once called by photographer Richard Avedon "the most beautiful woman in the world." China, like most of us, does not live within her income. She lives with her two daughters in a rollicking great apartment on Central Park West that once belonged to Ring Lardner. China was given to talking about going into television, or into the fashion business, reluctantly giving up the magazine work she loved simply because she had to earn more money. The day I was sacked, Mr. Deems gave China Machado the opportunity to improve her fiscal position by bringing in the turban-wearing Carrie Donovan from *Vogue* to replace her. Carrie was moved right into China's office, which boasted a single desk, and China was unceremoniously moved out after a dozen years at *Bazaar*.

The only note of style associated with the entire mini-purge was the arrival of a young man called Brick. It is not clear just who Brick might have been, but he accompanied Miss Donovan wherever she went, hung up her coat, coiffed her hair, answered the phone, brewed hot drinks, and shouted at junior editors so that Carrie did not need to raise her voice. Brick was not on the payroll, you understand, he was simply there, to serve and to wait. China Machado would later comment wryly that she now understood why she had never been recognized as a great fashion editor. "I had no entourage," she said simply, as if it should have been obvious all the time.

The following Monday Deems sent around a rambling memorandum that announced, in his fashion, my "resignation" and replacement by all sorts of people. Mazzola was to become editor, leaving *Town & Country* to limp along as best it could. Tom Loose of *House Beautiful* was named publisher. Phil Slater of *Town & Country* became associate publisher. Miss Donovan was named fashion editor and an aging, though loyal, saleswoman was put in charge of merchandising. In all, five miracle men had been named to save *Bazaar*, which even I had to admit was progress. A year earlier one miracle man had been deemed sufficient.

In his memo Deems seemed to be calling *Bazaar* the most prestigious, profitable, and authoritative fashion magazine in the country. Reading his remarks, you had to wonder why I had been canned if the magazine were all that good. Mazzola had something to say too. He told the staff that *Bazaar* was a "pioneer" in fashion journalism and would continue as such.

Among its innovations, he declared with pride, were the bikini, the synthetic wig, and the waist cinch. He saluted *Bazaar* for having had the moral courage to put a black woman on the cover. Six weeks later *Bazaar*'s fashion editors would be told they were using too many blacks, to cut them out. But that October, to be fair, Tony Mazzola may not have known this.

Honey Berlin, who had played such a vital role in the new order at *Bazaar*, who had been the first to recognize genius in Tony, did not attend the staff meeting at which her candidate was introduced. She sent her husband instead. Dick Berlin, there to lend solemnity to the event, had, in the words of an insolent young editor, "been inflated for the occasion." After Deems paid gracious tribute to me, Berlin rose, repeated several times the words "I distinctly recall . . ." and then, not recalling what it was he wished to recall, told an anecdote. Deems, who has a Nixonian flavor to his prose, made reference to "relief pitchers coming in from the bullpen," which thoroughly confused several of the more intellectual fashion writers. He noted, though no one else did, that there was great enthusiasm on the staff for a new and greater *Harper's Bazaar*. Within two months nine people in the room had been discharged and the Brady era was over.

Deems and I met twice more to discuss disposition of my contract. It was all quite diplomatic. Until he brought up the question of my charge accounts at various restaurants. There was one, from La Grenouille, which had apparently become the stuff of legend in the dingy offices of the Hearst Corporation. The bill was $2,501. Deems had the company accountant there, shuffling a stack of my expense accounts in his lap, poking at them with a yellow pencil.

"I note that you took out insurance when you traveled by plane," the accountant said while Deems stepped out of the room for a moment.

"Yes," I said, "I always do that on business trips."

"Well, you know it's covered already, in your company policy."

"How much money is involved?" I asked.

It was something like thirty-seven dollars. Deems came back in. The closing ceremonies were mercifully brief. We shook hands.

"Just a moment," I said. "There's one more item. John questioned my air travel insurance. It was thirty-seven dollars or so. I'll accept his arithmetic if you want to disallow it."

"Nonsense," Deems said expansively. As I left, the accountant was still there rustling his sheaf of papers. I felt I had been exposed to a small shred of what journalists called "the Hearst treatment."

Directly I departed the scene, *Bazaar's* new management set out to undo the "damage" I had done. Staff members were fired, the thirty-year-old "nine day wonder diet" was resuscitated and headlined on the cover as something American women had been waiting for deliriously. Such writers as Halberstam, Tom Wicker, Charlotte Curtis, and Chuck Mitchelmore were dropped. Instead, Tony Mazzola commissioned a piece on orthopedic shoes, featuring an orthopedic shoe company that had long fitted out his mother. Mazzola's office was enlarged by half again as the carpenters moved in and the editors were partitioned off from their chief. There were to be no more meetings in which all the editors participated, and the cover of *Bazaar* was altered so that it would look like *Town & Country*, the old-folks magazine Mazzola had run for years.

Now, more than a year later, the issues of *Bazaar* are even slimmer than when I was in charge, personnel continues to be reduced, the puff pieces about advertisers are back in style, and there are rumors that Hearst would be willing to sell the magazine if it got a decent offer.

Just the other day I was told a marvelous story about poor Mazzola which is just unbelievable enough to be true. It seems that a recent travel column about Venice contained the famous Benchley line, "Streets flooded. Please advise." In the margin of the piece, according to instant and local legend, Tony Mazzola scrawled, "who's Benchley?"